PIECES

OF

MOLLY

PIECES

OF

MOLLY

AN ORDINARY LIFE

JUDITH EDWARDS

KARNAC

First published in 2012 by Matador, Leicestershire

This edition with new foreword published in 2014 by
Karnac Books Ltd
118 Finchley Road
London NW3 5HT

British Library Cataloguing in Publication Data

A C.I.P. for this book is available from the British Library

ISBN-13: 978-1-78220-218-9

Typeset by V Publishing Solutions Pvt Ltd., Chennai, India

Printed in Great Britain

www.karnacbooks.com

To Christoph, and to the memory of my parents

'We are all patchwork and so shapeless and diverse in composition that each bit, each moment, plays its own game. And there is as much difference between us and ourselves as between us and others'
Montaigne

'The dead are never quite as dead as we think'
Hilary Mantel

About the author

DR JUDITH EDWARDS is a child and adolescent psychotherapist who has worked for over thirty years at the Tavistock Clinic in London. Apart from her clinical experience, one of her principal interests is in the links between psychoanalysis, culture, and the arts, as well as making psychoanalytic ideas accessible to a wider audience. She has an international academic publishing record and, in 2010, was awarded the Jan Lee memorial prize for the best paper linking psychoanalysis and the arts during that year: 'Teaching & Learning about Psychoanalysis: Film as a teaching tool'.

Names have been changed to protect confidentiality

Foreword

I first became acquainted with this absorbing and beautifully written book after some years of teaching psychoanalytic autobiography to MA students. I devoured this story eagerly and immediately incorporated it into the course. Like all the best autobiographical writing, it is centred on the child within the adult, and evolves its own way of weaving together the past and the present, the child's naive spontaneous perceptions, and the inscrutable secrets and mysteries of the adult world. The vision of the child, intoxicated by the desire for knowledge, is interspersed with that of the adolescent and post-mid-life Molly, who is still making discoveries—no longer about complicated family entanglements, but about herself as she was then and is now.

Molly was born at the end of the Second World War on the family farm whose fields reached the seashore and stretched as far as the eye could see, and her story is bound through earthy nature to the realities of growth and survival. It is also bound through history, poetry, and legend to representations of mental survival and exploration. Even the Viking ships that wove their way across the North sea to implant their gods and customs on East Anglian soil play their ancestral part in the total picture of Molly's world as she reconstructs it piece by piece. The web of perception is shot with gold threads. Hence the theme of tapestry restoration, presented in technical vignettes that link the chapters as they unfold—a weaving metaphor for the odyssey of the self which is indeed as old as Homer; though in the case of this narrative it has a special relevance to a mother who was queen of the Singer sewing machine, concocting clothes and household linens, and a father who furrowed the soil as king of the tractor and the combine harvester.

Molly's story begins with her gestation, in watery fluid echoed by the waves as her expectant parents, sitting with 'linked arms' on the clifftop, survey the sea beyond and ponder on their lives to come. The picture demonstrates how any true story must be founded on a voyage of the imagination. Later, those linked arms became crossed in other ways, whose 'shadows' or 'ghosts' Molly senses but cannot make sense of. Like her father, she is caught in a web of family frustrations, pinned between her talented but increasingly neurotic needle-sharp mother and her sexually expansive grandmother, possessor of soft pliable 'buns' in which all sorrows should have been buriable.

Chronologically, the story ends when at age eleven this 'swan', her parents' darling, is ejected from her childhood Eden and cast out to boarding school, the big wide world—the second ejection after the birth of her brother, or perhaps the third if one includes her own birth. It is a time-honoured route in spirit, whether or not the literal details are shared by everyone alike. Hence, the rightness of the subtitle 'an ordinary life', which may be taken to mean 'universal'; and, of course, it only achieves this universality because the idiosyncratic and particular context of an individual existence is so vividly evoked.

One of the joys of this book is the lyrical flow of its language, colloquial and at the same time studded with quotations from poetry, nursery rhymes, stories, and children's games. These counterpoint the author's voice in a totally natural way, making clear how deeply these influences are embedded in the structure of the growing personality. Current events of the time are recorded through glimpses of the popsongs, political manoeuvres, and scientific discoveries that locate the backdrop to any life and anchor it in its cultural context. If these snippets are the weft, the vocal warp is probably the underlying melody formed from remembered snatches of vivid homely conversation or silent recollection, which catch hold of lines such as Hardy's 'He was a man who used to notice such things' and give them a present meaning—in that case, the death of Molly's father.

Above all it is the life of the farm and village that gives Molly's childhood its foundation in reality: the hedges, crops, harvesting and marketing, the life and death of animals, significant to any child for both its equivalence and its otherness. Molly recognises there is no contradiction between the father who shoots rabbits for the cooking pot, and the father who says 'skin a rabbit' when pulling off the children's tight vests—both are signs of love. Then there is the gang of village children who 'knew so much more than she did' and initiate the first social-sexual explorations; the influx of summer visitors bringing intimations of life beyond the fields; and the old house itself which is destined for destruction by modern values, together with the 'cathedral of the great corn barn' and all the old rural way of life. In addition, her progression through the local schools provides a basis not just for academic learning but also for the extra-curricular widening of life's horizons, internal and external; but being sent to boarding school focuses her suspicions and she feels she has been 'stitched up' by mother and grandmother, sewing her 'trousseau' in unison as if to patch up their own differences, a pair of 'Viking queens'.

The key to any child's identity is inevitably the oedipal triangle, and their perception of it. Despite the temperamental mismatch between Molly and her mother, and her father's 'ladies' man' confusion between his own loves over three generations, the pervading impression is of a happy and privileged childhood, with its own inevitable sorrows and anxieties, but lacking in neither physical nor mental sustenance. Both her parents are keen to promote her education and make sure she has appropriate opportunities, not just a repetition of their own. They make the most of the rare opportunity that a farm provides for both parents to be at home and yet working at a family business whose successes and failures are evident and rational even to childish eyes. They also play *en famille* and celebrate—card games, bonfire night. The father tells stories, lets her ride the tractor, makes sledges, lights fires, adores, and is adored. The mother, despite her acerbic comments and her instinctive repulsion of Molly's attempts at demonstrative affection, works hard to run the house and family efficiently. With a mother's instinct she senses the time in later life when Molly is in 'deep trouble' and shows her understanding through a dream of a kitten clawing at her skirt. Only in her horror of religion does she seem to actively censor her five-year-old daughter's desires to catharsize her own guilty feelings by means of a rosary. In other ways, the children's liberty was uncircumscribed, as was typical in that era, allowing the world to be full of interest, with scope for self-expression. On days when the father was conducting business in the city, the children would be left to their own devices in the museum, which stood in loco parentis, containing Molly and her brother (not even quarrelling) by means of its fascinating exhibits.

When Molly needs a new direction to redirect her murderous impulses towards the new baby into constructive channels, materials are to hand in the form of red and green volumes from her parents' childhood—a 'spur to a new world'—and she becomes a precocious reader, 'counterfeiting growing up from age three'. Guidance is available too, despite her mother's characteristically spiky remark, on her first attempt, that she is reading the newspaper upside down. She is attracted to the hairstyle of one of her teachers because it is so different from her mother's perm, indicating her thirst for educational possibilities and (in psychoanalytic terms) for enhancing the qualities of internal objects. Rejecting her mother's flair for matters practical, she discovers instead the power of words through pronouncing the word 'bugger', which she had overheard being used in an all-male setting, and sets to work to become a potent wordsmith. Key to this is her love of punctuation, which opens out the possibilities of tracking and ordering one's thoughts. Meanwhile, the announcements of the station master complement her idea of fatherliness and of an 'honourable job', 'marking the pilgrimages ordinary people make' and, she hopes, helping to shape her own aspirations in life. And indeed, half a century later, returning to the rose-garden and knowing the place for the first time (as the poet says), this fascinating memoir is just such a pilgrimage.

It is in the nature of a good autobiography for the reader's own experience or life history to be brought to mind, often with a sense of vivid empathy. Reading *Molly*, I found myself reliving episodes from my childhood on the North Sea coast, and on my grandparents' farm, where my mother grew up. She was the first in her family to go to university, and in a book for parents of teenagers, she asks (writing I believe about herself), how can parents cope emotionally with a growing child who has become better educated than themselves? 'Fortunate—even if at times unhappy—are the parents with an adolescent in this state. They can help him or her best by saying "God speed!" and letting go. If they can manage this, their teenager will come back to them not under constraint but in his own way and with free affection.' Molly, whose mother never forgave her for learning to walk, was perhaps never let go—but she went on anyway.

Meg Harris Williams
Artist and writer on the relation of psychoanalysis, art, and poetry
Her latest books are The Vale of Soulmaking,
The Aesthetic Development, *and* Bion's Dream

Prologue

In the middle of the country is a dark wood, as the old rhyme says. In the middle of the wood is a dark path. Down the dark path is a dark house. Watch how you go. Through the dark door and up the dark stair. At the top of the stair is a dark room. In the room on one of the blank walls is a dark door. Open the door and there she is, in the cupboard. Well to be precise, there is the box.

I'm imagining a bit of a scrap of a girl inside there. Talking to ghosts, her ears straining to make out any replies. What are they saying? She thinks she can hear whispered shouts, broken melodies, stray syllables. Is this the same old chattering muddle of conversations, that old ferment that never stops? Maybe she's just mad? Or is she trying to make some sort of a mark on life from the beginning?

If you're free to, and you want to, you can go up or down between these worlds, the lift-shaft of many tensions and tenses, where past present and future characters in the old stories collide and complain, bluster and lie, jostling each other with a nip here and an elbow jab there like cunning old ladies at a jumble sale, as they push themselves forward with no attempt at orderliness, what a crew they are, the everlasting unburied dead. Where are we now? they ask. Are we nearly there? We all speak to our dead, and they speak to us, we live side by side.

Look into all the rooms, so that nothing is forgotten.

Molly has looked, and has salvaged what she could from the wreckage of a burned old house. You have to hold your nose and the ash creeps wispily into your eyes, into your ears, you pick your way through the mess and find very little left of value, your eyes sting, with tears but something else too. It's all blowing and going but that's only because there are universal rules here, try as you may to deny them. Blowing in the wind, there's a whistling of old tattered tunes which get thinner and thinner in the stern air. There are stories here too, yes there are, but muddled and twisted and linked and frayed and pulled apart and cut—there are loose ends fruitlessly trailing, trying to find a solution for themselves when there are possibly, probably, none.

Take what you can, and the rest, the unsaved things, the left things, the broken, helpless things, un-housed now, will drift and dawdle, pushed firmly on their way by the hard hand of time.

Is there a story here?

You'll just have to wait and see.

Who said that?

Did I dream?

Chapter One

In which Molly is born: one small and insignificant human being arrives with great difficulty in a village by the sea, and we meet her young parents, dancing from being a couple to a threesome with a baby. An almost deadly three-day labour threatens to cut this story off at the beginning: but Molly, unnamed as yet, survives, and so does her mother.

How can we conserve this stuff we carry round without distorting it? And would we know if we did? The conservation of an old tapestry requires a clear, cool stable environment. Whose tapestry is this? The needle, as the saying goes, though it has clothed many, remains naked. Naked perhaps, but not innocent.

Sometime in early November, one night maybe or one early morning before things started to get going in the outside world, one of a myriad of sperm lashed its little tail and collided with an egg—was it waiting, or was it just launching itself like people do down a busy street, anyway it was one of those unremarkable miracles which happen every millisecond of each human day on earth. The world began for one child as cell multiplication began, that night or morning in the nineteen-forties. Slipping through a gap in existence's framework, into a space not especially made for her, but one she took up and ran with.

Five days this first journey took, cells churning and developing on the way, from zygote to embryoblast and trophoblast, until the blastocyst found a home, as they do, in the uterus—what an odyssey, the greatest awesome voyage, stuff of myth and raw reality. Are we nearly there? The beginning of the atom dance for one, as they start what they'll do for a whole life long, dipping in and out of the same quickstep.

When Molly's mother was pregnant, she told her daughter, she and

Molly's father would walk over the fields and down to the sea. They sat on the cliffs, looking out towards the horizon, thinking about the future with their unborn child. Looking at the horizon protects you from seasickness, that's the usual view. Human flesh may well be made of stardust, as the nuclear physicists tell us. It's also saturated with hopes and dreams. For better, for worse: married to your parents' preconceptions. Flesh and fantasy inseparable even at the beginning, before breath.

So from a pin's head bud of an embryo, it all started. The little bang. Space, time and gravity getting going yet again for one small proton. Translucent, virginal egg meets lusty sperm. These little events happen punctually, for ever and ever, as the poet says.

While her parents sat together and talked softly as the evening light silvered the grey sea into night, on the mysterious cliffs, drifting each spring with scarlet pimpernels, and already beginning to slip, almost unnoticed, into the sea, the child was already a project in the making. Whatever your religious or spiritual or scientific take on it all, you must admit it's a huge performance that gets going in the visceral darkness. Just consider. Construction cell gangs team up, from those first three or four stems which can be used to make anything in the body, who's going to get to do what, gang? Slowly they raise the scaffold poles of the skeleton, gathering together in friendly cooperative colonies to make the heart, the lungs, all the fine grained tissues of life, a human child from a few cells, balanced on the head of a pin, angels or devils in the making. Nice work, team. The ear is the fastest organ to mature in the womb. Forty-five days on and it's a going concern, fully functioning, even before the heart . As her parents sat on the cliffs, looking out to sea, her mother fat as a wheat-ear, what was the first backbeat this small project was aware of apart from mother's heart, was it the surging in and out of the North Sea, gnawing at the Norfolk coast, mingled with the surging of the amniotic sea on which she sailed as they all do in blind faith?

I'm nearly ready, my makers, not long now and our meeting will take place. It's getting noisy and uncomfortable in here. How I long for our meeting time! I've already got a few thoughts, but they swim around like fish and I can't seem to hold on to them. But I can see now, opening my eyes, closing them, I'm practising you see, sleeping and waking, balancing and listening, sucking and hiccupping, sometimes even somersaulting just to show off a bit, ready to go, or just about. You're maybe ready too. Well I hope you are. I'm a baby in waiting...

And then like parcels at Christmas, the tinsel comes off, the present is unwrapped. They unwrapped her, and she unwrapped them, to see what they had got. Here. We. Are. The clock starts ticking in the birth canal, as what we call the foetus, in a timeless zone, turns into a baby. The doing is done, the being begins.

Where am I? Things were getting a bit too cosy, even a little stifling, no more stretching and moving possible, so I sent out the signal, time to go. Well maybe I was a bit late off the mark there, but I was still regretting cosy even when no room no room was being shouted in my ear. Go.

Everything slid into action, pushing, squeezing, slippery smooth passage it seemed, just a bit of last-second regret for the old home so I turned myself round to say goodbye. Well I think that's why I did it. No going back now. But that, I soon discovered, was rather a mistake. The pushing and the squeezing got totally out of hand, beyond any control I thought I'd had over it. I started to panic, I couldn't turn, I couldn't move, I was just impelled to endure something beyond my understanding. Open the door, dammit. Should I give up? Forget navigation, forget taking soundings, forget any thought of some grand planned entrance. So I did surrender but it made no difference, the pushing and the wringing and the pulling continued and then I did give myself up for good and gone. There were muffled sounds growing louder, groans, cries, bangs and steely crashes. The thunder of blood and fluid all around. Time had no meaning, and just as I started to embark on its measurements, space had disappeared. Things were grabbing bits of me and believe me by then I did need rescuing. Hauling, wrenching, dragging, raking, drawing, receding, returning, falling and losing ground, a long pull and a strong pull, a bloody ejaculation and a botched job, careening into a world where some wounds could never be bound. The tangled country of soiled sheets I had arrived into was murky and stained, drenched with weariness and disappointment. Birth may be the passport to freedom, but this one had been stamped with a black mark from the beginning. Parts of this baby were born in pieces, a little dead. Squeezed out, dragged to death. It took time even to scream in the usual and expected way. What's happening to me?

But I didn't mean things to be like this.

In spite of the parents' prospective optimism, the birth was a confusion, and Molly's mother suffered hugely. She lay in labour, groaning and crying, for three days, in the bedroom at the front of the old house where Molly spent some of her childhood years. As an adult Molly returned, remembering the original frieze of autumn leaves around the top of the wallpaper, and the feeling of warmth and comfort as she stared at the wandering flames of the fire which was always lit if anybody was ill and upstairs. She was a breach baby, and in those far off days, in the nineteen-forties, breach births weren't thought to be quite correct (and they certainly were dangerous). For three days, her ma recalled, on each of her daughter's birthdays even to the end of her life, rather overlaying happy birthday have a wonderful day, they gave her terrible, scouring enemas, and she felt turned inside out, they tried to turn the baby around and around with what she described as metal spoons. Stirring, scraping, concerned cooks wanting to bring forth the baby brew in prime condition. This mother was in agony giving birth. And as her daughter made this difficult exit, which bit was pulled out first you can wonder, she left behind a stomach stretched and swollen for ever, skin as puckered over the whole abdomen as a badly sewn collection of seams, a permanent reminder, to her mother, of her daughter's guilt. This original guilt permeated their lives, covered over by future guilts, but still alive under them all, the first footage for what came later. As it was in the beginning, is now and shall be, for evermore. The original movie. Script already written, but whose copyright might it be?

There are circumstances, so the theoretical physicists tell us, in which a disaster becomes inevitable. Infinitely compressed energy arises in an infinitely curved space-time, and a black hole, for instance, may be the outcome. Tiny fluctuations eventually trigger a disaster. But a black hole radiates energy too.

How could I do this to my mother, my container, my maker? If I kill her, who

will take up the baton and give me a chance? If I kill her, my dad will abandon me.
If I kill her, my dad will kill me. If I kill her, my dad will never in any case want
to look into the eyes of a murderer. If I kill her what remains for me is living death.
If I kill her. I lose her eyes, the eyes in which I could live and grow. If I shut mine,
will all this nightmare disappear? Or is there no going back?

The whole country was on daylight-saving energy conserving double summer time, on a par for once with Europe, but for this young labouring mother in her little corner it was a seemingly relentless torture of a never-ending night. The doctor asked the father who should be saved, and he said, and who could blame him, 'save my wife'.

Please save my wife, my life. His eyes shifted to the horizon as he made his plea, one life for another if that was what was called for.

She lay suffering, hardly able to speak, and he was kept out of the room, outside the panelled door, beyond her agony. He feared going in anyway, when he heard the cries and groans. Was this his youthful wife, transformed into a pitiable, screaming monstrous thing? What had she done to suffer like this? She was poised on the dangerous edge between life and death, and so was the child.

He too feels on the edge of an abyss of loneliness and terror and he scratches the door in his agony, tearing his own nails in identification with the child-wife's screams. She doesn't deserve this.

So-called 'primitive' tribes believed too that breach births were dangerous, but rather psychologically; the future people who didn't have the plain sense to choose a safe exit forwards would walk backwards and be contrary all their lives. Babies who made this fundamental error were indeed killed once they had negotiated their first journey, if they ever did. Molly was forced to admit the thought later, that this first mistake of hers had major consequences. She wasn't doing it right from the start, she needed to be helped to come out properly. Listen up, baby, do it our way. The going was bad, she'd left it too long. Being born was a struggle. Someone would get killed off. Someone would be chosen and someone sacrificed. The old ding-dong of your-fault-my-fault, who gets left holding the sticky end?

Ooh no she didn't.

Oooh yes she did.

Could she justify her existence? The daughter's right to be collided head on from the start with her mother's. Did she have the right to live and love, and be loved? What future contradictions could be explained in that first almighty clash? A persistent lower back problem got cured only fifty years later by the acupuncturist's needle. She spent a lifetime trying never to be late again. Just in case. This had been an untimely entrance, nearly as they say an untimely death.

It was a hot August, they told her later, and her father was harvesting wheat on one of the top fields, close to the sea. There was a harvest-time shirt, which he wore later, she recalled, matching the colours of the frieze of leaves on the bedroom wall. Bringing the harvest home. When she grew up, grasping for narrative where she could, this story was again confirmed by Gladys, the spare and tentative woman who was working in the house for her mother then, and remained there till her retirement, quietly cooking and serving up the lunch, a role quite separate from that of the women who cleaned the house from top to bottom each day. Mince turnovers she produced like little neat tents, pale golden brown, ('nip-rounds', Molly's dad called them) and caramel custards in glass cups, to be upended on the plate as the dark sweet juices cascaded down their sides.

Gladys cycled to the house each day, pushing her pedals slowly and rhythmically as she curved on her well-maintained old black sit-up-and-beg bike round the drive, stopping each day precisely in the same place, in front of one of the sheds opposite the back door, where she carefully hopped off her machine, and settled it against the inside shed wall on top of all the others, some working and some long rusted beyond use, in the corner opposite the door. Before she went in, she straightened her always thin brown hair over her narrow head, pushing at the Kirby grips which fixed a scruffy little bun just above the collar of her coat, just once more, to be sure it was all in place. She herself was a fixture in the house, and in the landscape through which she toiled each day, like a Chinese miniature, a landscape of flat fields, scruffy windswept trees and huge skies, sometimes magnificent, sometimes brooding with clouds like turbulent thoughts banging and grumbling on the horizon.

'Yoo-hoo' she calls gently, rather than ring the bell.

Gladys lived with her husband, the road-sweeper and bike-maintainer, and her two children, a few miles away, in a cottage nestling at the bottom of a small hollow in one of a farmer uncle's fields. Pit Cottage, it was called. Most winters the cottage would be buried in snow, and six-foot drifts had to be tunnelled through to make a pathway for this hardy family.

In spite of this, they loved their cottage, especially in spring when all sides of the little pit glowed like a tiara studded with daffodils and primroses, and they mourned its passing when the pit was filled. They had to move themselves and their few possessions to nearby Blundeston, like David Copperfield before them. When Gladys died, her daughter found she had kept tattered little letters sent from the Front by her reluctant soldier husband—I will see you very soon, my own sweetheart. I never knew my dad had thoughts like that, his daughter said. Well maybe we never like to think too closely about our parents' love, and the sex they had without us at all in mind.

Gladys was there, in the house, cooking as usual, when Molly's father was torn apart by the anxieties around those two harvests, wheat and family.

Later, this father, farmer, landowner and hero of Molly's first days, never grew wheat. She used to love looking at the fat grains in an ear of wheat in other people's fields; barley seemed more shrunken, bearded to hide its littleness, less fecund and full.

So this baby arrived at a busy harvest time, there were other things going on and you can imagine her dad, sweaty and driven and dusty, driving the combine harvester whose thunderous noise was mixed in his mind with his child-wife's screams, and wondering if she too might be dashed under the augur which sucked the wheat into the threshing drum. Would he end up with a broken woman or a murdering child? *All we shall die, though us like ill.* Horace had a way with words, over two thousand years ago.

Before this conception, they were a handsome couple, he fourteen years the elder. In the shoe box of photos Molly inherited, toppling in a jumble careless of time lines, there were two photographs in particular: one of her mother, on her twenty-first birthday, standing, 'posing' as she called it later, on the front doorstep in a long shiny dressing gown. She made it herself, she told Molly, of greenish-blue brocade curtain material. This was early in the nineteen-forties, and there was no other material available. It was two years before her daughter's birth. She looked unformed, but ready, on the doorstep, for life to unfold around her and within her. She had a curved, fluid beauty, with dark eyes liquid under dark waving hair, and a very determined mouth, and she held on to the doorpost in an apparently casual but determined way. Wife in her new domain, mistress of the gravel drive, the sloping lawn, the fields which led to the top of the cliffs already starting to crumble into the sea. She was going to help destruction on its way, but she didn't know it then.

You were a much wanted first child, Molly's mother had told her triumphantly. Everyone thought she had married at nineteen because she was pregnant, but the gossips had to eat their snappy little prurient words and wait four years for a happy arrival. And even then there was a wait: the baby was born pink and white and doll-like, much overdue, not red and wrinkled and on time. Not even apparently scarred and exhausted by that first calamitous journey. Apparently, but not everything can be seen, or dreamed of.

The other picture, of Molly's father, shows him, too, posing, but in a field of wispy seed-filled grasses, hay in the making, sitting with his head to one side, showing his handsome profile which grew more and more hawk-like with advancing years. Even in youth there is a chiselled symmetry about his features, a regularity and unsparing, even perhaps too painful honesty in his balanced deep-set eyes beneath heavy overhanging brows. He has his arms folded, a pose which seems to speak about his settled relationship to his own universe, governed by the weather, as well as his need for certainty in a changing world beyond the farm gates. It was a solid base for him, and it took Molly years to understand something about the land which exists inside the mind. But by that time she had been disinherited from the broad acres, partly by choice and partly by others' acts beyond her choice. He's wearing the kind of clothes she could still almost touch and love in that gentle memory of early touching: corduroy trousers, creased, faded and old, an open shirt. Who knows now, as we translate from black and white, about its colour, maybe a shirt of soft browns and blues like the spring around the hay-field. Over a hundred stitches you can choose from, to fix this memory now: tent stitch, half-cross, continental and basket-weave; straight and slanted gobelin, brick, mosaic or byzantine. A kind of benign embroidery. Not necessarily an exaggeration or a lie, though these may of course always creep in slyly however vigilant the seamstress, but a way of fixing something for a while.

He shines and glows with potential, this man who would remain rooted in his own land, who in his last years had a dream which he tearfully told his daughter. It was of a prize heifer that he had left neglected in a barn; he returned to feed her, and she was dying. He snuffled into his handkerchief, swallowed and gulped as he told the homely, deadly tale. The way life led him, driven by the determined person of his wife, took him slowly and inexorably out of his furrow, and at the end of his life she dressed him, and how could she do this, in shiny blue jogging pants and top.

A family video, one of those cruel records of what might be better forgotten, shows this old man, still hawk-like but feeble, demonstrating himself drained and diminishing, driving his invalid chair and smiling with wry uncertainty. Dressed in this hideous stuff. He bumps his way down the gravelled drive, to show his briefly returned daughter his geese. They lurk cackling in the long grass and lumber stretching their hissing long necks to greet their lord. King of the tractor, King of the combine harvester, King of the black bulbous Ford Zephyr Six, reduced to this. All he has left is his walking stick, which he still clings to as a memory of old strides, cut from the branch of a tree he had planted many years before. How did this happen? How did this happen? The old refrain.

That in't fair.

In her mid-fifties Molly wakes stunned on her own account, how did this ageing happen, so soon, where did they go, those other versions of herself? Which is the true one, and which the impostor? Is it now? Is it now? How can you understand this long now? Do you ever wake from a long dream, and become again who you once were, perhaps never stopped being? Such age old questions, yet we all repeat them. We make a line to help simplify the question. All these realities could exist side by side, a multiverse of possibilities, if only we had the eyes to see. Well it's an idea worth having somewhere in case of need, don't you think, Horatio? More things, more things in heaven and earth....

And the days are not full enough,
And the nights are not full enough
And life slips by like a field-mouse.
Not shaking the grass.

But in this first photo of Molly's dad none of that regret was written: instead you see someone on the crest of a life, simple, graceful, enfolded by his acres and his history. Always a ladies' man, flirting, so her ma told her, with the bridesmaids at their wedding, love children already hinted at, reputations dishonoured and yet only seemingly enhancing his own. Maybe for her ma there was triumph in carrying off such a prize.

Darling, will you be mine, in apple blossom time?
He proposes, down on one knee, at the crest of a railway bridge.
Sooner than that I hope, she says, inclining her dainty determined head.

She is just nineteen.

They get married on a crisp New Year's Day. The January wind-frost nips the wedding guests, and the photographer manages to fail with all but one photo of the happy couple standing and shivering in front of the church door. She looks like a little girl dressed up in her grownup clothes, as her new husband holds her arm, maybe to steady her on her high-heeled lace-up shoes as they start the marriage dance. Later in their lives they regularly go to a New Year's Eve ball, and circle the floor gracefully together, in a solo memorial performance of the Anniversary Waltz, as soon as the New Year chimes and toasts die. Mr and Mrs Wonderful.

They had met on the dance floor at a local ball. Dancing, especially the ballroom kind, is an art where the dancers seize the moment, not the last nor the next, but poised on the brink of the beat each timeless time, some intuitive space between the quick and the slow. Molly's parents didn't lean back to the last step, or leap to the next. They hit it right in some unerring centre, and whirled at least on the dance floor with poise and ease, a kind of eternal flow so at odds with what happened every day. Molly's father held his wife firmly, hand in the small of her small back, and she looked up at him and then around, sensing the applause, silent though it may have been to the rest of the world. They made the floor glide with them, it was a smooth and floating surface that they used to perfect their act, transforming the shining parquet floor into a moving carpet that they moulded to their desire. The family would all watch enthralled the films where Ginger Rogers was twizzled and twirled by Fred Astaire, who danced on pianos in his debonair carelessness, identified in all their minds with the handsome father and a mother whose beauty, their dad assured them, was greater than that of any movie star.

Years later Molly's mother told her that she had in fact been waiting for another man. He had, her mother found out when she was in her sixties and they renewed acquaintance, visited her old home, left a written message never delivered by her own mother, for her own reasons, and the disappointed girl had assumed him gone for ever. Those reasons of her mother's were about her own desires. No-one knew it then, but this was to prove one of those turning points, the plot device which sets a lifetime's path. Molly's mother would survive them all: her lover, his second choice, her second choice; fragments, fading, genes thrusting forward as the only record of these early failures and disappointments, branch-lines where one track was taken and another left behind for ever. Aspects of randomness, unpredictable and impossible to avoid.

So why did these two marry? Perhaps for Molly's father, the days of chasing girls had started to seem less attractive as he progressed beyond thirty. The young man who had thought nothing of riding on his potent motor bike to London for a hot party and returning the next morning was maturing, into a man who wanted to settle down, and to look after his own little girl wife. He once told his daughter fondly how shy her mother had been when they met.

She wouldn't say boo to a goose.

Well, but that wasn't for long.

For the child-wife, brought up in a much humbler way, the lure of the big house and the land all around it was a magic way out of what she considered to be origins which were really beneath her. She once recalled to Molly the horror she had felt as a teenager reading a book about life in Britain during the depression of the thirties, *Love on the Dole*. One family, or so she said, and this was what had stayed with her for all those years, had sat round a soft boiled egg, and passed the spoon around so everyone could share this rare delight. She told Molly when Molly herself was still quite a young girl, as the parents' fortunes began to change in step with the changing world around them, that her worst nightmare was to end up back in a little house, with nothing. But unlike the fisherman's wife in the Grimm's fairy tale, who asked for the sun, the moon and the stars and ended up back in a hovel, this farmer's wife, although just as tyrannical and demanding in her own way, stuck with her second choice and changed things from the inside, like a secret agent. Slowly and irrevocably, to fit in with her deepest desires. The shy little goose girl changed gradually into a queen, at least of her own small space on the earth, and ruler of her husband's heart.

And if there was a future irony, that she did move into a smaller house at the end of her story, she moved with money to cushion her against her most profound fear. Through a narrow rectangular window at the top of her new house, she could still see in the misty distance the ruined spire of the church where she had tied herself to her chosen destiny, I will but I won't, a lifetime ago, a spire still used by older fishermen as a point to sail home by.

Chapter Two

In which we see how this particularly difficult birth will echo on down the years. Some mistakes may never be undone, and this trauma reverberates until Molly's mother's dying day.

Freezing is probably or so they say not harmful to objects provided that condensation does not occur anywhere in the process. You need to allow the objects to re-humidify before they are handled.

So Molly was born, in the same room where her father had been born, and his father before him. Her ma was exhausted: the idealised child of pregnancy turned into a child attacker that nearly killed her, but came out pink and white, looking unscathed by the ordeal; by the doctors' calculations extremely overdue. That very year the Greenwich Royal Observatory installed its first quartz-crystal clock, ten times as accurate as the pendulum system it replaced. But something had gone wrong with their clock already, for this mother and her child who tried daily to cling to an iceberg, desperate as a little chinstrap penguin thrown up again and again by the Antarctic waves onto the frozen land. For these two the time seemed to be always a little out of joint. Babies are born in rhythm with the world, researchers now can show, but this was a tough call for both parties, and the lyrical phase ended rather than began with being born.

Her ma was sick for weeks, depressed no doubt, and why wouldn't you be, opened up and carved around like that, something had been posted with love into the box and then delivered in agony from the same place, an unwieldy, uncooperative parcel. Where was the mother's own mother at this time? She had her reasons for not being there. The baby cried unceasingly, slept to escape the sound of her own screaming and woke in terror to scream again.

You can almost hear Molly's mother thinking: I don't like her. I can't feed her. I don't want to feed her. How can I love her, she's hurt me much too much. And I didn't deserve it, I really didn't .

This new mother was born in pieces, too.

Erwin Schrodinger's famous cat was, he said, in a variety of states if seen from an overall vantage point. In some of these states it was still alive, in others it was already dead. When Molly and her mother took their space-time journey together, time collapsed. This tricky situation didn't make up for the fact that they had to get going afterwards in the ordinary three spatial dimensions, when things started up and would never stop quite like that again, for them.

Mother's milk from mother's breasts was out of the question. A nurse was hired, then fired, by Molly's father, who took on the task of trying to soothe and mother this perhaps too-beautiful, certainly frightened baby. Night after restless night he carried her up and down the landing between the top bedrooms in his strong arms. Mother's rivals both, from the beginning, the daughter enjoying father's embraces and the father in the mothering role. Molly's mother was done with carrying. She never really came back.

I don't like her.

But I don't want him to like her either.

Is that how it went?

Was it an oxytocin problem? Somehow, while the oxytocin receptors might have been primed, the love hormone didn't get through. It was there or was it, for the procreative act, but not for its result. The spark died. Love's first little arrow didn't leave the bow, after that deathly birth struggle. So the addiction didn't begin, the dopamine didn't materialise, the smelling and touching your baby didn't set up a platform for the sharp dive into love. It was to be a deficiency with a sequel. Maybe even hormones can be put off by pain, sensing in some dumb way that they shouldn't even try to put up a fight.

Go to sleep, my baby,
But what happened? What happened?
Close your pretty eyes.
What have I done?
Can I ever make amends?
Too late, too late, from the very beginning.
Where are you, mother? Don't leave me.
Don't deprive me of your eyes.
The cord was cut, yes, it was-but is that the end of it all?
Angels up above you-
Guard you till the morning fills the skies.

Her mother's milk had dried up. Maybe her breast was never offered: a question never asked. Why would you offer your breast to your tormentor? Perhaps this was the child's first punishment. Later the child had learned to suck her thumb as compensation; this was frowned on, it would make her teeth stick out the stated reason, and her mittened hands frustrated the bed-time needs to feel comforted. And even later, she gnawed her nails. Although it may be from the factual point of view a not too uncommon event, as the start to a life you could admit it's not too propitious. These facts were the structure on which another part of the future plot was hung. The magical, mythical pre-birth cliff-top curtain had been, it seemed, torn beyond repair, and the world rushing towards the new born child had arrived primed with that soured sense of disappointment—for them both.

Mother where have you gone?
How can I tell you how sorry I am, that I caused you such pain?
I didn't mean to, listen, I didn't mean to.
To be born or not to be born. It's a heavy question, hard to bear.
I thought I was dying to be born, then something died in any case it seems.

These old ranklings revisited another birth when it came to be Molly's own turn to perform on this tricky stage: what is it about the third day? In the days before the birth, spooky thoughts hovering wispily over the years brought a dream—would the baby grow up to be a murderer? On the third day after the birth of her son, far from rising like the fabled Saviour to the occasion, her mother rang to direct Molly to have her milk tested. It would be no good for him: hers had been no good either and that was that. Something poisonous here; a conviction that nothing good could come out of either mother or daughter, without being spoiled by disappointment and anger.

'Just ask the nurses' was all Molly's mother said, as her daughter leaned tearfully against the hospital wall clutching the cruel phone, receiving this coded message from her mother's past.

At the moment when this mother was at her most needed, she was at her most undermining. All her own old fears rose from the deep and spoiled anything that might have been better. She couldn't help her daughter to be a mother. Molly's mother, a first-time grandmother, met her first grandson for the first time in a hotel, halfway between their place in the country and the town where her daughter now lived. Breastfeeding, which Molly managed well despite her mother's discouragement, was just not on in a public place; the new thirty-three year old mother, somewhere still just three, was directed by the old mother to the ladies loo. Too late, Molly thought, to cry over that old spilt milk.

Nine of the twenty planetary rings of Uranus were discovered in the year Molly's son was born. Uranus, which takes eighty-four years to orbit the sun, is infinitely cold, with a rocky core and a cloak of ice five thousand miles thick. How could this cold mother, planet of Molly's life as one of her orbiting children, not have been touched by the birth of her daughter's first child? All too easily it seemed.

Molly was later to become once more the idealised child, not only the one who had injured her mother. She was presented, pretty in her little dresses, with fair-haired curls and a chubbiness which proved economic security, making her a small star in the contemporary canons of baby beauty. At nine months in one of those studied photographic portraits so beloved in the nineteen forties and fifties, the baby is sitting on the arm of a large arm-chair, the feel of that upholstery Molly fancied she could still recall. Her mother is sitting in the chair, beautiful, with her hair rolled up around her face. It was the style, and Katherine Hepburn led a million women down this complicated hairpin way. They're both looking at something that is in her mother's hand. If you look through a strong magnifying glass, you can see it is a small white flower, a daisy, she loves me, she loves me not, almost hidden from the camera lens. But although the photo has a classic feel, capturing a moment, it seems, but maybe just to Molly herself a lifetime later, a moment which lacks depth. The contact is, literally, at arms length, not heart to heart, nor eye to eye. The spark had died. Mother's hopeful little sparkler would have to find a larger stage. People take longer to develop than photos, but there may be clues here to what would unfold over a lifetime.

A baby's smile is supposed to warm a mother's heart, light her up, light up what are called the reward centres in her brain, as the brain imaging techniques now show. It's a benign beneficent cycle. When it happens.

The human eye, so the wisdom has it, possesses about 137 million separate 'seeing' elements, all spread out on the sheet of the retina. The number of nerve-lines leading from them to the brain gradually condenses down to little over a million, and each of these has in the brain, we must think, to find its right nerve exchanges. Those nerve-exchanges lie far apart, and are themselves stations on the way to further stations. The whole crust of the brain is one thick tangle of exchanges and of branching lines, going to and fro.

What were mother and baby looking at in this small snap of time? Did Molly's mother look at that baby and wonder what or who it was? Was there something else behind the picture, something not known about then and not able to be known about later? Something Molly can't see because of who she is? She twists it around in its tarnishing silver frame. Where can she place the camera now? What clever lighting might reveal something new? A new angle, unseen before. There's no rewinding the film, stopping it and starting it, slowing it down, speeding it up, jump cutting it, freeze frame enlarging it with great grainy blotches, all the technological tricks we now play with time, to compensate for what we can't actually do for one second in our ordinary lives. She has just this one image, and what it seems to shout out, underneath the classic pose. It was the forerunner of a million unrecorded fugitive moments.

Home is inescapably where one starts from. As we grow older and maybe a little wiser, the world becomes more strange, more complicated, and as the poet said, a lifetime burns in every moment, every photograph out there in the frame, and those never taken but still somewhere in the mind. In spite of all our hopeless wishing it's a one-take life, propelled by the force of forgetting for such a little time, until its end. It's a book that can be read, will be read, in different ways, joining one story to another story to another. Every second of every life can be both deeply meaningful and scandalously insignificant.

At least what the photo shows, Molly thought, is that they could look at something else together, but maybe not at each other.

After her husband died and Molly's mother moved to her smaller house on the cliff-tops, she made each day last and gain significance by baking in her immaculate kitchen, a kind of drive for meaning masking as devotion. 'I have to do something', was what she said. It was a true kindness performed for others, but somehow more difficult in terms of the generosity of giving and receiving, for both her and her only daughter. She made complicated plaited loaves studded with sweet dried fruit, and layered cakes oozing butter cream, then pressed them on her daughter in a way that felt not like giving, but some kind of nailing—take that, because I'm trying to be good. And Molly took them, of course. Mother, we made it together, she thought, but only just, I guess in the last reel, a mutual lifelong dance, approach and withdrawal over the years, trying to get the distance right, not too close, not too far away. It just never stayed right for long.

In her final months, Molly was awarded one dazzling smile. Her mother could knock the socks off you with that smile, even as she lay dying and denying in a hospital bed. But it was not meant for her daughter; 'I thought you were the nurse,' she said, and the dazzle vanished.

How come, Molly's mother asked her carer, whom she, during her last weeks, could love, it seemed without reservation, that I could never love either of my children? For her own unknowable reasons, the hardwiring supposed simply to be there between mothers and children had been cut. Yet this woman carer had been able, with ordinary salaried friendliness, to unlock the frozen secrets. The question, reported to Molly by the carer, was she supposed a twisted sort of gift. She had imagined herself unloved, and it was so, but maybe not, as she had thought, unlovable. The deficit, unexplained but actual, lay deep within her mother.

How can Molly get inside her mother's head, then or now? This was her mother, for heavens sake, impenetrable, quixotic and unknowable. She always was that way. You could slide off down an exterior slope of apparent calm, love even, hey isn't this just dandy, let's enjoy it, and end up in a crevasse, twists and turns and changes, no such thing as a stable point of view, from Molly's point of view, in growing up.

The only solution? Try to think about it in a different way, or so Molly thought. And yet if you haven't got a handle on the way a slope can upend like that, how can you begin to plot a different terrain, if one day, before you go out with your dad, your mother is feeding a kitten, small and furry and so very appealing, loving it and vowing to keep it warm and safe till it's a grown cat sitting by the fire, then when you come back later the kitten has gone, who knows where, maybe put down by a farm hand, or taken into a more welcoming household, not part of the picture any more, ripped out and the hole stitched over with apparent unconcern, we'll have our tea now, hurry up and wash your hands, how can you get to grips with that? Don't mention it, just carry on.

And that, a million times, was Molly's experience of an unpredictable mother, who dug a scary landscape for her so she never knew when and where the next pothole would spring. Motherland was a dangerous terrain, landmines buried minutes or months before could explode and she'd be limbless, speechless. She could well believe the old Norse legends, stories of their forebears, who thought that the world was created from a warring mixture of fire and ice. They invoked the spirits of heat and light to struggle with the ice-lords. Shiver and shake, deny and burn. Feedback wasn't what Molly wanted: it was feed-forward to save her from the carnage. And as Lamarck believed, if you have no eyes but still you want to see, you keep on trying to see, and you'll end up with eyes to get the picture. Part of her heart quivered in helpless, pitiful, contemptible despair, marinated in a stew of broken hopes. She developed a great talent for being satisfied with what little she got. Part of this same heart tried to polish itself defensively, to cultivate imperviousness. And it failed, as daily it was pierced by her mother's anger or disdain.

But nobody is the person she thinks she is. That applied to both of them in this one small instance of an unpromising partnership, and still does.

Afraid and wanting, Molly needed a code book to read her mother, and never found one. No wonder. Since Darwin made his attempt to classify the human heart, his own original six emotions have been elaborated to a breathtaking ten thousand. Researchers claim there are forty-two distinct movements that can be analysed to read a person's thoughts by the subtle way the muscles move.

A close-scanning electron micrograph can show you the iris and the pupil of the eye, magnified until you can see, like a piece of tapestry in itself, how the iris pushes and pulls at the pupil's perimeter, and how the lens is suspended in a radiating pattern of filaments. But no matter how much Molly kept her strenuously active eyes about her, she often didn't see what came, before it hit her.

How do you restore your mother's face, after she's dead? The tapestry here is as you can see in bad condition. Large areas of bare and broken threads have been cobbled clumsily together through the lining. Missing areas are re-threaded and pulled together in an awkward way. Was this impatience or ineptitude? It's such a crude, botched attempt at repair. As if the person doing the work really didn't care, or was to put it kindly only partially sighted. The overall surface of the tapestry looks like one of Molly's father's ploughed fields after harvest time, with many stubbled warp ends still out to scratch the unwary. It needs water, soft water, distilled water and nonylphenol ethoxylate detergent, fine spraying and suction to carry away the accumulated dirt, to reveal the facial features, to detach them from the heavy soiling of the years. Then the loose warp ends start to look cleaner, silk and wool threads begin to shine, the tapestry seems clearer and smoother. A face emerges from the blur. It is you could say something like a re-transcription of memory.

'Remember your Mama in a happy way' runs the old gospel song. It was a tough assignment. The melody Molly carried inside her was a melancholy one.

So is this the story? Unrequited love? Did her mother break Molly's heart?

When as a young adult Molly was in desperate need of help but felt she could tell no-one, her mother dreamed that same night of a kitten, clawing at her skirt, and knew her daughter was in deep trouble. This kitten she couldn't give away, even if she sometimes wanted to. She was undoubtedly good in illness or a physical crisis, knew how to plump the pillows and smooth the sheet, could bind horrendous gashes when the farm hands got caught up in machinery, and, unlike her husband or his daughter, who quickly felt faint on the injured one's behalf, was apparently unfazed by the sight of copious flowing blood. First aid, last aid… something missing in the middle. The inside gashes remained untouched; we need that soft water to float away the difficulties, warmth to melt the permafrost.

The Snow Queen sat for years inside Molly's head, vivid and unknowable on her glittering touch-me-not throne, surrounded by barriers of frozen snowflakes. While the diaries of those who went with Scott on his ill-fated expedition described a snow with rainbow shades, from deep pink and purple to transparent green, for Molly this compacted snow hurt with its blinding unforgiving white glare.

It was only when her mother lay dying that Molly could pity her. She had cheated herself of love, what Kirkegaard called 'that most terrible deception.' It was, he thought, a loss for which there was no reparation, either in time, or in eternity. The Ice Age ended, or began to end, after her mother died, when Molly could love her safely without fearing the daily sabotage of words launched with the precision of heat-seeking missiles targeted at the heart of hoping. All those years, born yet unborn, in the paradoxical way of it, still inside her mother until that mother was no longer there. Conversations then began that could never have happened in their lives together.

More cruelly visible with the devastations of old age, you could see with her ma how this skeleton was boldly emerging as the years went by, where it had hidden for so long under high heels and ball gowns. For every occasion, christenings, weddings, funerals and all the other little lesser happenings in her social calendar, she had to have new shoes, new suits, new dresses. Her wardrobes bulged. Some dresses were carefully packed away against moths, others lay in crumpled disarray on the bathroom window-seat. What finery it was, for her. She could never give up her imagined throne, but such a fragile little bony structure sat on it, brittle in a way that made you fear to break it by a sharp word, even though she delivered so many herself.

That's stupid, was one of her favourite tail-enders.

The night before Molly visited on her mother's last weekend on earth, she dreamed that her mother disappeared into a black hole. Not under the ground, but whipped away into an anti-gravity vortex. She feared too that maybe that's where she had consigned her. But her mother's mortal fear during that act of dying allowed Molly to help her over the threshold, perhaps not into a dark hole, but down the stairs and into the night.

Just moments before she died, Molly's mother nipped her caretaker hard on the arm. Take that before I go. How dare the world go on? Her efforts to outstare death in her usual imperious way were in that last instance a failure. Greedy for cream cakes, she who had always been concerned about diet and her admirable figure even as an old woman had gorged these confections daily, waving away more sensible offerings.

What the hell, I'll have a binge before I go. Which I'm not planning on anyway.

It was you might say the end of one chapter, and the beginning of something new. If, that is, you are of an optimistic turn of mind. Beginnings, middles, ends, but not in that order, ever.

This was how it went.

Woken in the night by one of the carers, Molly walks almost in her sleep to her mother's bedside.

She's not very well, says the carer, a large woman who sits heavily in the chair by Molly's mother's bed.

Well she is after all terminally ill. What does this mean?

Her mother lies there, eyes rolling, even as the carer assures Molly that her mother is not in pain.

But while the morphine may be taking away the pain, as the project is or should be, who knows what fearsome side-effects it may be having, are little men crawling out of crevices intent on killing her, are swarms of insects collecting around her wildly rolling eyes? Those who return to tell the tale report such things.

But I'm not planning to die I told you, this is a very dangerous message to be sending. It's not for me. This shouldn't be happening, not now, not ever.

Look how you're calming her down, says the carer.

Molly thinks her mother is beyond recognising anyone, as she buffets her way down this road she had never intended to take. Can you really leave dying till the last possible moment? What do you think as you die? This is an emergency, help me!

Dad will be there for you, Molly says. She isn't sure she believes this, but it's a way of bridging the gap. Whether there is indeed an eternal core at the centre of each human life remains questionable. Later in her mother's house Molly found two labels written in her mother's hand, as her mother had laboured over what to say alongside the flowers placed on the coffin at her husband's funeral. The bereaved wife, often so at odds with her husband while he lived, if he thwarted her will in any way, had kept even those. And all those little messages, on those ponderously named 'floral tributes' from family and friends, were then reprinted in the local newspaper, alongside an obituary for this old man. Whether he would be there waiting for her mother was another story. It was not a subject that could be broached. Far from being one of those people who wished to talk about their departure, this terminally ill woman refused her plight and challenged anyone to say differently. And why shouldn't she face Death the way she wanted to, cutting him dead in just the same way as he would do to her?

Gradually the storm passes, her mother's personal fade to white takes place. Or is it fade to black? For once, at least since the far-off days of early childhood, Molly can hold her mother's hand. Mother. Goodbye.

She's not really breathing, says the carer, it's just a habit, it goes on a little while, even after we're dead. Do you want to hold her in your arms?

Even then it seems not to be possible, without her mother's permission. So she holds on to that papery dead hand for a while, the liver spots her mother so hated, she notices, more prominent than they had been in life, and then she leaves her open-mouthed begetter to her everlasting state. It was as if there could be no transitional stage, dying preceding dead. She'd never been dying, never at all, what an outrageous idea. In short order, when she was gone, she was gone, and that was that. Molly's mother simply went, leaving not a jot behind. She got right out of it. She was ashamed of dying. No control there. Thinking abut this new state of being dead couldn't possibly have interested her. Maybe too this was because she wasn't called back to earth, not attached to any human being, as the Buddhists say. Like the death of a supernova, this was the biggest event in Molly's personal universe. Without that supernova death, as theoretical physicists tell us, at the beginning of time, we would not be here. It was a paradoxical circle that could hardly be grasped or understood. If Molly could have replayed the death scene with her mother, what would she have done differently?

Mother where did you go?
Where had you ever been?
All mothers die.

The stars were falling. Something new could maybe be born, but it was yet again an agonising birth. Time strangely stilled. If there was a sound somewhere, it was outside a vacuum, beyond the cataclysm. So this is death, even before one's own, Molly thought. And it's happening all the time. But not to me. The tears come later, when the days stop their whirling, and the trees loose their leaves. Then, she snatched up a few scratchy stalks of heather from her mother's garden, a healthy thrusting plant they had bought together when her mother had moved house, and she ran down the broken wooden steps to the beach nearby. Molly had been concerned, earlier, when her mother moved to the small house, about the state of these steps, but her mother had never been down them, and had preferred to preserve herself like a self-immolated Snow White behind the glass-fronted expanse of her last 'home'.

On the empty beach an assertive clack and clamour of gulls circle overhead. Molly is not interested in what they might be saying. The sand grabs her feet as she attempts to float over it to the water's edge. Maybe there's some music playing here. Is this a drama or a melodrama? She throws the heather into the glittering early morning waves and watches as the heaving singing sea moves itself to take the dry little posy, tosses it a bit in the foam of the next wave, then draws it, sucks it, swallows it, back into itself for ever. Mother's little wave had lost all its energy, and joined the general swell. Dispersing, dispersal. If the credits as well as the debits are rolling over this scene, forgive her the lump in the throat. Well you probably will, but still she needs to ask forgiveness. The end of the story is coming out of place here, but then timelines don't always behave the way they should. In any case, we often have to work backwards, picking up lost threads and making what sense we can as we go along, as Kirkegaard has said.

Now in common with all our numberless dead, Molly thought, nothing and nobody can help my mother. And neither can they hurt her. She's safer dead. It's too late to tell her anything now. But she can be loved without fear, in spite of all the difficulties. Death had indeed had dominion, finally. Her mother had to live her life, then she had to surrender it, however unwillingly.

But are the dead finally safe? In truth, not really, not at all. And unlike the living, you can't ever escape them.

According to family legend, Molly's first word had been 'button'. While she struggled as must we all to find consensual meanings from the powerful jumble of sounds which assail us, to find out about the strangeness of words, what they say and what they don't say, at least there could be agreement on the meaning of that little button. Bright as a button, forward, kitted out for success, but something fundamental not achieved, so that in later years the bond was edgy between child and mother, conditional, lacking in trust. Something already questionable in the family tapestry, taking years to un-pick, rework, alter the balance of the harsh shades, to restore, to conserve, to get in some sort of order, even if in telling the story embedded in the images you make some of it up, losing threads, finding them, losing them again, in translation from then to the never-endingly changing now. We must perhaps I suppose agree that invention can creep in at the very moment of recording, but it's what we have and what we work with.

In the battle between memory and pride, pride may override memory at times: a novelist in every mind. A truism because it is so true. Memory may be fallible but it is culpable too. Should you trust Molly's voice? Should she? The telling of self to self is always a fairly hazardous enterprise. Any thought bombarded by a contrary one, by the voices too of the undoubtedly dead who still hang around somewhere demanding to have their say. And why not? There will be no shortage of explanations, justifications, just take them off the shelf and choose.

Well I have very different memories.

You've got this all wrong. And you always expected far too much.

Who said that?

Attachment to her dad was a different matter, but again it was the seedbed for future difficulty and, dovetailed as it was with the love/hate affair with her mother, it was inevitably problematic. He adored his daughter, this man who wrote to her weekly all of the rest of his life, from the time she had been sent away to boarding school, this man who struggled to 'give her away' in marriage, and hated her, Daddy's Girl, for wanting to be given away, or his adored version of her, the one he held in his mind's eye even when reality might have told him differently. Though he had managed, on that, for him, hateful wedding day, to exhort his future son-in-law 'take care of her'. Courage in the face of his own despair.

He was the one who walked the landing, on the worn green carpet only transformed to deep-piled pink much later, in the wealthier years, soothing the wailing baby, that displaced refugee, trying perhaps to make up for the love that Molly's mother struggled with, and failed to offer, in the weeks after birth. He fed the baby, changed her, and later took her on car-rides with him all over the county, to cattle markets in country towns, to meet men in agricultural machinery depots, to help him jump the queue in shops, his charming little daughter on his charming arm. She was an extension of his potency, his charismatic way.

Even after his death, as Molly went driving with her ma, they would pass, on the road to the local city, a celebrated family spot: 'tinkle wood'. Here charming daughter, potty trained almost at birth and never known to have an accident, so they said, would demand to stop, and do her stuff.

Not for this little infant girl the supposed pleasure of a nappy full and warm on the body, only causing discomfort when cold. She had it seemed been all too ready to sacrifice that primary pleasure for the early desire for parental praise, saving them from her mess. And while she was so adept at holding onto her messes, she was fashioning precocious words coming out of an unstained orifice far above, delightful for her parents to hear. Maybe there was already a wish to be forgiven for the hurt she'd unknowingly caused her mother. She made herself up for her parents, as she went along.

Tinkle wood: just a little scruffy clump of tall trees, scratchy against the sky.

It must have been tough for her mother, this love-affair, and every parent of a daughter knows how that innocent girl longs to take dad from mum, to be the queen of his heart and have his babies. What immutable, immortal longings, which lie not too far below. That *meringue a trois*, that crowd of three. Before the statues topple off their plinths, as they inevitably do, father was right up there, potent and omnipotent, but this was not so easy for him to handle either. Even in her teens, he would embarrass her in front of her friends, as she sat lolling and wincing in her too-sensitive skin, telling creepy stories about men at the local ferry thinking she was a doll asleep in the back of the car, she looked so beautiful, how admired she was, how forward, how civilised. Daughter in Wonderland. But as Alice said: 'Now Kitty, let's consider who it was that dreamed it all. This is a serious question, my dear, and you should not go on licking your paw like that...' He was part of Molly's dream, of course, but then she was part of his dream too. It takes two.

How can you unpick and sew at the same time? Molly's father would tell her awkward smirking adolescent friends how her ma and she looked like sisters, how people mistook them for sisters, how much he loved them both...while Molly's intestines curled in gradually overheating shame, she still wondered. Was she really her mother's sibling, rival for her father's love? If they were to be sisters, then his daughter was still his woman too. Daddy's sweetheart, from the beginning.

Molly ground her teeth and made a resolve to be as unlike her mother as it was possible to be: a resolve based then on clothes and colours. Her mother, and didn't many of them then, wanted her daughter to dress in the same way as she did herself, a pigeon pair like those that smirked on the side of the soap packets. But apricot twin-sets made of some newly minted marvellous man-made fibre sent shudders all the way through her daughter struggling mightily to have a separate sense of self. Trips to her mother's hairdresser, where the obsequious man tried to find a lurking curl in rudely straight hair were a demand she finally refused, (how she grew to hate the roaring sound of a room full of cavernous hair dryers, hot air holes clasping the heads of women studded with rows of spiky rollers which held the promise of unfolding curls and dreams). The torture of once having her eyebrows ripped off in the name of beauty at the local department store (her mother had plucked her own almost into non-existence, perhaps in homage to the mystique of Marlene Dietrich) confirmed what might have been previously a shaky resolve. It was so important to be different, to call her soul her own.

This same department store sent out in a dark green van direct to the queen mother armfuls of clothes, to try on at home, 'on approval'. At home they would be left in casual disarray over the backs of armchairs and sofas, a stylish mess, and her mother would languidly try them on, over several days, swaying and bending critically in front of a long mirror, before sending most of them back. Molly wondered often if she too were 'on approval'—when would it be her turn to be a reject?

Sort it out, like with like, colour with colour, shades of doubt and disillusion. Underneath, as she grew older, she reflected, she perhaps grew more and more like her mother in some if not many respects, perhaps her son would know. But would he say? The truth, if there is any, is hard to find.

There was, of course, there was bound to be, a terrible future cost to this apparently unashamed paternal adoration. Molly struggled with it, and resentment grew elsewhere in the family plot.

We need to remember that future demands for knowledge may take quite different forms from those that appear to be of interest to us right now. Each generation asks different questions that in turn prompt even more. There's a constant process of editing, of discovering, of new understandings; the stories shift, change and float free with each retelling.

Holding forth again, are you? Don't you ever stop?

Take a deep breath they recommend, when you are interrupted, and carry on.

She has to work, as they say, don't they, in the available light.

Chapter Three

In which Molly herself enters the narrative, as a three year old, told by her adult self, or one of them, starting to become concerned about who she is, and how she is seen by others. Vestiges of war hover in her dreams, 'germs' and 'Germans' are hopelessly confused, and her hero father assumes grand proportions in her mind.

The question keeps coming—how can Molly work on these fragments, from the point of view of her child and adult selves? Display procedures involve the canny use of colour and light. Then damaged objects can deceive the eye of the casual observer into seeing them as whole.

Perhaps she should be allowed a little of her own voice? Will the 'I' tell us something different? She is struggling and straining, tapping and moaning a bit, wanting to get out of that constraining box. The lid's fixed down but she is rattling at the catch, and you can see part of an eye staring angrily through the tantalising fragment between the sides and the top of the well-made prison. She's more than ready to speak.

Oh, all right, just for a while, mind.

And by the way, although her name is Molly, it was Margaret at the beginning, after one of her father's favourite sisters.

But Molly ever after.

Go on then. Do a bit of holding forth.

The sarcasm is inescapable.

That's probably her mother talking.

So many voices, so many characters inside, milling around.

Hah! Out she pops from the box. The shock of air in the lungs, painful, searing, then the relief of a place to breathe...

Do I recall this deliverance before?

No, I don't need notes. I'll just pull and it will all come out.

A bit like a magician pulling coloured scarves from his sleeve?

But it's not magic, is it, just liberated bits and pieces.

It won't be very tidy, but why should you be in a box before you die?

My first months coincided with the tail-end of the war years. My parents' home, stuck out on the pregnant bump of Britain called East Anglia, the most easterly point of our island, scoured by the North Sea, was beyond the defence lines. We were unprotected, if enemy swarms elected to attack this unpromising coast. No Man's Land.

No Man's Land. First noted, like the house where we lived, in the Little Domesday book: *nonnesmaneslande,* unclaimed and unprotected. It took another thousand years until the First World War for a correspondent to take up this haunting phrase. The land between the lines, where a tangle of dead bodies from both sides lay draped across the swaying wire. A deadly strip.

Human beings had lived precariously on this coast for millennia—- nine-hundred and fifty of them, and counting. Early Britons, with their little sharp flinty tools for cutting and sawing at the precarious path of life, lived alongside sabre toothed cats and mammoths. Cave paintings deep in the heart of a mountain in France, inside mother earth's mysterious body, show how these early beings worshipped the strength and grace of the huge animals they lived alongside. Living outside of our historical constraints, and without our arrogance, they dreamed of taking on those qualities. The only human form in this huge temple of desire is of a woman being impregnated by a huge beast. *Homo antecessor,* otherwise known as pioneer man, left some of his tools in the earth, at a time when the earth's magnetic poles were reversed. He hung on in there as human beings do, while the earth moved slowly and without malice towards an ice-age. Pakefield and Happisburgh, close to where I lived, held some of the tools of *antecessor*'s trade.

The village on the edge of which lay our house, surrounded by its land, extending to the North Sea cliffs, had been an agricultural community, essentially unchanging for hundreds of years, until the latter half of the twentieth century exacted its toll. Its population increased only very slowly, as the drift away from the land to better paid jobs in towns and the importing of grain from America slowly put paid to the natural growth of flourishing generations. When I was a child, our own land was surrounded by that of my three uncles and one cousin, on their own respective farms, so that wherever you looked, the land was looked after by my family.

Unlike mid-ocean islands, Britain is called an offshore island, still linked under the sea to its nearest continent. Dogger Bank, in the North Sea, is a plateau only sixty feet below sea level, and it was dry land in relatively recent times. Undersea discoverers found relics of forests and the Stone Age animals that sheltered in them, as well as of our forefathers and mothers, struggling to survive the eastern blasts. If Hitler had invented the technology, he could have walked to the Britain he so wished for as the final prize.

While the worst of the war was over by 1944, there were still the final stages to withstand. There was an air-raid shelter in one of the farm's numerous yards; (the stack yard, the bullock yard, the horse-yard). This Anderson shelter, named after its inventor, with its sheets of corrugated iron, was sunk into a deep hole, in theory to withstand bombardment. Many a night I was, so I was told, bundled out and into it, as the enemy planes droned overhead. My mother told of snipers popping shots at her from their homeward-bound planes as she hung out the washing in the yard next to the shelter, on two beautiful long linen lines, holding a gradually increasing phalanx of pillow cases, shirts, dresses and handkerchiefs, with two tall forked wooden props made by my father to hold up their sagging middles as they swung in the wind. I've always loved the look of washing on a line, and can see my ma, bright skirts blowing and her mouth full of pegs, hauling up the sheets while I poke hog-weed through the netting of the rabbits' and the ferrets' cages nearby. Linen galumphing and dancing on the line with its own life, cracking in the wind and arguing with it, air and cloth going through the motions, knowing what has to be done.

While she shook, straightened and pegged, I would squat on bright days and smell the green angelica which grew thickly round the rabbit cages, competing with the nettles, and pull at the scrubby weeds sprawling from the cracks in the concrete beneath the linen lines. Next door to the rabbits, black, white and brown, in the cruel irony of captivity, lived the golden ferrets, which my dad took with him when he went shooting. Then the sky would rain with falling bodies, a shower of meat, and meat would be drawn too from deep rabbit burrows beneath the earth. Wings flapped in a steep rise of panic, and warm bodies were reversed by a shot into terminal free-fall. Burrows like ghettos were systematically purged.

Let the dog see the rabbit! Tails furiously wag, barks crescendo into the crisp blue air.

Let the ferret see him too! Tip the wily fellow from his bag, and he slides eagerly down the next hole.

Many years later I saw my brother as a young man weep when he took a sack of golden still-warm bodies from the back of his car. The ferrets had been killed by exhaust fumes. Something beautiful had died. His tears were perhaps about more than ferrets, as we shall see. The ancestors of these unlucky ones, when we were still children, could snuff the rabbit smell which came from the cages of their ancient prey close by them. The jills and the hobs, the bucks and the does.

My ma told me too about a Morrison shelter, designed by one Herbert Morrison, hip-high with a metal top, that stood in the large kitchen, 'like a monkey's cage' and of how she and my father would put me in it, sleeping in my carry cot, and go out the side door with the stained-glass panels to watch the doodle-bugs doodle-bugging by. These unmanned German flying bombs were destined for London. They made a distinctive droning sound, falling haphazardly when they ran out of fuel. You knew they would fall when the noise stopped. Not so much 'smart' in those far-off days, but exhausted. The last doodle-bug, chuntering its aimless way over the North Sea in March 1945, was brought down by anti-aircraft guns off the bleak Suffolk coast. The end of the war now seemed more than a pious hope.

After the war was over and I had sturdy legs to take me foraging around my territory, I found in the dust under the wooden stairs which led to the granary two gas-masks, like the husks of two long-dead monsters, witness to the fear of a silent, deadly destruction which might infiltrate the pure sea air we breathed. There were long months to be lived until the war ended in Europe, on May 7 1945. Then, one anxiety conquered, another would rise to take its place. The age of collective insecurity between the wars, and the concern about totalitarianism with its inevitable outcome in war, gave way to the age of anxiety about a new threat, the nuclear cloud. Is there never a way out? I doubted this, as with my own small perspective I dreaded the demons out there and the ones lurking and leering in my own mind.

'Germans'. Who or what they were I had no idea, but they permeated my thinking from that preverbal time when they ruled our lives and disturbed our sleep. My father had a camp of Italian prisoners of war to help him on the farm, bussed in from a local town each day, and he used to shoot rabbits for them to put in their stew-pot over the fire. He admired their cheerful resourcefulness, which had something in common with the more hopeful parts of himself. He was in the 'Home Guard', since as a farmer his war effort was to keep the acres productive. He was one of those left behind to till the land for whomever came afterwards, to keep the earth fresh and welcoming for new seed. He found it all a bit of a joke, and would plead calving cows as an excuse to skip drill. But nevertheless he was awarded a brass medal fixed on a red and black striped stiff ribbon, 'For Faithful Services in the Special Constabulary'.

While the country was heavily rationed, with eggs and jam, butter, meat, cheese and tea being doled out only in minute quantities on a strict points system, lorries loaded to the brim with bags of sugar would arrive in our yard, deals would be struck, and although my mother refused to eat corned beef ever after because it reminded her of those pinched and skimpy years, we clearly had a better time of it than many.

But she was not to be seduced by recipe suggestions for 'corned beef hash' (the very name denotes its desperation, a hash indeed). It was mixed up with onions and potatoes, formed into an omelette shape when 'nicely browned' and served, but of course on a hot dish, as if that might heat up this ghastly concoction, with a sprinkling of parsley to hide its essential loathsomeness. Even more outlandish, you could serve it with cooked peas on a bed of lettuce leaves, with a French dressing. *Non merci*!

For fear of the invasion and vehicles being commandeered by the enemy, people surrendered their distributor caps and cars were immobilised. But there was an agricultural petrol allowance, coloured red to show the difference, and my father's travels were not inhibited by fear of Germans. These 'Germans' hovered over my young later life however like an ever-present threat. I would fear a German leaping out at me from behind the great barn doors, hidden by a great grey iron helmet, bayonet at the ready. I had dreams of barrage balloons, looming like deformed eggs above my nightmare world. Later my dreams, emerging like the stars at night but always, always there, were of flying and falling, wading through mud in flight from the unknown enemy. In bed at night, strange contradictory sensations, I was huge, I was mighty, or I was tiny, dwarfed by the universe. Germs were mixed up with Germans, noxious and alien. The Germans I heard the adults talking about took up residence in the world inside my mind, and, like sponges, collected all my fears into a great quivering shivering mass. Shiver and shake, deny and burn.

Then after the war there came to our house the German *au pairs*, Frieda and Celia, whose stout smiling kindness made restitution, at least in my mind, for their nations' previous misdeeds.

The wider world too was then in turmoil.

William Beveridge's 'Full Employment for a Free Society', as well as the Education Act the same year, began a short period of social solidity coming out of shared suffering.

But 1944 had seen the publication of T. S. Eliot's *Four Quartets*. He complained of the slipperiness of words, breaking under the burden of what he wanted to say. Others too were in despair.

'I have tried to help others to understand life' wrote Edvard Munch, who knew so much about the silent scream. He died in 1944, even while popular songs were insisting 'Accentuate the Positive, Don't Mess with Mr In-Between', 'Swinging on a Star', 'Sentimental Journey', 'Don't Fence me In'. Munch's mother had died when he was five, and his older sister a few years later. Like Yeats before him, he remembered little of his childhood except its pain.

The screaming figure in his picture stands, hands over ears, with dead blank eyes and open mouth, on a lurid path beside the lurid streaming sea, waves bending and wavering in a terrifying sepulchral light. Only in the far distance lie calmer waters, and two other figures, perhaps of parents, are walking away. Even though Munch himself tied this moment to a specific event, and the two figures look male, his earlier history might lead a person to deeper conclusions. When he described his picture, he talked of tongues of fire and blood in the sunset. He saw the scream in nature, but it could have been a reflection of his own agony.

Henry Moore, by contrast, was already working on his 'Madonna and Child'. He called it a 'fundamental obsession', made in brown Hornton stone, after he had served his time as an Official War Artist. Eric Newton wrote that same year 'She, the Madonna, is not part of an art revival but a stage in art evolution. Therefore a century hence, whatever may have happened to Christianity, she will have lost none of her potency. She will be seen not as an example of Henry Moore's sculpture but of a deep seriousness somehow inherent in the mid-twentieth century'.

Although I sat balanced on the arm of my mother's chair in that early photograph, with my toes slightly curled, as if a bit uncertain of my balance even then, this child carved in blooming brownish solidity, sits squarely on his mother's lap, her right hand holds his shoulder, her left hand grasps his left hand. Perhaps Eric Newton was right: the very solidity of the pose is a mid-century certainty even in time of war. But in 1944 Primo Levi was deported to Auschwitz, and while my parents were eating corned beef, thousands of Jews and Romanies were being wiped out. 'Human memory', as Levi said, 'is a marvellous but fallacious instrument. This is a threadbare truth known not only to psychologists but also to anyone who has paid attention to those around him, or even to his own behaviour. The memories which lie within us are not carved in stone; not only do they tend to become erased as the years go by, but often they change, or even increase by incorporating other features'.

The past's not behind us, it's all around us, memories knocking, shoving, squeaking behind the door. We can be muddied by it, buried in it, suffocated by it, before we can be free of it, if we ever are. There is a constant interplay between our unreliable selves, and the characters we make up out of ourselves, and others.

The trouble in our family really started, so my mum told me darkly years later, when I began to walk. I was a late walker, not wanting perhaps to walk out of this renewed perfect bubble where I sat enthroned as the ideal little-girl baby, clean, dry, the babbling apple of the parental eye. Walking turned out to be a sin never forgiven. Sixty years later Ma could dismiss her frequent coldness because of the crime of separation. We all need to leave our mothers. 'But you went away' was what she said.

Yes. Partly I went to fulfil their hopes, but partly too to escape the life of fire and ice. My parents were also trapped between two ideas, pinched perpetually in the vice of that contradiction. A daughter stays at home, to carry on the family. Such a one must beware of being 'over-educated'—above herself. But if a daughter leaves, she fulfils her potential and other, different parental hopes. If I had stayed, I would still have felt an exile, from something which I felt lay outside the little world I knew. That old nostalgia for the cosy womb had let me down before. Yet I took my homeland with me, more than my parents could ever understand. Paradise is the world we leave. The fruits of the Knowledge tree open up new worlds, and in any case the Cherubim now guards the gate of the garden. No going back.

What would I have really made of life at home if I'd stayed? Would I have been stunted, even annihilated, by those grasping roots? I escaped, yes, from the too-tight bonds of this family place, to grow what I might have thought of as a true self. But I left a lot behind. As the old fairy tales tell us, leaving home is an honourable and necessary step, to 'make your fortune'; new discoveries get made, the quest for the 'something else' goes on, and if you're lucky you find out what that might be.

There is a cliché, one of those phrases you can slip in to your thoughts, convenient, prevents further thinking—an easy slide. And yet a cliché, an old printing term, has become a cliché because it was once, and maybe is always, describing something true. Does it take the first forty years to escape home, and the next forty to get back? Stepping out, and stepping back.

Walking is hazardous but essential for the expansion of the personal world. Before it becomes as automatic as any of our other later skills, it involves quite a lot of working out. My earliest memory, was it a memory, or maybe something just told to me, yet I've got the feeling, bodily, of how it was then, is of half-crawling and half-staggering out to the coal-shed where my dad was filling the coal-scuttle in the twilight. There was no electricity for us till I was three or four. There I am, crawling towards the object of my desire at the centre of my infant universe, with filthy hands and knees. I have a camera angle on it, tight-shot, almost floor level, as I look up at him, I seem to sense still how it was to be so powerless and so drawn to this hero of mine.

Many heroes, as Horace observed, lived before Agamemnon, but were unknown because 'they lacked a dedicated poet'. I told my cousin that my dad could kill lions; acting as hunter and protector in the unpredictable jungles, inner and outer. I believed he really could, although all I'd actually seen him kill was a huge rat cornered in the cowshed. He attacked it with a pitchfork, and in its brave and reckless terror it tried to fly up and bite him in the neck. As it died it screamed.

There was no contradiction for me between this fierce implacable father and the one who hugged me to his chest.

The rat-catcher used to come at least twice a year to set baits of Warfarin to kill off King Rat's progeny. But they multiplied notwithstanding, and in their last years that same poisonous Warfarin helped both my parents' blood flow less thickly in their veins. Strange to think poison too has its different uses, but either way it ends in death.

I needed to see him as warlike, although most of my memories are of his gentleness, the man who took bread and milk to the spitting wildcat kittens who lay in their warm dark litters behind the beams that edged the cowshed walls, the man who often came in holding something under his jacket; a kitten, a puppy, a chick, a bird fallen out of a nest, 'full floppers', he called them, no longer quite babies but not able yet to use their wings, flopping helplessly along the ground.

My ma had been apparently an only child. This was an unsolved mystery to me: did my grandmother have miscarriages or no sex? Or was her one experience of birth, which my ma said she did not know about, too horrific to persuade her to let the selfish gene have its way a second time? It was not until my mother's final months, when I unearthed a book of 'snapshots' left me by my grandmother years before, that I wondered something different.

There was a small shot of my grumpy mother, aged perhaps between fifteen and eighteen months, or even younger, seated at the foot end of a pram. The black fuzzy head of the baby at the other end drew no recognition from her old lady self; this was the only character in the whole of that lovingly collated little book that she could not identify. No searching of birth records provided an answer. Perhaps this child died before the record had been made, six weeks allowed in those days too after birth, and before official recognition as a member of the human race.

Had my grandmother left me that tantalising if fading clue? There was another small picture, in a silver frame, of my perhaps year-old mother, or so I thought, in her own grandmother's arms, next to my grandmother, who seems to rest her arms protectively over her stomach, in the way pregnant women do. In my mother's last confused days when I talked of the photo she said 'perhaps that baby was not me'. Was she still in the womb's private space? Or maybe this was the sibling who came and went, leaving her with a bewildered guilt that lasted a lifetime. These questions now can have no answers.

But when I asked, in those final days, about her earliest memory, she recalled walking with her own mother, helping her push a pram, and watching the gravel stones kicked up by the wheels hitting the shiny undercarriage with a throb and a rattle.

You raise a lot of interesting thoughts in my head, she said.

The she told me too of walking as a child in the warm summer meadow which lay beside the drive from their house to the road, seeing a white cat asleep under a tree, softly breathing. But when she got close, the breathing was a heaving, and she saw, not soft fur, but a writhing mound of maggots consuming the corpse. She left me stories, finally, but stories with huge holes in them, questions that could never be answered.

My father was one of fifteen, and those fifteen were only alive together for a little time. The second eldest was killed in the First World War when the youngest was scarcely three years old. William Robert fell in what they called the Great War, on May 21st 1918, and it's too late now to know where or how. Missing, presumed dead. Perhaps it broke his mother's heart. Before the battles of Ypres and Aisne, in late May, the Germans had launched their last great offensive, and 350,000 allied troops were killed in the first six weeks. Did he, like so many others, die with the word 'mother' borne on his last breath? 'I have slain none except my mother' as the Kipling ballad goes, 'She died of grief for me'. They died like cattle, so Wilfred Owen said. Did William fall at a single shot, or did he have time to die, slowly, much less prized than one of his father's bullocks? Yet another poet, Edward Thomas, called the whole enterprise 'one designed to turn young men to dung'. The village memorial to this young Lance Corporal records that he is buried in a cemetery in the Pas de Calais. But 'missing, presumed dead' is what my old aunt told me.

Maybe the fat lazy flies buzzed over his body, as he lay tangled with his battle-fallen friends in a gruesome and decomposing sculpture of death, one of so many un-named exhibits in that squalid gallery of war. An overwhelming stench still lies over it all, overlaying the passion and the always doubtful glory of war, even while some of the women folk back home were encouraging their men to volunteer. The feared white feather symbolising cowardice drove the men on, and there's no record to tell if William's family encouraged or discouraged him from his path to eternity. Did they say, stay home on the farm, boy, or did they admire his kit as he set off on his big adventure? How did his father say goodbye? Maybe just a strong pat on the back as his second eldest marched off down the curving drive, out of the farm gate and into the distance under an uncertain sky. The last of the veterans of this war died in the early twenty-first century. 'I've seen devils coming up from the ground. I've seen hell upon this earth', he said.

There were child deaths and early adult deaths, and it wasn't until the year of my birth that the first 'blue baby' operation took place, when the blood supply to the lungs of a female infant was replaced. Two of my father's sisters died in late childhood for lack of this operation, coming much too late alas for them. There were in any case too many children to help my dad feel cared about, even if he was. Laugh and the world laughs with you, he would say. Cry, and you cry alone. He used to joke that he couldn't remember all their names when I asked, avid for detail, about his family, 'Annie, Diddy, Benny, Bobby, Ikey, Ernie, Tot and Sid, Polly, Jack and Fanny'. Although in truth each child was given two solid Victorian names, the eldest only bearing his mother's maiden name, and this first child was born a decade before the twentieth century began.

Who was your favourite, Dad?

The one that got away...

It was this oldest son who, on returning home from Canada where he had bought a farm, after he had been sent away following the disgrace of a pregnant dairymaid, rescued my six-year-old father who was spluttering and drowning head first in the huge iron tank, an old ship's boiler, which gave water to the heifers in the cattle yard. I too would lean over its thick rusty sides, trying to see the one large goldfish, grown beyond the regulation small glass bowl size, sailing in mighty splendour around his dark domain. Did I want to be rescued? No, perhaps that simile doesn't hold water, but I thought about my little boy dad, saved by his hero.

This eldest son, a romantic faraway uncle to me, a mysterious 'black sheep', arrived unannounced when I was scarcely seven. He took me off immediately to admire the view from the old church tower; something normally strictly forbidden. The ruins of this mediaeval monument to God, dating from end of the eleventh century when the first monk was appointed to read the service there, stood in the centre of the village, surrounded by ancient gravestones, while the new nineteenth century church built after fire destroyed its predecessor, stood by the side of the busy main road at the other end of the village, a scarcely noticeable sign on the route from one town to another.

According to a contemporary nineteenth century account, it was early in the year, one dry and gale-torn January, when sparks from the old church's stove started a fire after the morning service. It roared through the church tower like a chimney, consuming everything, including a dozen coats of whitewash from the walls, revealing momentarily more brilliantly painted patterns underneath. Some fishermen tried at least to save the organ, but in their enthusiastic but limited zeal, they got stuck in the porch, because no-one had the wit to dismantle the organ pipes, and the instrument perished.

I used to wander in the old churchyard (you could carefully if sometimes painfully squeeze through the hedge from one of my dad's fields trying not to tear your skirt and knickers on the thorns) and pick buttercups to put on the tombstones of my dead grandparents and their already dead children. My own parents' silent disapproval of my uncle's transgression over the tower was an adequate reason for me never to climb it again. But the thrill of the rather limited view it had offered me that one time still reminds me nevertheless of the value of sometimes going beyond limits set by sensible people, just to see what you can see.

Dad's full floppers, ejected too soon from the nest, fallen and frightened, touched something in him, and he would put them by the fire and feed them. Many died. He was frankly paranoid about human beings. He told me early in my life to trust nobody, one day when a friend who was to meet me on her bike for a picnic didn't show up, me with my sandwiches hopefully packed in a red and gold biscuit tin strapped to the back of the bike. He saved his concern and understanding for animals. Sticks and stones, he would intone, can break your bones, but words can never hurt you. I could only wonder at how he had been so hurt by words that he'd forgotten what it felt like. This extravagant pessimism about his fellow human beings induced a correspondingly extravagant optimism in me, not always the best foundation for a realistic grip on life. Hope as a retreat, hope as a prison, hope which only made me feel helpless against implacable reality. It became a pathology, another trap, a desperate little boat to sail in. It was a hope that would be shipwrecked many times before I could acknowledge its inherent hopelessness.

But he also said , don't let the sun go down on your anger. Even then I puzzled over this contradiction, doubtful counterweight to the mass of his anger and despair. It was only when we ran and skipped together that I really felt some joy in him, surging up from his childhood, as he would grab my small hand in his huge one and plunge forward. 'A-deedle-de-deedly-de-de-de-dee', he would sing out, as we veered and careered down the curving drive. There we were, two delirious kids for a few minutes, with not a care in sight or mind

His tales, which I always meant to record, but never did, were wonderful. He told of horses, his father's speciality had been in breeding heavy horses, and dogs. There was the one about the fierce dog that no-one dared go near. My father simply got down on his hands and knees and barked back. The dog was subdued and followed him slavishly.

My father reached right down into the well of the past and brought up treasure for us. The jewel in his story-telling crown was the Bonzo series, tale upon tale of his favourite black curly-coated dog, a mixture of breeds but pure devotion in character. My hero father had motor bikes, a Norton, an Ariel, an ASA, and Bonzo would ride pillion. How was this so? How did this uberdog know to grip on? Did Dad have to go super-slow, or was his bike steady as an armchair as he rode up and down the country roads? Bonzo was his constant companion and, unlike human beings, he never let him down.

Over and over I would ask for the last story, the day that Bonzo was too old to live. Tears would roll down my cheeks as he told it, how Bonzo, old, weak, almost blind, almost too tired to eat, was given his favourite last meal.

He slowly drags himself to the dog bowl. As he puts his head down and begins to eat, my father levels his loaded shotgun, his own eyes full. Bonzo lifts his great head, looks at my father directly in the face, then carries on eating. They had been partners in life and Bonzo, my father thought, was still honouring the partnership. He buried him in the meadow opposite the house, where later, after rows of caravans in the nineteen-sixties, stood rows of 'commuter homes'.

Dad like the Ancient Mariner was compelled to tell and retell his stories over and over, compelled too by his children. Tell us again, dad, tell us again. The repetition magnified each event, and it would become larger and more powerful each time. Stories are there to be told, to be changed, and that will never end. It's the human way, to decorate our lives, to gather together our sadness and our conflict, our grief and our joy. We never tire of the old, said Kirkegaard, and if his stories tied Dad in some way to inevitable death, as Freud suggested, and isn't that a typically pessimistic view, they also gave him continual life. They seemed to take care of us all.

His mind was peopled with individuals we didn't know, still ranged inside to be called on at the appropriate time. If we dropped something 'throw it down again, old Siddie!' he would chant in amusement, but who clumsy old Siddie was, we never asked. 'Out of the way, Buckie Hoy!' he would teasingly say as he made room for himself with his elbows at the kitchen table to butter some bread. He had a nickname for most people, Dick Spit, Wizard, Rabbit, Uncle Perkus, so that to me at least, our lives had a story-book feel, where we, of course, were the main characters.

Our village seemed full of a vivid cast of people, with names ripe for translation into myth: the Steptoes, the Snowlings, the Godbolds and the Windsheffles, the Catchpoles, the Kettlasses and the Proudfeet. I learned at school about the way names had been attached to trades: the Bakers and the Butchers, the Millers, the Carters, the Drivers, the Weavers, the Thatchers, even the Walkers. We didn't seem to have any of those, but the village had survived without them, it seems, built from a more vividly named cast of everyday heroes.

He had had extravagant ideas, this old man, some prescient too. He was an H.G. Wells of his small time and space. He talked of covered holiday centres for tourists to be protected from the weather, commonplace as an idea and actuality now. He even applied for permission to put up a huge store, forerunner of the carpet of hypermarkets covering the country. This, he hoped, could be built on a collection of our barley filled expanses. 'No demand', was the verdict of the planning committee, and Dad turned back to his own world and away from these larger visions, of great machines which could harness clouds for rain when you wanted it. This was another of his big ideas, and was of course a farmer's dream.

When he was an old man in a hospital bed, he lay fiddling with his bent and mottled old fingers in some complicated intricacy.

I watch for a while.

What are you doing, Dad?

He smiles, weakly, almost with apology.

I'm making a halter, he whispers. The whisper still echoes somewhere.

His fingers continue to move, but more confidently now.

He was trying to reconnect, it seemed to me, with the old life on the farm, where he knew what to do and when to do it. This was his search for his old authentic self, his place. He was a bit like John Grout, in Ronald Blythe's portrait of a Suffolk village, *Akenfield*. Grout was a farmer's son who ran away to London for what he hoped would be a better life, but he hated it. 'There was a place in Broad Street Station where you could stare through the arches and see the stars. That's the only thing I remember about London'. Loss permeated my father's life, too, and it accelerated as he aged.

Dogs remained a vital part of his life, and all our lives. He had a profound respect for their differing personalities, their sensitivities, their intuitions and their needs. There was George, a beautiful dalmation dandy so highly sexed he howled on the end of a leash, until the vet's knife cut out his passions. There was Nixie and her progeny down the line, she a gentle little wire-haired terrier, so unlike most of her breed, who seemed to me to have a similar temperament to our dear Gladys, who cooked the lunch. Nixie looked after a succession of demanding puppies with a kind of amused resignation, as they snuffled and butted around her dugs. And there was Bill, another Beau Brummel with an impressive pedigree, passed on from a family where they hadn't been able to manage his impulsive ways.

Animals for my father became invested with characteristics he clearly found it harder to discern in human beings, for his own reasons. He told of the cow who was in love with my mother: and used to cry huge real tears until she came out to stroke it. There was a string of cats, whose names, once so vivid in my memory, now escape me utterly, who did marvellous things and were devoted to their master and mistress. 'Greylugs' comes into my mind: but what he did and why he was remembered by them, I no longer know.

After the death of Bonzo, although we had so many other dogs, only two seemed able to enter my father's heart. There was the gentle Nixie, the good mother, the only dog allowed indoors, who sat under the table and licked up the remains from my father's plate, and there was Tiger, a feistier Jack Russell who was the last in this long line, before my father was persuaded by my mother to give up his identity as a dog-owner. Maybe that was the beginning of his own end. Unlike it had been with Bonzo, my father was then too old to take the responsibility of what to do. Tiger, still a healthy dog, was put down by the vet and my small son Sam was devastated at his first encounter with death.

No! He waves his hands dramatically, then lets them fall, helpless in front of something he knows now, for the first, real, time.

He had spent happy hours sitting beside Grand-dad in one of his series of little sheds, built with flair and skill on open ground round the back of the farm, from his own daily scavengings on the beach. Tiger was always at their side. It felt, Sam said, like the place on earth it was simply good to be.

No! Now he waves his arms to wave the news away, to try and stop the changing world, his own death, and the death of those he loves.

The bones of all these whispers of life lay around the farm, buried, remembered, now forgotten. *Lion, fish and swan Act and are gone Upon Time's toppling wave*. Isolated incidents remain in my memory, like the time when the bull trapped one of the farm men behind a five-barred gate and tried to gore him; when my father had to subdue Stormer, the huge heavy horse, last of the cohorts of previous years, as he reared and tried to stampede in the walnut meadow. There was a chaos of huge flailing hooves, and my father, small in comparison and fearless, stood steadily talking and calming him down, whispering into Stormer's ears, as his father had taught him to do, as all horsemen did, hardy old sorts that they were, often living to a great age. An Alsatian went mad one day, frothed at the mouth, and had to be shot. It was a breed my father had never trusted and we never had another. Just after that, I saw my father peeing in the nettle clump that stood by the old railway carriage he used as a workshop, where heaps of untidy nuts and bolts and nails and screws grew and multiplied, accumulating dust and oil, speaking silently of new enterprises perhaps some day, or at least a solution to one of life's minor problems, and with a smell I've never forgotten. I hadn't seen him pee outside like that before, and I was shocked as well as admiring of this open display as he stood with his back to me and sprayed a controlled arc into the green tangle. Flies buzz above the maze of nettles; buzz and buzz.

And then there was Nip, the ginger Manx cat with a stubby inch of tail, with whom I used to share my Easter egg each year as I sat in holes in the hawthorn hedge on warm spring days. Nip had a pink nose, covered with minute dark freckles. He seemed like a human being to me, so knowing and understanding. In the summer, Nip used to go walkabout, leaving the farm for the open road, taking his chances and having, I assumed, grand adventures. Yes, you can tell winter is coming when the clocks go back and the evenings start at teatime, but for me winter had not arrived until Nip appeared one autumn day in a ginger halo on the outside kitchen windowsill, rubbing himself up and down the glass, deigning for the winter months to be dependent on kitchen scraps and the inevitable standby bread and milk, which my father, too, used to eat for breakfast; cutting great chunks of white bread and eating it in a bowl of hot milk with spoons and spoons of white sugar. Pussy Cat, Pussy Cat, where have you been? Then, one winter, Nip did not return.

Each winter Dad entertained a tramp called Rodney, who stayed a few weeks in one corner of the huge corn barn, with sacks for bed covering, before wandering off again. My father respected Rodney, and told me that if ever my mother died, he too would take to the roads. In this scenario, what would have happened to his children evidently didn't figure, and somehow I didn't resent it. One winter, like Nip, Rodney with his red scarf bag and his knobbly stick failed to return. Dad always gave the time of day to Wry Nick, whose mother still looked after him even though he was an adult. Nick would garble something back, jerking his bony head on his thin shoulders. Dad had a soft spot too for Gordon, also a relatively young man, who walked with a stick and cast wild looks around as he talked to invisible companions. 'Not right in the head' the villagers said. 'A bit touched'. Touched by what? Well he was certainly different, but who was right, I wondered, really right? Gordon still lived with his mother, Mrs Steptoe, in a tipsy little cottage with an untidy garden opposite the old church, riotous with orange nasturtiums in summer time, and it was his sister, Edie-Beedie Button Boots, my father called her, who would come to baby-sit before my parents considered we could manage the job ourselves. Gordon rather frightened me, and his incessant conversations seemed as threatening as the gabbling of the geese, though in truth he hardly noticed me. Rodney, Gordon and Wry Nick seemed to represent to my dad separate states of existence: that of having no mother, or of not being able to leave her. Was that being 'not right in the head'?

My dad had always wanted a mother to himself. In his old age he let my mother take over his life and his powers to make even simple decisions like what to eat in a restaurant. 'My wife orders for me', he would declare grandly to the waiter, as he fingered his tortoiseshell reading glasses lying beside the unread menu. This short speech was delivered with pride, as though this lordly relinquishment of his own capacity to choose were a triumph of civilised behaviour. But there was another side to this. He ate my mother's food, her 'concoctions' as he called them, sometimes with a grudging declaration of enjoyment, but there always seemed some resentment underlying his compliance, as he moved the food suspiciously round his plate. In truth he preferred a simple dish of bread and milk.

In a train one day, as I travelled down from the city to see my parents in the time-honoured way, I sat opposite an old couple. The man read the newspaper and gently allowed himself to be mothered. His wife poured the powdered milk into his tea and stirred it, opened the biscuit bag and gave him one. This old lady in the train seemed to be ageing alongside her husband, companionably, and he could take what she offered in a less oppositional spirit, whereas at the end of their lives my parents were locked in a more desperate dance of to and fro, proffering and rejecting. On the train, this man's old hands, mottled and brown and gnarled, reached right into my heart.

'*So all day long the noise of battle rolled*', as my dad used to declaim, from Tennyson's *Idylls of the King*, '*among the mountains by the winter sea*'.

Why do we call a stroke a stroke? Where is the gentleness? Our old man was stroked by death and went obediently into his kennel. Heel. Just like that only slowly, blood on the carpet and three days dying from that magisterial command. 'I shall always think that he died at home' rang out my mother's icy voice at the hospital bedside, and he finally got the message, creeping with resignation into that cold place, leaving his dropped dead jaw to be tied up and tidied away. Such a brief episode in the record of last hours. She gave him the orders, even then, and part of him in any case, if he had stayed at home, would indeed have liked to die, if die he must, in the same bed onto which he had been born.

When the family stood on the shining parquet floor in the front hallway and the hearse came slowly down the curved drive with my father's body, that mute dead thing which destroyed our dailiness with its harsh reality, I thought how much he would have preferred to be mingled with Bonzo's crumbled remains in the old meadow before it had been consumed by the thrust of development. But he was carried unresisting to the grave in the churchyard whose position had been chosen by my mother, facing the setting sun, and my mother in her defiantly white suit covered his coffin with rose-petals before it was covered with earth. 'That was so beautiful' said the funeral director, as he walked sideways, thin back aslant to face my poised iconic mother, after the ceremony was done. But to me it felt kitsch, unreal, a play which denied the underlying earthiness of my father's life.

In Irish tradition the dead are buried to face the rising sun. This contemplation of the sunset chosen by my mother seemed to me to be about people looking at the setting of their culture. But one William Russ, a gravedigger, told Ronald Blythe, as he records in *Akenfield*, that it was only the priest who was buried facing west, dressed in his priestly robes, so that he could greet his flock when the resurrection came. While my father was dressed in his best suit, sent to the undertakers by my mother for his laying out, when my mother joined him, she was perhaps wrapped in the usual shroud, as I had not been on hand to chose her last dress. Unless she had left instructions with her carers, who she seemed to love more than either of her children. This is a painful thought, that I didn't deck her out as she might have wanted, in a beautiful dress, a petticoat, sheer stockings and one of her necklaces of pearls. It was another missed possibility which fell deep down into the family split.

Nick nack, paddy-wack, give a dog a bone
This old man came rolling home.

Most days I still remember something this old man did, or what he said.

To bring the dead to life, as Robert Graves said, is no great magic. Blow on a dead man's embers and a live flame will start.

Thomas Hardy wrote his own eulogy, celebrating something of a life fundamentally connected to the natural world, with its hawks and stars... *He was a man who used to notice such things.* The world may be a different place entirely for those who can insert themselves into the natural order we largely ignore now in our love affair with technology. 'Authentic' is the word that comes to mind. Though that's a state easily lost as well, when warring thoughts carry on sparring, in the day and in our dreams, which carry on regardless day and night. Like brave Sir Bedivere at Arthur's death, so Tennyson declaims, I would have spoken at the old man's funeral, but I found not words.

He fell, he died. The law of gravity ends in the grave. No levity can escape it. Born and falling, into this world, within this world, under this earth.

But here I go, barrelling on ahead: the baby slow to walk is leaping over the years too fast, rushing headlong into childhood, mixing my father's memories and mine. Years later there was a dream about a baby on a railway line and a fast-approaching train: slow down, sundown, all you really need is time. But the question remains, is there a story here, and to whom does it belong?

Well, should we clap now? That's definitely her mother, metallic tones bright and sharp in the cutting air.

She's been talking so much I can't hear myself think.

Why can't she just be normal?

She thinks too much.

And maybe that's true.

Chapter Four

In which the fourth character enters the family drama. It was a shock in different ways to Molly, her mother and her father when Molly's brother was born. Although Molly learns to live with him, the stage is set for the gradual build-up of sibling battles over a lifetime.

When you are trying to repair and restore this old tapestry, you have to unroll it section by section, so that each piece can be brought to the front for detailed working.

So here, as Freud would say, we have a classic scenario. There is the beautiful child-wife, the heroic husband, man of the land, and the bright button daughter. Can this last, you wonder? Molly's mother was putting on weight, and she went to her doctor for advice about her diet. What did he tell her? That she was pregnant. (Maybe she really didn't know: her periods had always been erratic). She was appalled, aghast, depressed, suicidal, refusing to be tortured again in the service of the implacable gene. And maybe depressed about something else besides. What an awful pregnancy it seemed, though apparently healthy, for Molly's mother and for him, Molly's future little brother slowly and inexorably growing towards the day his reluctant mother so dreaded. This birth was dreaded too by Molly's father. He would gladly give up the idea of a possible son and heir if it meant having to choose again who should live and who should die, as he had been asked to do before. Save my wife, please save my wife.

Even though she wasn't told, did Molly really know somewhere what was going on, didn't she see her mother's changing state? Was this little girl who was usually so eager to see all, hear all, understand all, wilfully turning a blind eye here? Molly was a plump child, with dimpled elbows and dimpled knock knees, fleshed with nourishment and invincibility as well as decorated with blonde come-hither curls which grew in apparently artless wisps framing her chubby cheeks. Her blue eyes challenged the world to contradict her. At least, that was then. Maybe others too were keen not to look, to think, to wonder about something which might have been a problem for them all, each in their own way.

In the event, the birth was easy, 'like podding a pea' Molly's mother said afterwards. Molly had been sent to her aunt's house, at the other end of the village. 'Just for a holiday' her Dad told her, 'You'll be back soon'. So Molly took a little bag packed with toys and books, and off she went. It was a pleasant-enough time, she liked her aunt and uncle and her slightly older girl cousin, who had toys she herself envied: an early Lego building set, taking up one whole corner of the dining room in splendid disarray and a very fine dolls' pram, but no books to speak of. This cousin had a baby brother, James, but he slept in his cot in a corner of the kitchen and didn't seem to bother anyone much. 'You'll have a little surprise when you get home', her aunt said. Oh yes indeed. Surprises were usually fun, and Molly was rather looking forward to this new one. She tumbled with anticipation out of her uncle's open-topped green Jaguar car with the shiny leather seats, grabbing her bag, so glad to be back home.

This is what she sees. She runs through the door, and down the hall, waving something in her hand that she wants to show her dad. She turns right into the dining room, and stops: she stands on the little step before the parquet floor begins. The stone of the step is worn into a curve in the middle by the feet of the generations. The floor beyond seems to ebb away to a new and unknown land. Her heart is beating fast and she doesn't quite know why. Her hand falls from its bright wave.

Come and see who's here. Come and meet your new little brother. This is the news!

Her what?

Over on the other side of the room, far, far away, stood a carrycot on a brass topped table. Out of the carrycot came cries and shrieks. Around the carrycot were clustered—who? Molly no longer remembers, but for her this was a total outrage. He looked scrawny, wriggling, horrible, she

52

thought, when she peered with distaste into his rumpled cot, at his crumpled scarlet face. Slowly and icily words formed in her mind: 'how could they want him when they've got me?' The universe was changing shape.

At Manchester University in that same year something new and revolutionary was installed: a stored-programme electronic computer. The story goes that a moth got into the circuitry, causing the machine to fail. That first real moth 'bug' was the actual ancestor of all the other succeeding metaphorical 'bugs'. Molly's brother was a bug for her: small, insignificant, and yet huge, wiping out the received wisdom of being the only one. This was the cue for the uncertainty principle, and the reality principle.

That was when she decided to be a grownup. This was the end of the line as a child, and the only solution was to skip the difficult bit. She was destined for adulthood, and she was about to take the fast route. Knowledge was power, she recognised that. Grownups had it, she wanted it. They retired behind the pages of the newspaper each day, and it clearly held truths she would steal as quickly as she could.

Her dad is reading today's newspaper, and yesterday's is already stowed in the stick basket to light tomorrow's fire. Molly retrieves it quietly. She spreads it out on the kitchen floor, right in front of the stove, centre stage to show off her 'reading' skill, acquired instantly, by magic. Someone, maybe her mother, very probably her mother, points out that the paper is upside down. Molly shoots her down coolly, 'It's not'. Inside she feels humiliated at least for a moment.

Soon afterwards she was sent to nursery school, though in her own mind she probably thought she herself made the decision, and she determined she would study her way out of this impasse. On the first day her dad took her in the Ford Eight down the bumpy green lane to school. Later her dad could sometimes be persuaded to take her on one of the tractors, to the admiration of her little peers, but on the big first day, only the noble Ford Eight would do, whose shiny green bodywork reflected the overhanging trees as they made slow but steady progress down the lane.

Once arrived, Molly found letters of the alphabet all around the ceiling frieze. She knew she was in the right place, dressed for action in her liberty bodice, a new blouse and skirt, and socks that never stayed white for long.

Molly shared a double desk with a girl called Jackie, whose father was the owner of a chain of local bakeries. This desk wobbled when either of them moved too quickly, and its seat was very hard. But to Molly the shared long seat felt almost like a throne, a place where she would devote herself to the tough new task, and she realised quite soon it would be work and not magic. Once Jackie wriggled so much that Molly fell off her end, but she just climbed back up and carried on. Jackie could write her threes the right way round, but Molly's somehow had a mind of their own and refused as yet to obey their three-year old mistress. Number three was curvy, though tricky in its own way, but number four was altogether different, angular and straight. This number four would be even more of a problem, since the family number too had now increased. She worried about whether she would be able to pull this new trick off, and she drove herself sternly on, determined to rise above the despair she felt when she thought of her rival at home.

In 1543, when Copernicus put forward the shocking idea that the earth moved and went round the sun rather than vice versa, Martin Luther spoke for the outraged world: 'This fool wishes to reverse the entire science of astronomy, but sacred scripture tells us that Joshua commanded the sun to stand still, and not the earth'. For Molly, her parents were the fools, and she, like ousted Joshua, felt so very foolish too. 'Before John' turned into 'After John', and there was no going back. She stood on the brink of a new and uncharted world, and the whitest of socks weren't really of much help.

It was perhaps not so surprising that her parents couldn't help her; the despair was all hers to cope with. Her mother, apparently, had been an only child, never called upon to struggle with the problem, whereas her father, born somewhere near the end of a long line of fifteen children, had simply given up and lost his faith in human beings, and his brother Albert, born only fifteen months later, had left him so little time to be the baby in his mother's lap.

While little Molly had not in the event murdered her mother by her birth, now, she was murderous, and several years later did, (again, apparently), try to push her brother John off a hay-stack. She had also given him, so she was told, many sly pinches as he lay still helpless in his pram.

Tip him out of the pram. Bash him and bash him and bash him. Smother him. Sit on his face and stop him breathing.

Well cats are supposed to do that, they're probably jealous of babies too.

When one of her grand-daughters had a second child, Molly's mother was convinced that the first would murder her new baby sister, though her grand-daughter was sensitive and aware of each child's needs. Hindsight led Molly herself to wonder whether it wasn't her mother's own murderousness all along, deep and forgotten, echoing down the generations as she tried to get rid of it through others. Would there have been a dead baby in that tiny part of history which stamped Molly's mother's early life? It was at least a possibility, as photographs revealed.

It seemed at any rate that Molly's parents' little girl with the curl and the mole in the middle of her forehead had truly changed from being 'very very good' to being horrid. Her jealousy was given no tolerance, not understood nor forgiven, and it lay inside her like a shameful deformity. In the little pink 'Birthday Book' given to Molly by her aunt, there was a rhyme she took quite seriously:

'I've scrubbed so hard to move away
My brown offending mole.
I fear to scrub another scrub
In case I make a hole'

She did scrub off the mole, so her parents said, as she stood on a chair in front of the bathroom mirror, using the stiffest nailbrush she could find, but not the badness that she thought might be inside it, tunnelling away inside her mind.

Bash him, pinch him, push him, kill him. Underground chatter which never seemed to stop. Oh yes she did. Oh no she didn't. The pantomime went on inside—watch out, she's behind you, just wanting to finish you off.

She was in any case tried and found guilty by the judge and jury of the parental court, and whether she would ever be let off for better behaviour was a worry to her. While those still deceptively innocent blue eyes pleaded not guilty, her heart already knew better.

When Molly's own son was a baby, his half brother Daniel, left with him for a short minute when Molly went to fetch a vest warming by the fire, pushed him under the bath-water and crowed anxiously on her return 'I'm teaching him to swim!' The baby lay, curious but somehow not afraid in his new element, with open blue eyes under the water. She snatched him up and shook him to shift the water from his lungs. He coughed and continued. Another ordinary murder had been avoided.

Molly wondered how her own mother had felt towards this apparently unwanted second child. When he was still a baby, John had to be sent to a nursing home because he refused to eat the food his mother offered, just as her husband as an old man would refuse the food she pressed on him. Molly could see her mother, from her own position as a small girl beside her mother's chair, holding the baby on her knee, trying to get him to eat something from a spoon. Resolutely he turns away, mouth clamped shut, implacable, he turns back, bobs up under the spoon and hits his mother inadvertently on the nose with his head. A painful blow. It was a desperate game of chase and dodge.

I don't want it.

I won't have it.

I don't want him, he doesn't want me.

Molly's mother collapses in tears. Baby John is already screaming. Molly is shrinking under the chair, to escape the drama as the decibels increase. This was a weighty moment, a small tragedy repeated over and over as it is in many different lives, often having no place at all in the official family myth. In the end, it seemed nobody could accept Molly's mother's food. Molly might have done, but it had not been offered, at the start of life. Each mother is on her own, with each child. And each child has a different mother.

A few days before her mother's death, Molly was feeding her, as she lay in her bed at home, surrounded by a team of carers who nursed her round the clock.

'That's funny', said her mother. 'You're feeding me now, and once I fed you'.

But not from the breast of her infinite kindness, Molly thought. That had never been available. That's how she remembers it, a different memory from her mother's.

So here again was a beginning weighed down with powerful feelings; the little brother didn't want to take in the thought that he was unwanted, such bitter food to swallow. And it was after this birth that Molly's mother refused to leave the doctor's surgery until he had agreed that she could be sterilised.

Over fifty years later when Molly chanced upon a picture of her brother at his own son's wedding, with a look of someone other than their dad about his face, she wondered too about the shock of his parentage and his birth, and her mother's demand for sterilisation which would guard against any sort of future shock. By God I will never go through that again, Molly's mother must have vowed. Dismay at pregnancy can of course be felt when there is guilty doubt about the baby's father. That's another blank hole in the tapestry here, filled only by a question.

It was during her mother's final weeks before her death that Molly's cousin James said to Molly 'we always thought that Johnny was a misfit'. John's pain was something he could perhaps never release, so he passed it on.

When Molly pictured her brother as a little boy, she remembered his touching knees, two perfect knobbly grubby shapes, and his wish to do cruel things, like tying kittens by the neck to the handlebars of his tricycle, and cutting up worms in his barren garden patch. He relieved Molly from doing anything cruel herself, as she might have wanted to do, and she thrilled with indignation at his acts. He would pile the wormy pieces, some still moving, all up together until he got bored and walked away to find another pastime. Well, as the rhyme says, all little boys do these things, at least in our minds. There is even a picture left, small and faded grey, of this imp with the engaging smile, carrying three wicker egg baskets in his chubby arms.

What are little boys made of?
Snips and snails and puppy-dogs tails.

The puppy-dog's tail she saw when they were bathed together; it was proof of their difference, his otherness. Somehow in her mind it made him seem more vulnerable, this tiny tail which looked as though it could so easily be damaged: damage which in any case she may have wanted to do.

It didn't, as far as she could recall, seem then to be something to feel lost without. Perhaps for both of the children, ejected as we all are from our mothers' bodies, this little 'tail' was less than impressive as an alternative to being inside. Molly's own tentative self-explorations were firmly stopped by her parents, in those oppressive late 'forties days, branded as 'fiddling', and expressly forbidden. This was her parents' idea of a mortal sin. 'Pinwood'! Molly's father would declare firmly at bath-time, as he grasped first one and then the other of them by the hair to wash out their ears, after they had climbed that wooden hill, which led so inevitably to Bedfordshire. It was a process he called 'fying out': and it felt as it sounded, pretty thorough.

When Molly's favourite cat Daisy got her leg caught in a rat-trap she escaped, and trailed her severed leg still attached by a tough thread of skin for weeks before it dropped off. While Molly agonised, her brother taunted Daisy's humiliating affliction and the cat went to hide under a shed. He would eat his own Easter egg or bag of sweets, and think it was then his wheedling right to share his sister's too. Molly had to creep away, outraged yet also somehow still guilty, to enjoy her own treats. But John would find each hiding place, and she would have to scramble out of a hole in the hawthorn hedge to find another spot, down by the pond maybe, or near the turkey pen, because they frightened John even more than they did Molly herself.

She learned to live with him, unlike though they were as Mendel's smooth and wrinkled peas, and she would nurture them both with clumsily made sugar sandwiches when their parents went out, to 'the flicks' maybe, and left them alone. 'Don't eat all the sugar!' their parents would sing in concert as the door was closing. They would leave the children with the TV as a babysitter, and Molly as elder guardian. It was at other, secret times, when she wasn't required to look after him, that Molly would wrestle him to the floor, sit on his torso and threaten to spit in his face. This little boy John, perhaps unwanted from the start, had a lot to struggle with.

The TV had appeared in order to keep John from roaming the beaches, where he loved to watch the fishermen at their lonely sport. He was evidently looking for something. The children watched a glut of American comedies on this marvellous new machine: 'I married Joan', 'I Love Lucy', and they particularly loved the antics of the raucous Sergeant Bilko. They knew by heart all the early commercial jingles for butter, soap powder and boiled sweets.

On one such parentless evening when John had finally taken himself to bed, Molly watched with appalled fascination the pictures of piled-up bodies taken at the liberation of Auschwitz, bodies naked and abandoned in a way which made gaping holes in her understanding of human nature. The son of their old family doctor had been present there, at the liberation, but Molly did not know that then. These naked bodies were the dark side of what Goebbels had called 'the *via triumphalis* of living bodies' that filled the halls at Nuremburg as Hitler found willing ears to hear his rallying call. They entered the theatre of Molly's dreams alongside the other characters already stirring around inside there.

When their parents took them to Norwich, that fine and noble city, where their father would go the cattle market for an afternoon's exhilarating talk with other farmers and flat-capped auctioneers, and their mother to the smart department stores, John and Molly would be left for thrilling hours alone in Norwich castle, which had been turned into a museum. They had a bag of sandwiches, apples, and a drink to share. The children would tiptoe in silent awe past the rows of knights in armour, go to the top floor and hang over the edge to see the sheer size and distance of the entrance hall where incoming visitors looked remote and unreal, and sit beside the glass-walled section of a honey comb, where the worker bees toiled unceasingly. It was a place where they never quarrelled. When their father walked through the vast castle door at the end of the day and called out to them, they would hide away, just for a minute or two, before obediently trailing down from the top floor.

Despite bullying and resentment, out in the open acts as well as secret desires, John and Molly often became allies against the common parental enemy-for-the-day, later to be found sleeping with their arms around one another. They presented a largely united front to the outside world of relations and other vaguely interested adults. Neither of them really cared to remember who had written with their mother's best red lipstick on the airing cupboard floor 'Mum is a fool'—only discovered when the cupboard was taken down to make the hall wider. They shared in silent guilt the knowledge that they had once, but only once, remember, called their mother 'unnatural'. In the world beyond the airing cupboard, these words remained stillborn and frozen. 'Someone is looking for a smack'. 'One, two three, four, five'… The threatening parental countdown which succeeded every time in taming a rebellious act.

At times they were both faced long after lunchtime's end with a detested plate of cold fish and caper sauce, or spongy yellow parsnips, served on the Royal Doulton Countess dinner plates, whose green garlands interspersed with bows and flowered medallions seemed only to emphasis the pallor of the cooled down food glaring without pity from the plate. They would giggle and hide their faces behind the softly-woven kitchen curtains, of a similar green, playing a game where they were 'distant relations'. This was a strange prefiguring of what would eventually happen to them as adults after the reading of their father's will. 'Talking to the wa-all'! they would shout defiantly at each other when they wanted to ignore a jibe. When Molly began to learn French, she taught John too, and at the end of each day they would shout from one bedroom to the other '*bonne nuit, garcon!*' … '*bonne nuit, fille*'.

But something, somehow, entered her brother's heart, as it had her mother's, like a sliver of ice, so that as an adult he couldn't honour his father's final wishes in his will. That was the end-point of sibling struggles, as estranging as the conflicts in their father's generation, and as seemingly un-mendable. Just as with the sweets, John wanted it all, and this too is not such an uncommon story. Molly crept away to heal and sustain herself as best she could in a rather barren little land inside her mind. She couldn't 'play hell and chop sticks'- her father's vivid description of a tantrum. She kept it all inside, not even asking why, in the jumble of little questions that plagued her each day.

Perhaps again the crime of separation, of difference, was John's justification. Or did both John and his mother, in some strange union despite their unpromising beginning together, protest all their lives against Molly's father's unashamed behaviour towards Molly, his favourite? Pride of place on Daddy's lap had its price. Molly probably gloried in it too, and in the end got hanged by her halo. Daddy dearest, she might have called him, but such extravagances of endearment weren't often used in her family. He admired her forwardness. 'I can't wait for you to grow up' he'd say. But unlike the story of the talents in her delicately fraying bible, Molly discovered, using them as opposed to burying them would have a bitter cost.

Or was this brother simply born ruthless, like the blind cuckoo chick programmed to turf out the competition in the nest? The roles were certainly reversed, in later life. If he had felt rejected from the start, he would plan to oust his sister for ever from the family picture, she whose pudgy studio portrait had been framed and hung by adoring parents in the dining room at the old house. Her brother's version of events would inevitably have a very different flavour.

Bonne nuit, garcon.

In any event, the sibling world of two held fewer and fewer moments of warmth over the years. Although she learned to live with him, Molly shut in a cupboard a smaller girl who came to tea, listening with satisfaction as whimpers turned to screams behind the door, sounds well worth the inevitable smack. Molly could at least control this girl's fate, and she told her dolls off continually as she seated them in a floppy and reluctant row in the playroom.

Jemima Jane, go to the back of the class.

Stand in the corner with a book on your head.

Hold out your hand. Smack, smack, smack.

They were the failed pupils she could control and punish and she became a regular doll-basher. Her faded green copy of Charles Kingsley's *The Water Babies* had two names in the front, neither of them her own: they were the names assigned to her backward students, Susan West and Carol-Anne Mann. The first few pages were blemished by words alternately underlined; 'Once <u>upon</u> a <u>time</u> there <u>was</u> a <u>little</u> chimney <u>sweep</u> and his <u>name</u> was <u>Tom</u>'. Molly's lack of mastery of number three was forgotten as she pointed mercilessly at the words her silent pupils failed to read.

When she was still at nursery school she wrote a poem about her brother, which a visiting teacher used in his Radio Three talk about children's verse: 'Little Johnny's gone to bed/In his tiny cot/There he'll rest his baby head/And maybe sleep a lot/In the morning he will wake/And make a lot of noise/He keeps on shouting let me out/I want to get my toys!' Did she really write those little lines? Or did her parents shape them to help her, if rather belatedly, with her difficulty? The poem catered to Molly's wish to triumph and be her parents' best and brightest, to forget all those other unacceptable feelings which didn't sit at all well in any of their minds with her accomplishments.

She also won prizes at elocution competitions, declaiming poetry in her mightiest blustering voice as she stood, a tiny figure with sensible shoes and stumpy legs planted firmly on a wide, echoing stage. 'The King asked the Queen and the Queen asked the Dairymaid: *Could* we have some butter for the Royal Slice of Bread?' Miss Serious Socks gives it her all. The King went into a decline because the cow had gone on strike, but it all came out well in the end. And while her brother John clamoured to be let out of his cot in one room, Molly played her own private radio games in another, head smothered voluntarily by a pillow to get the authentic boomy sound of her own voice taking all the parts, as she thought she had to do. She was still making it up, for them, and for herself.

It wasn't until later at boarding school when she took a course in 'Public Speaking', that she developed the idea of an audience out there, not just locked away in her head under the pillow. The age-old art of rhetoric, with gesture, voice projection, articulation and the often unnoticed use of pause, subtle as well as dramatic, came naturally to her, the little show-off. At last there was a stage where it was permissible and even mandatory to give it your all. Liking the sound of your own voice, a sin in her mother's eyes, who nevertheless admired her own, became a less shameful vice. Not the only pebble on the beach maybe as she had learned in the inevitably hard way, but still a little pebble with a point of view.

Her favourite sharp-tongued aunt, nicknamed 'Old Acid' by Molly's father who also loved his elder sister dearly, wrote a letter the little girl found later, tucked behind the back of a drawer in the old roll-topped desk. When Molly's risk-taking teenage father had been dying after a motorbike accident, it was Old Acid, already on a healing mission in her early twenties, which would end when she became chief matron of a major London hospital during the Second World War, who nagged the doctors and her little brother into reverse gear and into life. He always valued what she said.

Old Acid warned Molly's parents against trusting this daughter prodigy too much. 'She'll no doubt burn herself out early if you push her', Molly read with guilty fascination, before stuffing the paper covered with her aunt's spidery handwriting firmly back to its hiding place behind the top drawer of the desk. But push they did and continued to do so. Of course, for Molly it meant that she could bathe in their continued admiration, even if she and they had driven underground the mortal blow delivered to her pride, when her brother was born. It was a doubtful blessing to be cast as mother's brightest child.

Yet for Molly this blow of a brother was the spur to open a new door into a new world. Reading was from the start a consolation as well as a pleasure, and the loss of place was more than made up for by books. There was never a shortage of them in the old house, to read as she chose. Old Acid's always impeccable choice of birthday gifts started off the great adventure: although all the characters in both *Wind in the Willows* and *The House at Pooh Corner* were male, except for Kanga, the mother of baby Roo, the situations spoke as they did to many children of that generation, of the age-old tension between independence and the need for security, of the power of a group to control individual desires. Bumptious bouncing Tigger came to his miserable senses when he got lost in the foggy wood. How much more hopeful they were than the old books inherited from her mother; like *What Katy Did* where, what a cruel twist of plot it always seemed to Molly, the poor girl actually broke her back because she infringed a parental rule, and just by swinging too. The swing's chains were faulty and like rock a bye baby, poor Katy did indeed come down with a terrible fall. Truly this Katy seemed like a descendant of the original Eve, sinning just to push a boundary or two. Why not? It was a question that had set the world free, you could say, from authoritarian control. Swinging was also one of Molly's own favourite pursuits. Then there was *Little Women* where you either got married or died of consumption. Beth the consumptive one, Molly realised, was the passive, accepting member of that fictional family. It was better to be more assertive, even if you might be in danger of breaking your back, she reckoned.

Molly identified with Jo, as did all strong-spirited young women of her own and her mother's generation. But there was also Amy the narcissist. Harder to see in oneself, indeed, but she returned in a dream, this Amy March, as Molly's mother was dying.

There was of course the question at that time of when her mother would actually die. There was no doubt, except in the mind of Molly's mother, that she would, but when? The doctors reserved their judgment. Molly's dream of Amy March breaking her back as she fell from an icy toboggan gave her, she fancied, the answer. That and a brief image of a broken clay pot, with the liquid draining out of it onto the hard ground. Was this a wish or a premonition? Sooner or later, as ancient Horace wrote, the urn is broken. In a final irony her mother died on Mother's Day, one sunny March morning, surrounded by flowers. There were orchids from John, cut and already wilting bulbously in a glass vase, and a pot of peace lilies Molly had brought with her to her mother's bedside. 'I like your choice of flowers' said one of the carers, who had been a witness to the family drama which continued to the end.

Molly's mother woke one morning and told one of her carers that she had dreamed of her children arguing over her grave. It was the first time she had acknowledged she might die, and it also showed that somewhere she knew too how she had fed rather than calmed down the feuds which had grown over the siblings' lifetime, preferring to divide and rule rather than unite.

The only book Molly's mother recalled from her own childhood was Prescott's *Conquest of Mexico*. In her old age she still mourned the little green book which had somehow disappeared down the long years, and which had perhaps spoken personally to her of bloody triumph and vanished glory.

Halfway up the backstairs to the bathroom was a good place for Molly to read, so was the hawthorn hedge round the garden, with Nip the cat as a companion, and so was the silage heap in the old bullock yard, where Molly used to sit and sniff the heady odour of molasses and rotting vegetation, nose half in the smell and half in the book. Smells could seduce her, this little girl who stuffed putty up her nose and had to go to hospital for its removal. Linseed oil smelt so sweet: she rather envied builders who used it as a matter of every day course. She wondered briefly if this is what she could do too when she 'grew up'. Whenever that was to be.

There was no censorship as she roamed about her parents' bookshelves. Walter Scott's novels were all early devoured, Harrison Ainsworth's wonderful and bloody *Tower of London*, and *Our Dearest Emma*, a novel about Nelson's mistress. Molly didn't know what a mistress was, but she couldn't help admiring the spirit of a simple village girl, little Emmy Lyon, who climbed out of her poor predicament via men, and ended up striking 'attitudes' to seduce them as much as they seduced her. Molly had puzzled over the stoning of the poor woman 'taken in adultery' when her parents for some strange reason took her with them to see one of their 'flicks', *Solomon and Sheba* . In her own house, Molly's mother was queen woman, but Molly could see that it wasn't necessarily so in the world beyond. Her one treasured book of poems: *A Child's Garden of Verses* by Walter de la Mare, told her that '*The world is so full of a number of things, I am sure we should all be as happy as kings*'. Molly wondered about that, but recited it like a mantra at difficult moments.

Then there was her much-loved collection of stories from English history. She felt as many children do for the characters in the history books, and their various fates. She could see smart old King Canute with his throne planted at the edge of the sea on her own beach, trying to teach his courtiers something about the vanity of power, because even he in all his majesty could not control the tide. She could picture Boudicca smeared in blue woad and filled with bloodlust yelling her mighty challenges and driving her chariot with its canny wheels studded with knives, just at the top of the cliff. As Cassius Dio the ancient Roman historian wrote, 'Boudicca possessed far more spirit than is usual among women'. Molly admired her, hugely. She found out that this proud rebellious leader of the oppressed had attacked London, and burned it to the ground. Molly was proud too of her Norse forefathers, who, despite their propensities to sack and erase, their own version of modern shock and awe, had another softer side. When they took off their horned helmets they had skills in leather, in wood, in iron, while their seafaring raids brought to Britain fine imports of amber, silk and silver. Molly had her own inner vision of a Viking woman, standing by her warrior man. She could identify too with the deflated and battle-weary Robert the Bruce, sitting in his mountain cave, watching the spider throw her web out time and time again until she managed to fasten it on the far wall. But webs could be dangerous things too. Robert and Molly both admired the spider's persistence, and her artistry, but Molly remained less in touch with the spider's mission to weave harmful traps, though her mother often wove them at home.

Molly's perhaps regrettable and certainly over-inflated passion for metaphor was satisfied again and again when she read the old and fragile pages of *Pilgrim's Progress,* a book which had belonged to her long-dead paternal grandmother. Molly could so easily transfer the faults and frailties of Bunyan's hero and see them in her own small life as a sinner. Christian's adventures were rooted in a country sometimes like her own, and she accompanied him on the long road which Bunyan traced. His odyssey offered her a world that was already encoded in her caravan of dreams; the fears of losing, and finding, failure and success. Bypath Meadow sounded all too tempting. While the Delectable Mountains might shine off in the distance, Molly was much more often an inmate of Doubting Castle, imprisoned by the Giant Despair. Bunyan caught and pinned down her floating terrors, and she found it comforting to know that poor Christian had them too.

Her mind was often full of the stories of the grim German brothers Grimm, locked between the green leather covers of an old book which might have been her father's. These tales seethed with sadism, with witches trapped in glowing ovens, vain people rolled down long hills in barrels full of nails, and shoes which squeezed narcissistic feet into an everlasting dance of pain. Grim they were indeed, and fascinatingly so. Molly was always less impressed by the reward side of the equation: little 'good girls' showered with silver apples, around whose heads doves cooed under the bowl of an eternally blue and cloudless sky.

Left over too from her father's boyhood was a battered copy of *Swiss Family Robinson,* with the detailed engravings that Molly loved. She admired the resourcefulness of this shipwrecked family, as Tolstoy too as a boy had been enthralled by them. He had experienced the painful dislocation of puberty when he could no longer play at 'Robinson' with his little sisters. When Molly tried to interest her own son in this book it was a failure. He didn't seem to have the same wish to salvage something from a shipwreck.

The books were beautiful to look at as well as into: green leather binding on the Harrison Ainsworth, Walter Scott triumphant red, some like *Swiss Family Robinson* with gold pictures stamped on the front, and then there were the scarlet-bound book club books Molly used to sneak off to read in the bath. She would lie in the cooling water, turning the pages with wet hands which left water marks on the cheap covers and stained the bath-water red. 'Haven't you finished yet?' her mother would shout from downstairs. Molly would hastily pull the bathplug and wipe her pink hands on her flannel. Her skin would be wrinkled and pink too, and she would realise that the bath water was nearly cold. She only half or less than half understood these adult pot-boilers, where the sex was hinted at rather than explicit as it would later be. *Gone to the Pictures, Forever Amber...*food for her curious hunger. On summer nights she read till her eyes hurt, under the sheet even in the broad evening light, always alert for the step on the stair, and the caution from one or other parent that she was ruining her eyes.

There was one place to read completely undisturbed and that was in one of the two servants' bedrooms, now deserted, which lay at the top of a steeply rising narrow staircase above the back passage and the dairy, and a further maze of little cramped rooms already empty when Molly was a child. At the bottom of the stairs on the wall outside the main kitchen, hung the old iron bell, which had once called the maids to their duties. These old rooms had a breathless, airless quality of emptiness, so that even when Molly took an egg-cupful of daisies up the stairs to put on the dusty windowsill in the hope of brightening the gloom, she couldn't lose herself in a book, however thrilling. The rooms lost her living presence as they had lost the others before her. They seemed as dead and dry as the cellar seemed damply alive, where mould clung to the walls, and discarded cobwebbed bottles tumbled around on the flagstone floor along with the pram and the playpen determinedly put away for ever when her brother outgrew them. Her dad would hump things down the stone stairs at his wife's command, and the heap of items no longer fit for use upstairs grew larger. There was a barred metal gate at the top of the cellar stairs, and Molly thought that if you looked in quickly you would perhaps catch a glimpse of rats and ghosts as well as empty bottles, old ladies whispering and whistling through their dead teeth.

Something echoed on, remnants of the now absent servant girls who had lived two to each room in those cramped quarters. In her old age Molly's ma still talked of 'Annie's room' when preparing a room in her new home for her live-in carers. And it was in 'Annie's bed' that Molly was sleeping when she was called to her mother's bedside on her last night on earth. Her carers had taken up Molly's old bedroom, and Molly could see the irony in that.

Who was Annie? Molly pictured her wary and withdrawn, a forebear of dear Gladys, ready with a duster or a pair of stout arms to tackle what needed to be done. The old iron bell to which she had responded hung for years from a shelf in Molly's bedroom, redundant but honoured, occasionally rung just to rouse the ghosts a little. There was a succession of maids who cleaned the house when Molly was a child, Ivys and Aggies, Ellas, Adas and Mabels. While Gladys endured, they passed through the house and then out again by the back door, unremembered and unsung. One even fell and broke her hip, poor thing, on the parquet floor she had shined so hard, while Molly sat reading by the window.

Eating was part of Molly's reading ritual. Devouring books and sweets; liquorice laces and sherbet dips or bits of bun sneaked from the kitchen, or gob-stoppers laboriously worked on down to the last aniseed in the very centre. And you notice something here? Nothing recalled about learning the process, of being read to, though this probably was a part of her life at bedtime when she was a small girl. But Molly wanted to leap right over the struggle and land clear out the other side, a reader and a navigator of new worlds.

In an old and battered book there lay the tale of 'Ameliaranne Stiggins', eldest child in an orphan family of eight. She stole cakes from a tea party by hiding them under her umbrella for the poor little ones at home, but unfortunately it rained just as she left her hostess's house. It was only the kindly father of the house who helped her in this moment of mortal embarrassment as she stood helpless under a shower of buns.

At intervals between bullying him, Molly gave her brother not cakes but stories. They are, after all, the universal currency. She couldn't tell them, thrillingly, like her dad, but she could read them. John was late to read, which must have been an added shame for him as a contrast to his 'bright' sister, but she used genuinely to enjoy, as did he, sitting for hours reading him *Prester John*, *The Black Tulip*, *She* and *The Return of She*, and *King Solomon's Mines*. They were thrilled by the terrible delights of the Hall of the Dead, where the seated bones of the departed were reigned over by a fifteen-foot high skeleton holding a monumental spear, and they too were stopped and breathless at the door of Solomon's treasure chamber by a mass of ascending stones. 'Truly the universe is full of ghosts, not sheeted churchyard spectres, but the inextinguishable elements of individual life, which having once been, can never die, though they blend and change and change again for ever'... Molly believed that then, and later too.

These nineteenth-century books, remnants of her parents' childhoods, bound in dark red and green solid boards, held all the things, Molly thought, we ought to know and think about. She would read to John till the light gradually left the corners of the play-room, and it was time for tea, down the long cold front hall into the even colder back hall and then into the warm kitchen.

What's for tea, mum?

Sardines on toast.

Lots of Lea and Perrins for me!

They sat around the kitchen table always strongly lit directly from above. Molly sometimes felt she was on a stage, and sometimes in a courtroom, accused of an unknown crime, that the whole world knew about except her. Body on trial, head still back in the playroom, filled with little lines of print. Oh please may I get down? You opened and shut these worlds at will. Inside the covers the characters' suspended lives wanted to spring out like Jacks in boxes, to capture your interest. She imagined them waiting, impatient to be freed, to live again in the old exchange between eye and mind. Her silver owl book mark, another of Old Acid's presents, froze their crises, and sometimes she could hardly bear to leave them there. At other times she deliberately, with casual cruelty, left them hanging suspended till she chose to allow them to have a life off the page again.

What would happen, she wondered, if the characters could squeeze themselves out from the tight-closed pages and climb from one book to another, what would bouncing Tigger think of boisterous Toad, or serious Badger of the pontificating wise old Owl—both puffed up and pompous enough for two in any case. Moley and Piglet would be firm friends, she felt, and maybe Ratty and Rabbit would find a lot in common. If Dearest Emma and her lover had been shipwrecked, they would have been relieved to meet the thrifty Swiss family who could have taught them how to survive—and Emma's Attitudes could have entertained them all. Why Emma hadn't been stoned, though, like poor Sheba, Molly never worked out.

When Molly went at ten to boarding school the other kids ribbed her for her 'grownup' use of words, which had gradually seeped into her from these nineteenth-century texts, as *Wind in the Willows* made way for more adult narrative. 'Speak English' said the Eaglet in *Alice in Wonderland*. 'I don't know the meaning of half those long words, and what's more, I don't believe you do, either!' But she did.

And then what did the teachers and the house-mistresses and the governors of what is good for you decree? They chose an hour each Sunday, between three and four, for 'Good Reading'. Now Molly was forced to read as a task and a chore what she had once absorbed into herself joyfully. The minutes gave up their glorious rush as she pushed the chosen book around the dark confines of her little prep-desk, secretly organising wars among her little phalanx of china woodland creatures, a group of strictly counted 'ornaments' trying in vain to give a homely touch to an institutional space. She soon gave that sort of 'good reading' up.

Back home, she pressed, painted and classified the flowers growing in the meadows around the old house and on the cliff-tops. Larkspur, scarlet pimpernel, shepherd's purse, purple loosestrife. Ragged robin, lady's mantle, woodspurge and fumitory. Ploughman's spikenard, devilsbit and stinking aster. Surrounded by a cast of thousands, she stage managed them between pages of blotting paper, and named them with the obsessive zeal of a fledgling Linnaeus, though she was at that time unaware of the naming of their sexual parts being part of the story.

She had been given at somebody's birthday party a tiny book, hardly bigger than a book of stamps, where on every page a painting of a butterfly filled the space, with just enough room underneath for each splendid name —the brimstone yellow, the brash red admiral, the painted lady, perfect in her mascara-tipped wings. These she could see, flying for their brief but glorious day, in the garden and the meadow beyond the lawn's hedge. Her sense of wonder was both religious and scientific. She loved the names of the little squares of colour in her water-paint box: the thrilling spills you could imagine and then cast down of crimson and scarlet lake, the infinite space of cobalt, cerulean and Mary Mantle blue, shading to ultramarine and purest emerald green. Each little square, like the covers of her books, held in check worlds you could unlock with the trembling of a poised paint-brush in pure water.

Sometimes she paints herself reflected in the mirror at the end of the hall. She sees, who does she see? She's really not that sure. Is she this rather plain little girl face with mousy hair? Not a princess at all, then, as she had fancied, abandoned in a poorer home to be discovered by her nobler family.

I never want, said George Orwell, completely to abandon the view of the world I acquired in childhood. 'So long as I remain alive and well, I shall continue to feel strongly about prose style, to love the surface of the earth, and to take pleasure in solid objects and scraps of useless information'. The solids of the world, ranged around the farm, as well as the scraps she collected in her mind, made Molly too, want to write, robustly, about her passions.

Chapter Five

In which Molly describes the exciting world of the farm, where pigs eat their young, her three year old brother learns to shoot and kill, and her parents struggle with the weather as well as with various farming projects, many of which fail. Molly even manages to see a chicken lay an egg.

Good conservation results in as little interference with the historic object as possible, and this makes the briefing of the conservator of the utmost importance.

Again Molly batters her fists against the sides of the constraining box. Can she, will she, be heard in the tattered scribbling of voices which lie at the margins of every life? These voices come and go. Where is there room in all this cosmic babble for the noise of one little individual ordinary life?

Well, she's going on so much, let her have another say…

Going on. Well, at least she did. As we all try to do. Molly's mother's elegantly plucked eyebrows are raised at this point. They may well stay that way.

So there was the world inside my head, vivid and exciting: there was also the world of the farm and the land and that was powerful too. Not till years later at boarding school when I read Wordsworth's letters did I find outside words for my experiences, on any old ordinary day. I could merge with the sky and the grass and the stones and the wind, walk into the cathedral I could see in the dandelion head. The trees seemed so human that I could picture Odin, Vili and Ve, the old Norse god brothers shut between the green and gold covers of my book on legends, walking along the seashore, where they transformed the ash tree and the elm tree into people with hearts and bloodstreams, upright beings right away, thousands of years before Darwin's breathtaking idea of man descended from the apes.

Wordsworth used to bang his head against walls to 'come down' from his trips in the landscape. 'The sounding cataract haunted me like a passion', he said. He, like others including my young girl self, took refuge in passionate attachments to nature because the world of human beings had let him down. I was lucky living in the country, but town kids too must hang on to the spider which climbs to where the ceiling joins the wall, or the butterfly which gives up its flight to end on the window-sill of a city room.

I would lie in the meadow and look at the sky, hear the skylark rising on a tide of joyful song. You never saw the bird herself, hidden in a sky of blue. I would see a grass-snake slither away at the edge of my vision, look at him straight and he was straight away gone, or smell the hay and the now disused leather of the bridles and cart collars in the stable (where we used to play dusty hide and seek). These things seemed to have been there for ever. Any minute, I would think, I'll just disappear into all this. Van Gogh in his asylum would calm down the too-painful joy brought on when he read Shakespeare by looking out of his tiny window at a blade of grass or a branch of pine. Both Wordsworth and Van Gogh had that painful sensibility which is often the lot of an ordinary child, especially one who feels solitary. They see a lot, they think a lot, some of it they get wrong, but some they get painfully right.

I sat for hours by a particular cupboard, made of walnut and built into one alcove of the dining room, where the electricity meters rolled on and on once we were lit up when I was three, and think that any minute I'd get smaller than Alice and pass into another dimension, through a little door. 'Oh Kitty, now we come to the passage. You can just see a little peep of the passage in the Looking-glass House, if you leave the door of our drawing room wide open, and it's very like our drawing room as far as you can see, only you know it may be quite different on beyond'... The mirror near the cupboard held for me all its past images, and a reflected future just beyond my understanding. I seemed to crouch between these worlds, waiting for the magic to happen. It was a space neither here nor there but on the brink of both.

Fresh air, Monet maintained, is violet. Outside the house there lay the world of the farm, standing firm against the violet back-drop of the sky and the sea. If you stepped out of the back door you could see the row of small sheds which often held pigs, behind a flint-stone and red brick wall which curved away to the left to become the main drive, continuing in an arc down to the small 'main road'. This ancient wall built of carefully curving bricks once had to be mended, and my dad got his three-year-old daughter to write 'Molly' in the cement. When years later the mend had to be touched up, although the workman faithfully wrote 'Molly' again, my dad mourned the childish letters now lost beneath the new mortar. Much as he declared that he could hardly wait till his daughter was 'grown up', another part of him found the changings very hard.

Though the pigs smelt high in their sties, my dad said that pigs were as clean as people, it was the way you kept and looked after them that made the difference. The kitchen swill, potato peelings, cabbage leaves and apple cores, were stored in a bowl under the sink. Once a day they were given to the pregnant sows, poured like a river of bounty into their circular iron troughs. My mother had a vegetable knife which had got slung out along with the slops by mistake, and its white bone handle was scored with chewing teeth marks. These pregnant creatures lolled and rolled in their confined spaces, then gave multiple birth, often with some dead, or lain on or eaten, oh yes, eaten, I was appalled to learn. I saw some of these births, where one after another the little blood streaked parcels got shat swiftly out, (or so it seemed to a child still rather mixed up about the various and fascinating human openings), then got up gamely for a suck and a go at life, however short, as they mostly then got sold for bacon.

After the war, rationing continued for many years. I remember a pig being killed illegally in one of the rooms at the end of the quaintly-called 'back passage' beyond the scullery, where loomed the massive and rather threatening presence of the clothes boiler, to be cut up by my father and the local policeman. I fancy I remember the screams.

The dead porker was then hauled up onto a thick wooden trestle table. It required a lot of heaving and ho-ing, and Bert the Bobby breathed in and out huge hot gusts of air as he struggled scarlet faced and mightily, alongside my hero father who never looked as though these things presented any sort of major difficulty. This cutting up seemed like a second killing to me, hovering as I was behind the scullery door. It involved carving and filleting and great sawing motions performed by Bert like a cumbersome ballet dancer, lumbering to a solemn silent music, hollow and menacing. Huge bits of limb hovered and then fell to the floor. Francis Bacon, oh what an ironic name, wouldn't have needed any additional flourishes to paint the scene. It was a theatre of cruelty which put me off pig, at least for a while.

Pig-curing and its by-products take up a whole one and a half columns in my Ma's old recipe book. He was an unwillingly generous provider, the screaming pig. You could cook his brain with his kidneys, his feet and ears with parsley sauce, his head as a pudding with eggs and nutmeg, and even his entrails could be used to contain his own meat for sausages, with mace, just a pinch, and breadcrumbs. We had so much of this fat pork that Ma once decided to omit the breadcrumbs. We were disappointed with the result. It seemed she had gone to such trouble, washing all those small slimy entrails and scraping them until they were transparent. We all agreed it wasn't worth a second try.

But she rendered the lard, tearing the two large fat sheets from his ribs, and baking small cut-up chunks in a moderate oven. At the end you also had the cracklings, and these were kept too for making puddings. The centrepiece of all this industry was the pigs' brawn, which my father loved. In a recipe passed down the generations, were listed all the steps to produce this festive dish. You cut off his ears, took out his brains, and left his feet and ears to soak for a week in vinegar. The cooked halves of the head were flattened, but kept in pig shape as much as possible, so that his ears and his feet and even his tongue could be tied inside it, boiled, and then pressed with weights for two days. It then appeared on the table, much to my pained disapproval.

The pigs' screams picked up the silent scream in me, I spent much of my childhood in passionate identification, like my father, with animals, but particularly with their sufferings. The runt of the litter was the one I cared for, the scrawniest kitten, the sickliest calf. I mourned the heifers sent to market and lay down in the newly vacated straw in the bullock yard remembering their sad brown eyes and their huge soft tongues which had licked curiously at my winter coat. Later, I would run and shout and wave wild arms to scare away the blackbirds sitting innocent in the oak tree, when my six-year-old brother had his air rifle cocked for action. A stray air rifle pellet found its way through the scullery window, narrowly missing my mother's breast, who knows whether by accident or design, and the gun disappeared, but only for a while. As a young adult this boy would become one of only a few people in the shooting world who could kill two swift flying woodcock with two barrels.

My brother's lust to kill needed to be fostered. There was a photograph of this sweet and still sensitive two year old boy in an endearing all in one suit, being taught by my father to bite the head of a dying pheasant rather than marvel at the passing beauty of its brilliant feathers.

Come on, son, this is how you do it.

Two trusting brown eyes look up at this vision of fierce tearing, as my dad bites the pheasant's neck.

One of Dad's retrievers beats its tail in approval, sitting on the scrubby land next to the hedge. You can almost hear the low sigh of the waves just over the cliff.

My dad knew he had to catch him young. He was teaching him in the way he knew, man to boy and growing man, a lesson about the hierarchy of needs. Yet years later, soon before he died, Dad wrote in one of his weekly letters 'I haven't seen John but he went shooting yesterday, he shot about twenty birds and had a grand day out. Poor little birds'. It was just another thought added on, that maybe he'd suppressed all his life for the sake of the grand days.

There was a little shed nearly opposite the back door, next to the bike shed, one of a whole line of sheds which were separated by the cob-stone wall, where the faded feathers swirled in rolling heaps on the floor, a few days after a shoot. The birds were plucked and hung on hooks. My father could have got one of the farm men to pluck them, but he always did it himself, with a black rubber apron tied over his work trousers, sitting tilted in a sagging old armchair and sometimes sneezing and smiling in the dusty air.

To the right of the pigsties was the milking shed, long and always wettish, cleaned down with a snake of black hose after every milking time. There was a man hired to do the milking, to put the mechanical suckers onto the cow's udders, to push them and kick them into line as they mumbled and grumbled over their hay rations in the wooden manger which ran the whole of one side of the shed. *Hub*back! *Gid*dover! were the perennial cries. Their tough hooves slid on the brackish floor; they set their obstinate flanks against their tormentor, who of course was also their saviour, relieving the bursting discomfort of their udders. This stubbornness was at odds with the patient glaze of their liquid eyes. As they chewed their hay and let down their milk, they seemed to me to be machines themselves, clamped onto suckers which sucked their lives away. In a symphony echoing around the whitewashed walls and cold stone floors, the suckers rasped and sighed; and so did they.

When they were not being relieved of their milky burdens, they grazed in the meadows surrounding the house. They lived this uneventful life, broken only by the twice daily demand, and occasionally by unexpected drama. One day I was in the meadow with my father, watching the cows, when one suddenly stopped her chewing as she rambled, fell to the ground, rolled over, and lay still. It turned out she'd walked over a broken electricity cable, just beneath the surface of the field. This picture remained in my mind, a lesson on the powers of unseen energies.

I also saw a calf, reluctant to be born, drawn by the labouring vet from the body of its moaning mother, on ropes attached to its feet. In the event, both died. Maybe it chimed with something deep in my mind about my own reluctant entry into the world. Both entrances weren't of the right sort. I hadn't died, but something had, and it was a dark and lifelong backbeat to my life with my mother.

These cows were Friesians, black and white and often dingy with their own and others' dung which splattered onto the concrete floor. But we always had a Jersey house cow for family use. She was called in successive incarnations Daisy, or Honey, or Caroline. She had a separate privileged shed and privileged life as a beautiful aristocrat, milked night and morning by my dad, who took the little three-legged milking stool and the shining pail from the scullery and meditated together with Daisy, or Honey or Caroline, to produce a stream of creamy milk. He would sit with his head buried into her flank, talking and singing to her, touching her cow-soul to get the best from her.

K-K-K-Katy,
Beautiful Katy, You're the only one that I adore
When the m-moon shines over the cowshed
I'll be waiting by the
K-k-kitchen door.

My mother would pour the milk, more whole and rich than anything dreamed of or allowed in later fat-conscious years, gushing like a satin river into the wide-mouthed milk bowls, till the thick Jersey cream rose for skimming: for butter, for whipped cream to be eaten with scones made with any milk that had by chance gone sour, and strawberry jam. Sumptuous teas of scones and strawberries and mountains of whipped cream would be served up when the friendly family doctor who had brought me into the world came to visit, and we children sat with dangling legs round the big dining room table, on chairs too high for comfort, but which emphasised the grandeur of the event.

The King asked the Queen and the Queen asked the Dairymaid.

Could we have some butter for the Royal Slice of Bread?

Later, my father reared calves, and I was 'given' one to cherish. I mixed up the dried milk powder in a huge galvanised bucket and, staggering under its slooshing weight, carried it out to the calf-shed, where 'my' calf would plunge his eager nose into the froth (they had to have their noses held into the mixture at the beginning, when they still missed their mothers' milk.) But 'my' calf started to dwindle, he developed a huge bulging hernia in his stomach and had eventually to be put down. I felt the pain of being a failed mother, but my Dad took it philosophically. It could all be mended, he thought, and he carried string in his pocket as if to prove that life's problems were simply a matter of fixing things. He could make a halter out of binder twine for a calf or a horse in no time at all.

When he died and my ma and I sent his best suit for the laying out, we found some string and hairy binder twine too in the trouser pocket. We left it there, in case St Peter's gates needed fixing, or in case he found some other use for a piece of binder twine as he journeyed to the after-world. If it can't be fixed with a piece of twine, he always said, you might as well throw it away and get a new one.

His hands bore witness to the essential roughness of what he struggled with, palms crossed with great cracks and lines, which every night he slathered with the Vaseline standing on his bedside table in a huge jar. His arms were hairy and hard with bunched muscle. Go on, bite me, he'd say to me and my brother, and we would sink our teeth into his clenched and triumphant forearm. He would hug us both together, tightly, and as you pressed yourself to his chest and hugged him back, you could smell him under his earlobes, in the space between the soft skin of his neck and his shirt-collar, sweet as a warm biscuit.

My parents slept side by side in twin beds, but it was into my father's welcoming bed that we kids would creep in the morning, to be taken in to his rough gentleness, as when he sat with us both crowded on top of him in one of the battered green leather kitchen armchairs.

Beyond and to the left of the cowshed was another row of outbuildings, tiles climbing in red ridges to the skies of my world. There was a huge barn, not the main corn barn but also with a vital use. This one was used for storing machinery, with doors you couldn't push open without an adult's help, and a cavernous cobwebby interior still heaped with yesterday's junk telling yesterday's stories, old tools hung high on rusty nails, tools on the floor half hidden under more dust than must have confronted Methuselah when he woke from his long sleep. Skeletons of old ploughs, designed as simply as the constellation in the night skies, lay next to a tangled mass of harrows and rusty rollers, some of which still got hauled out each spring to play their brief part in the annual dramas of the farming world. Inside on the left were the steps to the granary where my mother kept her chickens: they were hardly steps, just a long plank with wooden ridges, difficult to manage if your rubber boots were wet or too big, and your feet groped their hazardous way upwards in the semi-darkness.

Underneath this primitive stair was accumulated more fading and now irrelevant clutter: old number plates, tarnished forks and spoons, rusty billhooks and hedge-knives which had outlived their usefulness in the slashing and topping and digging involved in the time-honoured skills of maintaining the hedges and ditches of a working farm. And dust, dust everywhere, dust which had been there when my father was a boy, when his father was a boy, dust which had accumulated and woven itself into a huge hairy tangled blanket, binding and hiding who knew what.

In the granary above this barn were the chicken pens and their nest boxes: it was fun to climb the ridged steps and go egg collecting, putting them carefully, some still warm, in a pail of straw.

Mind how you go.

Don't crack the shells.

There was a ghost in the granary too. One day as she collected eggs, bending over the nesting boxes, my ma heard my father's step on the wood-slatted stair. The door opened, but when she looked round, with a smile on her face and an egg in her hand, there was nobody there. We felt it was a friendly ghost; perhaps my paternal grandfather, come to watch the daughter-in-law he had never met go about her serious chicken business.

The mysteries of the egg! Ovoid enigma, sometimes soft-shelled, often partly shit-covered: the egg-laying place so close to the waste-place. It fascinated me and was the source of much confusion about how babies were made. *Love and creation have pitched their mansions in the place of excrement.* Once, by the pond, I managed somehow to crouch in a bush underneath a hen's makeshift nest and actually see the egg emerge, while the hen strained to push out her cargo. It was an awesome experience. I told nobody, but felt that I had witnessed a powerful rite which bestowed some special knowledge on me: chicken and egg in some vast mysterious loop, sustaining the fragile world. I didn't yet properly know where babies came from. But at least I had seen my breakfast enter the world.

Chick- chick- chick- chick—chicken, Oh, lay a little egg for me.

More than a century ago, William James, brother of Henry and father of the term 'stream of consciousness', talked of the world as sculpture, made by each and every being in a different way.. 'My world is but one in a million alike embedded, alike real to those who may abstract them. How different must be the worlds in the consciousness of ant, cuttle-fish or crab!' The world of the hen seemed to me at once marvellous and pathetic, this holy egg-layer had sisters who screeched and pecked one another raw, bullies and bullied cast inexorably in the hen-house, fixed in hating and being hated, for no apparent reason that I, a non-hen-being, could fathom. And not so different, as I would discover later, from the lives of human kind. Once a hen had been cast as victim, there was no escape, she would cower and hide her scarlet neck pecked raw by her sisters, as they came at her over and over, till Ma would ask my father to wring her neck and put her out of her misery.

The floor of the granary was uneven. There were gaps in the floorboards partially hidden by mounds of hen-droppings, and flecked with feathers and grain. The room was filled with a stale and overpoweringly heavy smell. When I read in one of our impressive red row of large encyclopaedias, grandly called Books of Knowledge, about whole islands made of bird-shit, it was no surprise to me. The lids of the nesting boxes were heavy, and when you lifted them, outraged hens would cackle and run, unless they were actually laying: then they would give you a baleful eye and toss their horny yellow beaks. China eggs were left in the straw to encourage them or, more truthfully, to deceive them into laying more. It was a mean trick, I thought, but I kept that thought to myself. Occasionally, an egg-eater would betray herself by leaving a yolky stew in the box, and she would be tracked down and eliminated with no mercy. We gathered cuttlefish shells on the beach and left them for the hens to peck: the calcium strengthened the eggshells. They were fed grit too, for the same purpose, so that they would produce their own daily pearls.

Eggs and hens were my ma's passion, for a time, and they seemed to dominate our lives. She raised baby chicks, imported in a van by the hundred and then left to stir around under infra-red lights. One night there was a power cut and they all died. I had my Wellington boots hastily pulled up over bare feet, and cold legs, and my nightdress tangled round my thighs, as we stumbled up the slatted wooden steps to bear witness. Don't count your chickens, my dad used to say, and I thought he must be right. Even after hatching, life was a risky business for them. Then there was disease: the dreaded 'coccidiosis', a fowl pest which caused slow and painful death. The hen-houses were emptied of the corpses, and disinfected with a fearsome-looking red liquid.

Then came the transition from deep litter to battery hens, who lived in metal rows in a small building next to the implement shed. They sang to my father when he went in to give them their daily rations and collect the eggs which rolled down a rubber belt as they were laid. Cra-aa-aak, he would answer back, and I was enchanted by their melodious but mournful dialogue. Shit, too, rolled down a rubber belt, and the whole place had a musty unhealthy aroma. Years afterwards, the empty cages, still decorated with the odd whispering feather, were left to gather more of the millennial dust which seemed to creep out of the walls and settle softly and inexorably on each lost endeavour. But when these crumbling outbuildings were knocked down, and the slates sold for hard cash, the ground underneath flourished with vibrant flowering weeds, from seeds buried for who knows how long beneath the walls.

Beyond the battery shed and the bullock yard soared the grandest building of them all, the ancient corn barn. A mighty grain-palace thatched with Norfolk reeds, dark and magnificent as a cathedral, stacked after harvest with layer upon layer of barley sacks, soft to touch and sweet to smell in their mustiness. You could sink into their contours, slip down behind them, crawl dangerously under them, hang upside down from them, absorb them, become them, not know where you ended and they began. It was post-harvest ecstasy.

There was a tale told of a boy who had drowned in a grain hopper, as it sucked the barley down and along the pipes to be dried and bagged. I imagined him often, saw his desperate disappearing eyes, as I peered down into our hopper, and got yelled at by Dad or one of the men if I peered too close.

Dad was the one who drove the machine that cut the corn. It gushed into a huge hopper on the side of the harvester, where Ginger guided the streaming grains into the wide mouths of huge hessian sacks, and knotted them securely with fraying binder twine. Bill would drive the tractor round the harvest field and Harold would load the sacks which had been pushed down the chute off the combine. 'Watch yerlegs!' was the shout to me as I rode down the swift sharp-sided slope of the combine on a sack, and landed with a thwunk on the ground.

I'm watching!

The sudden plunge down the chute and the stop, over and over, I never failed to be breath-shaken by it. Then when I'd had enough of that I'd pick myself up and join Bill for the next stage of the journey from field to farm where the massive sacks were winched off the trailer, swinging dangerously in the air from a thick iron chain, and stacked giant-high, by the heroic team who managed the harvest spoils.

Bill. I see him now, solid and handsome, brown cheeked and brown haired. I sit beside him on the throbbing side of the tractor, a joy no longer allowed, by law, and he sings, we sing together. 'If you were the only girl in the world, and I were the only boy, Nothing else would matter in the world today, We would go on loving in the same old way, If you were the only girl in the world, And I were the only boy'. Above the noises of the tractor and of the combine as it sweeps by, driven by my godlike father, dominating the swathes of heavy-headed corn, the singing thrills me, as I balance ecstatically on the tractor's edge in my sandals with the toes cut out to make them last till the end of the summer. Bill patiently taught me to whistle too, and I would lie in bed at night striving to purse my lips as he did to blow out a blackbird aria up into the endless sky.

Long has paled that sunny sky: Echoes fade and memories die: Autumn frosts have slain July.

Fifty years later I stood appalled, at the sight of the still smouldering ruins of this mighty monument to agriculture, the ancient corn barn, listed as one of the nation's historic buildings. (As had been our house, until my modernising mother started making her unofficial *ad hoc* additions, a sun porch over the front door, a sun lounge instead of servants' rooms, designed by a leading architect of the area it's true, but these additions quite ruined the house's classic face, and so it lost its place on the list). The corn barn's thatch was apparently set ablaze by a spark from a welding machine nearby, and the whole mighty edifice was reduced to black splints and rubble in less than an hour.

Thatch is one of the most ancient ways to keep yourself and your possessions dry; a well-thatched roof, made of hazel spars and Norfolk reeds or straw, fastened to the rafters with strong iron hooks, can last many decades. In these long and ceaselessly revolving years, birds may pull at the thatch ends for their nests, and rats may follow, dancing along the joists and burrowing, so that once the mighty roof begins to slump you need to call the clever thatcher back to work his way steadily from the eaves to the top ridge, stripping the roof right down to the oak rafters and starting again, starting at the bottom and moving upwards till he reaches the crown, fastening the straw bundles as he goes with hazel rods he's cut the previous winter. At the top he makes his own signature pattern, writing his name in thick and solid thatch. Now one little spark had destroyed the work of so many generations.

Fine egg whites and horsehair were mixed together, or so they said, to build Suleiman the Magnificent's Balkan bridge over the Drina, a sixteenth century masterpiece of dazzling stone to mirror his power and strength. But in the late twentieth century this heart-stopping arch was destroyed by artillery in yet another war against the Other. 'It's just an old bridge' said the general who destroyed it. Later our old house too would become a helpless victim of such indifference.

I was at least thankful that my dad had not lived to see this final destruction of his world, the burnt remains of the magnificent storehouse for those harvests brought home by him and the generations before him.

Village children came to chase the rabbits that ran terrorised from their hiding places in the barley at harvest time. We all made houses from the straw, piling and burrowing and tumbling and flying, and by the end of the three or four weeks, my legs were a mass of raw red stabs from the stubble, as we hopped and skipped and raced from end to end of the rows of plundered broken stalks. Lunchtimes had a kind of sparkling golden timelessness: tired and sweaty hired men drank beer and ate sandwiches after my ma had arrived in the car, bundling over the bumps with a huge laundry hamper full of food. One year she catered to us all most royally with a hot roast chicken and china plates, carefully wrapped in tea-towels, but mostly there were satisfying chunky beef sandwiches, with fiery mustard for those who wanted it, with currant buns and apples and lemonade for the kids.

There were highs and lows at harvest, days when the grey and brooding skies brought heavy rain and my father paced up and down measuring the moisture content of his crop. Damp grain goes mouldy and is un-saleable. He would look up and scan the passing clouds: *mackerel sky—not long wet and not long dry.* The subtle movements of the elements, indifferent to human hopes and needs, were recorded on the face of his round barometer, which he tapped each morning with a gentle finger. They were a back-beat to his whole life, sometimes hopeful, sometimes mournful, as he recorded in his diary.

Dull, glass backing, we live in hopes.

At pressures below twenty-nine mercury inches the sky is cloudy and you can expect rain

Glass still falling.

Steadily decreasing air pressure indicates deteriorating weather

Glass well back.

In summer a sudden rapid fall indicates the approach of a thunderstorm

Glass still low.

Glass moved up a bit.

But at twenty-nine the weather is changeable, bright spells followed by frustrating showers

Better luck tomorrow, but the glass won't move.

Glass falling again, raining hard, a wet night.

Mercury falling below twenty nine point five, rain is a certainty

Glass rising a wee bit.

Glass rising, but sun too white.

Glass rising.

With air pressure of thirty mercury inches you can at last expect dry weather

Whether the weather be cold, whether the weather be hot,

Whatever the weather we'll weather the weather

Whether we like it or not.

My father like an ancient bushman could smell the rain coming, lifting his flaring nostrils sideways to the wind when he went outside the back door into the yard, and nodding his head as the first drops came to herald a shower or a storm. He could unfailingly read the riddles of the sky, or so it seemed to me. Here comes the rain.

Then there were days when all seemed set fair and yet at some unpredicted moment the combine would cough and give up. Another event in 'the chapter of small breakdowns' that Dad described in his diary. Long half-hours or even hours would be spent looking for the distant speck of the mechanic's red van, stuttering over the field all the way from Oulton Broad. Then there was the roar and the triumph and the relief when the combine throatily leapt back into action. On those days Dad wouldn't stop for lunch for more than a few moments, as Ma walked alongside the slowly moving monster, handing him sandwiches and something to drink.

When Dad was young, the sickle had in its turn had been replaced by the corn reaper and then the corn binder, pulled by three heavy horses. They too gave way to the tractor, and it was clear that someone would think eventually of marrying the two. Each development cut down on manpower; eventually Ginger gave up his bagging job and the grain poured straight into a hopper driving alongside the harvester.

As several functions were joined in the one machine, so human beings became cut off from the process. Once upon a time my father's handsome dust-grimed face had sat at the helm of his machine as he skilfully drove the swathes of corn under the binder. But this was no happy fairy story. New designs and safety strictures produced the cab and headphones to cut the driver off from the noise and the fumes, but also from the fundamental connections with the land. This was a relatively swift progress in two hundred years, from when Jethro Tull had advocated horse-hoeing husbandry as being the best way to till the soil. While my father's plough turned up stone-age axe-heads and flints sharp as the wind that cut over the high fields, the thrust was always forward, to the unimagined future.

In the evening I heard my parents debating barley prices. The rhythms of harvest and their link with the unpredictability of the weather lay deep in my father's bones. Forty years later, long after he had made his last run around a harvest field on the huge harvester, he wrote to me in one of his weekly letters, 'Harvest won't be long now, in fact some barley has been cut around here. Winter Barley of course, that means 'twas sown last autumn and after a mild winter 'twas early harvesting. All Dutch, maybe, sorry dear'. I felt his sharp pain at what he'd lost. One day when my son Sam was young Granddad took him for a walk along the green and muddy lane that led to my old nursery school. Granddad put down his walking stick, and they sat by the tangled hedge among the nettles and the hawthorns and the blackberry bushes. Then Granddad cried. 'It's hard getting old, boy'. Not for him the romantic music of twilight.

Time and the bell have buried the day, The black cloud carries the sun away.

Chapter Six

In which Molly at last gets to read her father's diaries and account books, which give the backdrop to the more intimate family life gradually eroding over time. Her parents work hard in their different ways, and Molly begins to learn something about the separate roles of men and women on the farm, as well as carrying on her researches into life and love .

Old repairs which are ugly and distorting the original tapestry should be removed. Cut the threads of the repairs with sharp scissors or a scalpel blade and pull free.

When Molly's son was young, her dad used to send his grandson pictures cut out of the *Farmer's Weekly* and the *Eastern Daily Press*. They stuck them all in a scrapbook. He sent pictures of heavy horses, jingling with polished harness and brasses, sheep farmers leaning on their sticks in front of their flocks, with faithful dogs alert at their feet. At the beginning of the book is glued a letter.

Sam boy, I hope you keep these pictures I send you. As I see the future, we will not get anything like this in say twenty to forty years, and in your life time that's a very short time. All these lovely pictures will be grand to look back on, and perhaps you will think of me. Granddad xx

It felt like a message to both Sam and his mother. Think of him. When did Molly not? She still looked for his strong hand and his muscled arm on dark nights. Those memories of his were downloaded into Molly, who developed a passion to pass them on.

In her son's first story book at school, there is a pencil-drawn picture of Granddad shooting a hare. In the picture it's not clear where Granddad's hand ends and his gun begins, and that was probably the way of it.

He had been born near the beginning of the twentieth century, and he had seen such change in his life, too much to manage, so he hung onto the old truths until he died as the millennium approached. It was the onslaught of the new which heralded the old man's slow decline. Houses were built in an adjacent field, and for the first time in his life he felt overlooked, crowded. Yet he had only one address during his whole life on earth.

Granddad often talked of having a shot at things; not just hares. Things indeed could be done, he thought, 'like a shot'. In his old age, ancient stories bubbling up from the family stew-pot overcame him, resentments and injuries from the past, and one day he held a gun to his wife's head. His son swiftly came and took the gun away. The gun cupboard was locked for ever.

There existed an ancient account-book covered with marbled green paper, documenting the farm's history when Molly's father's father was still alive, and carrying on until the 1950s. Here the old field names rolled solemnly in order of acreage: Gapstile, Rats' Field, Cliff Piece, Pond Meadow, Old Woman's Piece, Sourhollands and Molehills. Old Woman's Piece needed two tons of ground chalk per acre to lighten its heavy clay: fourteen tons on just over seven and a half acres. Here were set out the annual cropping plans: Hay, Barley, Sugar beet, Potatoes and Wheat. Cropping returns were also faithfully recorded, and lists each year of machinery held to farm the two holdings, one in a neighbouring village. Four drills, one hay-rake, three ploughs, one cultivator. Four tumbrels, five sets of harrows, two tractors and a trailer. All you needed to make the most of what you had, and coax riches from the soil in an understandable world.

Payments were made in cash to those on whose labour the project depended; to 'regular employees including domestic servants', to 'casual farm employees', including one 'old girl Frankie'. What a picture her name evokes: a feisty woman, perhaps of late middle-age, with a mouth on her as well as a stubborn propensity for hard work, doing the backbreaking 'tater picking' and singling out the sugar beet with a cunning hoe. Then there was rent for land subleased, under the heading 'other privileges'.

In that same year, there is a list of 'Stock in hand' included the bull (worth forty pounds), ten store cattle, four fat bullocks, twenty-five store pigs, ten heifers in calf. There were milking cows too, with names like Spitfire, Fill-pail and Nancy, Polly, Dolly and Rita (all served by William the bull, named Molly assumed after her paternal grandfather who had sired a considerable brood of his own). The figures for milk yields crowded the page in her dad's strong rounded writing, a solid declaration of his worth and a surety that there was goodness for him in the world of the farm (until a few years later when he hurt his back, had to lie prone for months and feared that he would have to give up what he knew).

Molly's dad had a 'Licence to Sell Milk by Retail', signed and stamped by one Sidney Foster, General Manager of the Milk Marketing Board, who sat in an office in London's Millbank, a world away from the dank cowshed. The East Suffolk War Agricultural Executive Committee in the local town of Woodbridge sent an urgent request in the year of Molly's birth, for a cropping forecast return. While milk production remained a priority, the farmer was reminded that the acreage of crops for human consumption had to be at least up to the level of the previous year. Flax was also an essential crop; its fibre was used for making parachute harness. This Woodbridge Executive Officer noted that now barley flour was included in the National Loaf, it too should figure large in cropping plans, alongside other essential items such as wheat and sugar beet.

Molly's dad kept a cutting from the *Eastern Daily Press* about top dressing for cereals, roots and hay. Seedbed feeding with sulphate of ammonia, nitro-chalk and nitrate of soda is recommended, rather than this being left till later growth. A spring top dressing for winter-sown wheat, said the pundit W.A.B., is established as good practice 'except on land in extremely good heart'. In spite of all these chemicals, her dad did indeed keep his land in good heart, going against the growing trend to burn the stubble, which he insisted on ploughing back into the earth.

There is a poem in the book too, a strong blank verse lament about a failing tractor, in the form of an application for a grant:

> *My tractor has done three years' hard work and is very much worn*
> *Using a great deal of paraffin and a colossal amount of oil*
> *Knocking when pulling a two-furrow plough on the Low Farm*
> *Which is stiff land.*

As the bearings are bad
I am afraid the tractor will let me down
And I cannot afford to be without it
So I have made this application.
There's no record of what happened to his touching plea.

The seasons rolled onward, and the family rolled with them, and once a year only went to church at Harvest Festival.

Don't you realise that all the wars in the world have been fought because of religion, said Molly's ma when Molly asked, in love with Catholicism at her convent primary school, where the little girls about to take their First Communion stood on chairs and pirouetted in front of the class in their stiff white dresses, please may I have a rosary? Molly had of course been christened, white gowned, laden with silver trinkets and sewn in to the myths of the Anglican church, but over the succeeding years her mother's true feelings overcame the tradition she had clearly gone along with before she felt the swelling of her own power into a force that could shape her universe. The slightest whiff of divinity made her purse her sceptical lips. Was it god or her father who had let her down?

Molly's own father had been a choir-boy in his youth, but his wife had clearly weaned him of whatever loyalty he felt towards the Almighty. *We plough the fields and scatter the good seed on the land.* In the church were baskets of flowers, walls of carrots and parsnips, beetroot and marrows, little regimental rows of jam which lined the sills of the windows, bunches of flopping corn which caught your legs at the end of every pew. *But it is fed and watered by God's almighty hand.* Molly tried to hang on to this conviction in the face of her mother's assertions which assailed her faith in divine generosity and forgiveness, just as her father's lack of faith in any good in humanity had threatened to undermine her hope, and simultaneously nourished an unrealistic optimism.

All is safely gathered in,
Free from sorrow, free from sin.
That was a puzzling thought. Who had sinned? Not the barley, Molly reasoned, and anyway she had long abandoned the idea of a world free of

sorrow. She knew she was a sinner. Didn't everyone sin? And how come everyone was sold on good? If everyone was really so good, how did the evil stuff get done? As usual she had to live with a buzzing barrel of unanswered questions.

After harvest her father invited the tired farm hands indoors to drink a few victory beers. They all crowded together, a close and awkward group pushing one another and smiling shyly, into the room beyond the scullery, and Molly's brother was invited as well to this all-male gathering. It was after one such event, as they emerged unsteadily into the back yard, that Molly, the excluded one, hanging about just outside the back door, launched the word she'd heard them use to test its power—*bugger*, not in a sentence, just the clanging word. Her father was shocked and she was indeed herself impressed by the strength and potency of it. A reckless utterance. Later she writes it, with beating heart, many times on a page, to feel again its unknown strength, its singular timeless force, then she tears up the paper and throws the tiny bits on the play-room fire, where they melt into the flames and make the chimney roar with new energy.

While those forbidden scraps were consumed immediately, in her mum's cookbook there remained three flimsy bills from the local wine, spirit and beer merchants, for the year that Molly was three. Eighteen half Guinnesses for the men were billed for sixteen shillings and six pence— the same price it seems as for half a bottle of rum, and a bottle of vermouth. Seagers Cocktail was a little dearer. You might wonder what sort of a potent mix that was.

In the late summer gangs of 'Scotch girls', as they were called locally, came down on the train from their northern home-towns to gut the herrings; huge gluts of fish whose scales still glittered as they poured in helpless, vivid dead streams from herring baskets carefully made in willow by local craftsmen. A sea packed with herrings had ensured that since Roman times the fishing tradition had thrived. There was a tale that so many fishing boats were often stacked edge to edge in the harbour that you could walk across their decks from one side to the other. Old men still remembered it.

Long lines of these 'Scotch girls' unfolded round the harbour standing behind trestle tables, and Molly's dad would exchange bold greetings with them when the family went to buy some of the bounty for pickling. Molly was fascinated by the deft way the strong gore-covered hands of these often rather mature 'girls' slit and eviscerated the fish, throwing them in the bloody baskets, while the gulls wheeled and shrieked above in anticipation of the best feast of the season. She was also fascinated by her dad's charisma, as he drove slowly by the long trestles, pulling at the girls' concentration with his easy smiles. The girls' aprons were stiff with blood and guts, and their voices, harsh and with a different accent from the Norfolk tones to which she was used, barked at one another as they guffawed their way through their long and bloody task.

Fifty years previously, the fleet of herring boats had been a thousand strong. The smoking and packing industry surrounding them ensured that huge cargoes of fish were sent each day to European destinations. Molly's dad would have been shocked to learn that, scarcely more than half a century after his flirtatious marketing, this once-famous fleet was reduced to one remaining vessel. Defiantly painted blue and red, surrounded by still hopeful gulls, it makes its way over the choppy seas into oblivion, because of the rise of the cod fish finger.

Bonfire Night always heralded the beginning of winter and the dark days, when at the end of the barley harvest in a newly-ploughed field a bonfire ringed with old car tyres blazed away, and all the village children came to let off bangers and roast chestnuts in the melting smelting singeing mixture of wood-ash and rubber, as good old Guy Fawkes toppled off his perch for another year, the flames died down and you could allow your scorching face near enough to pick out the nuts and spuds. Then the stubble ends from harvest time were ploughed back into the soil, and again Molly was an ardent passenger on the tractor. This fiery machine fascinated her, one day she put her hand over the pipe where the steam emerged from the uncapped radiator, and watched in fascination as her skin bubbled before the pain began.

Autumn blurred into winter, when the rows of animated and teetering swallows had organised themselves on the telephone wires across the yard before starting their anxious and courageous flight off to Africa, and it was down the drive to the bottom vegetable garden with finger-less mittens to pick the rock-hard sprouts off their unyielding stalks. Good old Jack Frost, who some say dates back to the days of Molly's family's Viking ancestors as Jokul Frosti, the frosty icicle, painted intricate landscapes on the playroom window. Layer upon layer of ferny shapes, which Molly and her brother then altered in their own way with warm, stubby fingers, breathing on his artistry, making huge black holes in the fabric of his fractal paradise.

They had sledges for the snowy days, their dad built a huge one and towed it behind the Zephyr Six up and down the winding roads, with Molly and her brother clinging half terrified and half joyous on the back. The registration numbers of those first cars! The Ford Eight and the Zephyr Six, the numbers still recalled from so long ago, ONG, BGU. They were friends, these cars, and when one was sent to the garage to be replaced by another, there were tears. They seemed to be so casually exchanged, and maybe it resonated with the children's own fears of being supplanted, ignored, forgotten, transplanted into a new and different space. How could the grownups do this? They played games with their own and other cars' numbers on the long journeys to market. Better Give Up. Our Nice Gran. Are we nearly there, Oh are we nearly there? The river of the speeding road fell away behind them. 'Help! We're being kidnapped!' was a sign they used to write on any old paper scraps left lying on the back seat, and stick up on the rear window to be read by the car behind. But their giggling faces put paid to that dramatic story.

They built snowmen, with sprouts for eyes, not coal, and Molly's hands chafed and went bright red as they thawed back into aching life afterwards as she sat by the fire.

Molly's dad was an artist when it came to lighting fires indoors. It was almost a sacred ceremony to watch him carefully build a fire in the dining room grate, paring bits off the side of kindling sticks with one of his many penknives, each one with a pearl handle, breathing slowly to match the rhythm of the ritual, so that when he finally lit the match, the whole edifice burst into life with a premeditated grandeur. Then he and his awestruck daughter would both sit and follow the flames as they raced up the chimney in a river of sparks. He made hooked rugs with the same graceful dedication, canvas draped across his knees after a hard day's work and after tea, while the family listened to the radio and played cards: Canasta, Bezique, Snap, and glorious games of Cheat, Cheat, Cheat.

Bezique was complicated, played with two packs of cards, with a scoring system presided over by their mother. Four kings were worth more than four queens, Molly was outraged to know, and a Bezique meant a queen and a jack of any suit together, worth forty points.

Canasta too was played with two packs, but the suits were irrelevant, the cards were matched by rank and number alone, like the army. While Bezique was only for two players, so at least one child was excluded, Canasta was for four. Still it was complicated for the children, despite Molly poring over the minutely printed rules on the black and white box in the hope of beating the grownups. A hand was only over when you had played all your cards. Far simpler to dribble them nonchalantly into your lap when they finally got to play Cheat, the ecstasy of a cheating roll, cards pouring into your lap unnoticed by your family of opponents, and the triumph of victory!

If Molly's father was king of the combine harvester, her mother was certainly queen of the Singer sewing machine. A century before, hand-sewing had been revolutionised by the invention of this device, another stone in the slowly-built path of progress and one first destroyed by rioting tailors in France. But for her ma this spelt liberation from drudgery. Molly could remember her mother's anger when as a teenager she brought home from a second-hand shop an exquisitely hand-stitched Victorian night-gown. 'You think it's beautiful, but I was the one who had to sit on a stool and not speak till the seams were perfect and the embroidery done without a false stitch'. Clearly Molly's mother did not feel herself to be in an honourable tradition of tapestry makers, sewing the world together from the beginning, as the old Norse myths said.

Isaac Merrit Singer, God bless his soul, had taken his place as the largest manufacturer of the tailors' enemy. His curved eye-pointed needle moved up and down carrying the thread forwards and backwards through the material, while underneath a second cunning little thread on a shuttle caught it, embraced it, interlocked with it over and over again. Molly's mum's machine was black with gold, green and orange painted patterns rather formally done, like those on a Persian carpet, running across the length of its strong body and down its one leg to the variety of feet to which it could be attached. It lived in a handsome wooden case with a scrolled metal handle, on the top kitchen shelf.

Molly's ma was like a wizard with her familiar, she and the machine seemed to sing magic rhythmical songs together, as they went about the serious work of creating clothes for all the family. She made Viyella shirts and corduroy trousers for her husband, and for herself she made a series of ever more stunning evening 'frocks', beginning with a white lace calf-length dress, made from curtain material when there was nothing else available as clothes coupons were still in force, which she wore to the first Farmers' Union Ball, with strings and strings of baby jet beads. She used whatever was to hand, parachute silk following the end of the war, and once even a dress made of maps printed on slightly stiffened fabric, maps which had been issued to the forces, and then discarded.

When restrictions lifted in 1949, she made a daring pink, blue and silver strapless floor-length gown, crossed over at the back and falling in an ocean of princess pleats to the floor. From a lake of shimmering electric blue French velvet, she drew up under her machine's magic foot a shining Grecian column, draped to perfection, which she wore with a diamante buckle on her hip.

She like countless other women fell in love with the new post war romantic style, pioneered by Christian Dior, with its wasp waists, full skirts, plunging necklines, silk and embroidery and coloured beading, dazzling contrast to the meagre years of gabardine suits. The New Look. It redefined entirely the silhouette of the desirable female form.

The winter of 1946 was the coldest on record in Europe in the twentieth century. Siberian winds cut across the continent, and the lowest temperatures were logged in Dover. Monsieur Dior, a previously unknown designer, announces to a Parisian audience still huddled in austerity clothes when he launches his first magnificent collection: 'Girls can safely feel they have all the trappings of a fairytale princess…what do the weight of my heavy velvets and brocades matter? When hearts are light, mere fabric cannot weigh the body down'.

After the privations of wartime, this was a return to femininity and a kind of infinite glamour that had never actually been abandoned by Molly's mother, who was in no way put off by the president of the board of trade's grumpy comment; 'if women are going to buy these skirts, they are going to have to buy fewer of them'. In his dreams.

Until she could afford to buy top quality ready made, and she aimed for nothing less, she had a cunning way of sashaying into something she had run up herself which gave the impression somehow of being covered with feathers and rhinestones, made in scarlet silk and taffeta, silk organdie and embroidered sequins. No princess was she, but a queen. Though she was destined to be dethroned in a way which she had certainly never anticipated.

After her death, her wardrobes still overflowed with evening dresses, from the wealthier post-war years, each bought for one occasion and seldom worn a second time. Molly was overwhelmed with so many conflicting feelings, and sold them all for a knock-down price to a vintage clothes shop. In the dank smelly basement of this shop, the dresses glowed as each was held up critically by the sour buyer, accustomed to drive a hard bargain, as she did with Molly, who left them there and fled the shop, never daring to walk past the window again in case she saw her mother's old finery on display. They would both have hated that.

First out of the suitcase is a long navy dress in heavy crepe, with long sleeves, lavishly embroidered with light and dark pink sprays of flowers. It has a sash, and a skirt cut to sway to the floor. It had seen, Molly is sure, at least one Anniversary Waltz. Gold zig-zag patterns cover the green crepe dress which next flows out; it has its own matching embroidered jacket with sweeping trumpet sleeves. There's an empire line dress with a pink and grey crocheted top, where pastel flowers float vaguely below the bust, in matching colours of pink, and grey, and brown. Then comes a violent contrast: a long loud dress crashes out of the case: bright orange and black swirls on a white ground, complete with a wide white fringed sash. Never could Molly have worn it, but not so the black pleated organza number that comes next, a skirt to die for, but one she leaves there with the rest.

Fifty pounds the lot, said the buyer. She had a ring in her nose, lanky hair in desperate need of a wash, and an air of supreme indifference to the history here. And why not. Fifty pounds was what Molly was offered.

I'll take it, she said.

But they were not so easily left behind, even though she had no room at home to keep them all. They lingered in her mind, the long dress in pleated pink, with ruffles at the neck, the silver and dark red column made of heavy stuff which fell from shoulder to hem in an unbroken line, the silk spotted suit, green on navy, with its sassy knee-length skirt and matching jacket with three-quarter sleeves…and pictures of her parents, dancing. It was too soon to say goodbye to them all, but she did.

Molly's party dresses too were always handsomely home-made, green or blue crepe, heavy with smocking; organdie skirts like pink whipped cream, puffy gathered sleeves to show off plump and fashionably dimpled arms. Dresses in which to parade around phalanxes of alternately placed chairs, to fly anxiously and triumphantly to an empty one when the music stopped… dresses in which to whisk under the linked arms of the boys, hoping even then to dance with the one you liked best, or disliked least. The old carousel had already started for Molly at her nursery school, when secretly she loved Antony Matthews who didn't seem to notice her, while Malcolm Tuck who clearly loved her was pitilessly ignored and pushed away. In and out the windows, in and out the windows, in and out the windows, as you have done before.

She loved these games, but dreaded them too. The most anxiety-provoking one was 'Farmer wants a Wife'. A little boy (of course) stands in the centre of his circling peers, and he chooses a wife as they all stand around him in a ring. The Wife then chooses a Child. The Child chooses a Dog. So far so good. But now the Dog wants a Bone. The next chanted line is a covert invitation to a bit of bullying: we all pat the Bone, we all pat the Bone, ee-ay, ee-ay, we all pat the Bone! No matter how pretty your dress, you feel crushed and humiliated if it's your turn to get this 'gentle' punishment. Of course the adults don't tend to notice.

Her ma had an ingenious little device, a canister filled with chalk which could be raised or lowered on a ruled stand. Molly would perch high on the kitchen table for the hem of the latest pretty dress to be got just right, and her mother would puff out the chalk with a rubber bulb to give a perfect line, then move towards permanence by fixing it with a row of pins which she held meanwhile between her pursed lips. The hero father comes in from the farm and stands amazed at the industry, waltzing his daughter or his wife and sometimes both round the kitchen table, scattering the pins. *Oh Rose-Maree I love you! I'm always dreeeming of you!* Molly's mother, three-quarters through the enterprise, would have a final fitting and insist on his presence. *Hold my hand! I'm a stranger in Paradise...*he would sing out in admiration. *Champagne and Brandy give life a much brighter hue, So have some handy, When I come calling on you...* Another stirring scene in the family soap opera

Molly's ma could be fun too, but you never knew when that would be. She allowed Molly to bring her skipping rope into the kitchen when it was a craze at school. The rope thwacked double time on the floor under Molly's mother's small feet as she showed her daughter how to do the bumps, her eyes shining with triumph after each bump.

One-two-three

Mother caught a flea

Put it in the teapot and made a cup of tea

The flea jumped out

Mother gave a shout–

The fun was unpredictable: great while it lasted. She could strut brilliantly like a penguin when she felt like it, acknowledging her children's shrieks of glee with triumphant eyes, had been known to have currant bun fights, when they went whizzing across the table, and once as Molly plagued her about something as she walked across the kitchen with her hands full, she poured the cold strained cabbage water down her daughter's neck. Molly laughed and laughed, glad to be sharing such a moment even at her own wet and smelly expense. She really was a stranger in this Paradise. Eagerness, probably painful for her mother to see, if she dared, would brim up in Molly, but it was short-lived and always spoiled by the foreknowledge of its own swift ending. Once in a blue moon, her ma would say. It meant almost never. The blue moon came as a second full one in a month, like the feeling of happiness, such a rare occurrence.

Then Molly's love would grow too intense, for both of them. Once Molly kissed her mother full on the mouth, and she drew back in anger, unable to translate her daughter's thwarted passion into a desire for ordinary mother-love. She interested Molly, absorbed her, this mother with her untidy heaps of clothes and makeup who found it tough to get up in the morning, so that they were often late and her father had to chase the school bus to the next stop in the car.

Molly was fascinated too by her mother's douche that she found in one of her secret prowlings under the sheets in the airing cupboard, relic of the old fertile days, and by the dark triangle of pubic hair she once fleetingly saw when she went into the bathroom by mistake when her mother was there. She looked just that once, and knew not to do it again. Such a complicated fascination, a mixture of blood and tears and lack of understanding. Maybe she wanted to get inside her mother, to be her, but she wanted to love her and for her to love her daughter too. Molly wanted in some strange way to be her mother's child and to have her child as well.

Her husband too was clearly enthralled by his wife's remote and untouchable mystique. When Molly was still a little girl he told her how he would watch his wife in the morning gracefully pull on her stockings, standing on one leg with the other pointed and outstretched, in front, behind, to make sure the seams were absolutely straight. She was his own version of the fabulous Betty Grable, whose legs it was reported had been insured against injury, apart from those, one supposed, which time would inflict. She was his Sonja Henje too, Norwegian winner of ten world ice-skating championships, who then became a film star like Grable, skating with her own ice show around the world. No accident, Molly thinks later, this choice of objects for his admiration.

His wife's ice show movie, where she was the most beautiful of all, fascinated all her family, but they were ultimately shut out of it. She grew the most lush and thrusting houseplants, because she knew that they like her thrived on their own reflections, so they were placed in front of mirrors all over the house. But they had to know their place as well. If one of them grew too flourishing, too shining, tall and beautiful that it might eclipse its mistress, out it went, to collapse and die in the cold yard.

Molly's father's dear Betty/Sonja knew her own power, was clearly conscious of her effect. Molly could recall a harsh tone entering her father's voice when she, innocent bubbly daughter on his knee, said she thought her ma was fond of one of the agricultural seed merchants who visited the old house, and he was fond of her. Something was clearly brewing, though not clear at all to Molly at the time.

Molly struggled with love, with doubt, with curiosity, wanting her mother's approval, which seemed always just out of reach. A small photograph shows the little girl with strictly plaited hair, hugging a doll under the old oak tree while her brother sits expansively smiling on a plastic tractor nearby. The plaiting could have been a time of closeness and attachment, but what Molly recalled were brisk pulls and tugs, watering eyes and strained hair too tight over a tingling scalp. Later her hair was cut, and there was much disapproval when as a late teenager, keen to practise opposition rather than appeasement, she elected to grow it again. It was as if she were a mini-Samson, whose power had to be controlled by cutting these unacceptable tresses.

Molly's mother could eclipse the sun on any and sometimes every day. When the children looked at the eclipse through smoked glass, one summer day when Molly was seven, she shivered at the underworld light which crept over the whole world, it seemed. She also recognised it. Molly lived in terror of her mother masking the light in her own daily life. It was impossible to escape. She was sucked into her mother's singularity, annihilated, done for, over and over again.

Oh don't overdo the drama. Do you really think this is clever?
It's easy for you to talk.

She dreamed of exposure on a bare hillside, and the sun suddenly eclipsed by the moon. She prayed to God, just in case he was there, listening to a sinner like her, to bring his light to bear on this terrifying twilight absence. Isaac Newton had discovered the rich bands of colour released from white light passing through a prism. If white light could reveal its hidden colours, an idea rejected by all Newton's peers except for the poets, what does absence of light portend? In Molly's life colour could easily be drained away, leaving only the greys.

Come into my parlour, said the spider to the fly. She was eaten many times, stuck in her helpless happiness, a wingless victim. She never really knew whether her mother loved her or hated her, or her own personal and complicated mixture of both.

'I've loved you all along', her mother said as an old woman, when Molly knew there was precious little time to ask the question that had been on her mind for so many years. 'But maybe I haven't shown it'. A week before she died her daughter dared, for the first time, since she was a child, openly to declare her own love. Her mother looked around, her huge blue eyes now inhabited by a watery vagueness. Let us not hope for tears.

'What are you looking for, Mum?'

'I think I've found it'.

And she told Molly she loved her too. 'But'-

But what? 'But I often think you're an idiot'.

Mrs Stonyheart refused to quit the field, even then. Swallow and carry on.

Molly wondered afterwards whether this was a reflection of how such simple feelings, simple at least for most people, made her mother feel foolish and vulnerable. If the ice melted, she would no longer be the mistress of the world, and she might end up sitting in a puddle. John Donne, writing four hundred years before, gave that fearful foolishness words, and any one of his scornful mistresses must have induced a similar feeling in him: '*I am two fools I know, One for loving, One for saying so*'.

Deep inside Molly's mother there lived someone who would spurn her, or so she thought, if she really declared herself. Loving means at bottom relying on someone else, feeling helpless, and she couldn't have borne it. It was a terrible loss for her children. Molly's passionate search, her unrequited love, took every atom of her energy, for many years. These atoms danced, dazed and bumping one into another, in a frenzy, leaving less attention for other things, but still, enough to carry on.

Her mother was queen of course of the kitchen, where for Molly 'learning to cook' meant keeping her mouth shut and her legs alert to fetch what her mother needed. This small girl didn't get to stir the bowl as recommended in the childcare books but she got to lick it out, though this too was accompanied by stern warnings about getting worms if you ate uncooked flour. Scones and cakes were her mother's forte and she was less certain with pastry. She made sausages and pork brawn, and pickled walnuts which the family had collected green from Stormer's field. She got her recipe from Elizabeth Craig's *Economical Cookery*, published in 1934. 'What kind of cook are you? Do you shine when you've got to make a shilling do the work of two, or do you only make a good show when you can buy what you please? There's nothing much to be proud of when you need never count the cost of your ingredients. There's nothing much to be proud of when you can have as many eggs and as much butter and cream as you want to cook with. Rather something to be grateful about'.

Elizabeth Craig said you had to prick the green walnuts before the shells hardened, all over with a darning needle. You had to leave them for a week in salt and water, then take them out and leave them in the sun until they turned completely black. Then you put them in a great big pickle jar, poured over a wonderful aromatic liquor of vinegar and all the spices of Arabia, and left them for six months till you could eat them with any variety of cold meats; something to be grateful about.

Elizabeth also had some helpful tips about 'how to use up scraps of pastry'. She suggests brushing them with white of egg, sprinkling them with caster sugar and cutting them up in 'fancy shapes' for baking. These fancy shapes could be topped with water icing when cooked, or raspberry and apricot jam, and whipped cream. If baked without a sugar coating, they could be used to garnish leftover ham, or boiled fowl, reheated in a white sauce. This all sounds like fun Molly could have had, but the Queen never suggested it.

Her mother pickled the herring bought from the brawny 'Scotch girls'. Molly never liked pickled herring, with their wispy bones you worried might stick in your throat, but her father did, with a passion. They had already been gutted on the quayside, and then they were salted and peppered, layered with cloves and allspice, vinegar and sage, into earthenware crocks. They were sealed tight both with a plate and a thick crust of dough, and boiled for hours, slowly and aromatically, on the kitchen range.

The economical Elizabeth offered advice on budgets: when a wife had to cook for a husband, herself and one child on less than thirty shillings a week, she could only use two and a half pounds of meat with a little fat. Life was better in the country and she tells her readers that a wife cooking for a husband, herself and four children in the country can get by splendidly on thirty-three shillings a week, she can have four pounds of meat but even so when the hens aren't laying she may have to use egg powder, or 'if hens are not kept, One dozen when cheap'. And of course in the country and certainly in Molly's house there was the free food from the hedges and the woods.

The year Molly was married, her ma copied out for her a neat page describing 'Your Great-Grandmother's Christmas Pudding Recipe'. She always used this recipe herself, and truly Molly had never tasted such puddings. (See Appendix). The potent mix of fruit and spices, brandy and old ale had to be tied up in a pudding basin with an old cloth (her mother used worn-out sheets), and the ears of the cloth used to lift the basins into boiling water, where they had to stay for nine hours in the beginning, and a further three hours just before you ate them. Molly only made the puddings once, leaving them to bubble and murmur in a large iron saucepan on an Aga, but this recipe remained as a gift from her mother.

Little Jack Horner sat in a corner, eating his Christmas pie.
He put in his thumb and pulled out a plum
And said what a good boy am I.

In later years Molly's mother graduated from the traditional recipes of her childhood to more swanky food, and she had a huge collection of cookbooks and part-works dedicated to the art of cooking Italian, Danish, but her favourite was French, dishes 'to delight your friends'. She served these dishes up with triumph and then a good deal of the resultant meal time was spent discussing the dish in question. She feigned, or so it seemed to Molly who perhaps was envious of her mother's talents here, an anxiety about the taste, the texture, the balance of ingredients, in order to have praise given and repeated and given yet again. It was the kind of food which Molly's father always ate obediently rather than with relish, with a grudging admiration, forced out under his wife's stern yet somehow desperate glance.

Molly's dad shot innumerable rabbits to contribute to the family table, and he hung them by their feet in the scullery till he skinned them ready for the pot. First he would lay them on the slate draining board of the huge scullery sink, slit their bellies right down the middle and take out their stomach bag. Sometimes if his daughter was watching he would slit this open too, to show her what Bertie Bunny's last meal had been, then he skinned him, loosening the skin first of all along the slit edges of the abdomen, then pulling it right back, slooowly and carefully—oh that pink pearly skin, traced with blue, revealed in all its nakedness—over the hind legs, cutting the tail as he went, and the first joint of each leg. When either of their parents was undressing Molly or her brother, and it came to the vest over the head, they would sing out 'skin a rabbit!' Her dad pulled the skin over, right over the rabbit's head , and this was where Molly had to abandon the notion of dead Bertie and concentrate on the process, the un-rabbit like corpse produced as her dad cut the ears off with the skin, and took out the dulled eyes, all with his scarily sharp knife. Then Bertie got soaked in salted water on the trestle in the scullery gloom, until the time came to truss him up for the stew-pot. It was an abundant universe, animals there for the eating.

What have you got for dinner Mrs Bond?
here's beef in the larder and ducks on the pond
Dilly, dilly, dilly-dilly, come and be killed

In the scullery too was a huge circular copper where water was heated up with a fire underneath to do the weekly wash, and the great iron mangle, whose handle John and Molly could barely turn together, as they helped with the vests and liberty bodices, flattening them with the huge rubber rollers, taking out all the water which had seemed to give them life even off their bodies. It was a noble iron construction, with a gold lion rampant on each side. 'Mind your fingers!' they were warned. Molly once heard one of the farm men talk about 'tits in the mangle', and even though she was yet to have them, she knew what their fate would be, life flattened out of them like the vests, the first blooming of air inside them expelled with a helpless 'pouf' for ever. Gradually the rubber rollers began to perish and flake, and a washing machine came to replace the copper.

Chapter Seven

In which we are introduced to another of Molly's heroes: Steve, one of the village boys, the same age as Molly, but who knows so much more than she does about things she can only have an inkling of. She wants to find out, but feels guilty too, and steals to make up for the lack, or so she feels, of her mother's love.

To join the lining and the tapestry together a guide line of thread is first placed across the width of the tapestry. Match a marked grid line with the tapestry line. Fix with pins. Chain stitch can then be worked in a line to hold together these memories.

If her dad shot more rabbits than were needed, he gave them to the farm hands, who lived in the village, and with whose children Molly and her brother loved to play. But there was unease not far beneath the shouts and the laughter. Those village kids who came to join their Bonfire Night fun were a source both of pleasure and of pain. There was Steven and there was Jimmie, and Rosie whose granddad, old Mr Bearton, lived over the road from the old farm house in a cottage belonging to their uncle's farm at the other end of the village. Rosie had a brother but he was younger than John, almost too little to count, and then there was Carla, whose mum, always in her slippers, lived next door to the Beartons. Even at four or five or six, with her fuzzy blonde hair and her gap-toothed rather vacant smile, you could see she'd grow up fast, that Carla. Sure to be pregnant at fourteen was what Molly overheard one of the village women say. And of course she was. Had more pricks than a pincushion, was what they said later, when her stomach bulged. The village gang let Molly and John play, but they made it quite clear too that it was a bit on sufferance: Molly and her brother lived in a big house and they were 'snobs'. The kids didn't venture up the drive to knock on the farm house back door and John and Molly certainly would never knock on theirs either, but they just drifted casually down the curving drive, kicking the gravel up in a show of nonchalance and hoping the little village gang would be there. These kids seemed to know so much that Molly didn't know, and they radiated for her a kind of louche glamour which spoke of worlds without the restrictions she chafed at in her own.

Opposite the Beartons' house was the farm pond, and just outside the bank around it was an iron railing, where these two disparate groups used to meet, and the girls used to do endless somersaults over the rail, trying not to, or not trying not to, show their knickers.

They played skipping games in the dusty road, who's in, who's out, over and over. You could tie one end of the rope to a tree so that only one person had to turn (but it was really better to have two turners when you could persuade someone to take the other end), while the others stood in a line, bodies and heads bobbing anxiously to the rhythm of the swish of the rope, until it was time to rush in, breath held, and start to jump. Or, even harder, you had to wait to hear the relentlessly chanted month of your own birthday, rush in to skip your age, and then leap out again without stopping the flow.

This might lead on to 'Piggie in the middle', if there were only three of you. What a strain it was, and a pain too, to try and catch the ball that whizzed over your head between the other two. It was even worse if there happened to be an audience of others queuing up to play. But you forgot all that in a heartbeat when you managed to get the ball, and change places with the one whose throw you'd managed to intercept.

They played complicated up against the wall ball games with devilish rules, involving increasing impediments to the actual task of catching the return ball as it skewed off at unpredictable angles. You could end up trying to dart at the ball left handed, one-eyed, needing to twizzle round twice before you even began to launch yourself towards it. This constant pushing of the boundaries of ability thrilled as well as sometimes defeated Molly, perhaps thrilled them all. They could only play this game when Mrs Bearton let them use her front wall, but Molly couldn't recall a shattered window.

They mastered hopscotch on grids chalked on the fading tarmac, where the odd passing car would scuff up the frame, and they would recreate it in their stubborn triumphant way. Clapping games were there for mastering too. Clap and slap your partner's palms, 'my mother said', clap and cross and slap again, 'I never should', first right then left, 'play with the gipsies in the wood, if I did,' clap, 'she would say', clap, ' naughty little girl to dis-o-bey.'

Wolves were in the wood too, out to get you. One person turns to the wall while the rest of them tippity-toe up behind.

What's the time, Mr Wolf?

He says one o'clock, or three o'clock, or seven o'clock, and then when the voices get closer and yet closer, before he can be tapped on the shoulder and caught out as the old fraud he is, he rounds savagely on his tormentors, fangs bared, and shouts 'Dinner Time!'

The village kids rode John and Molly's bikes and trikes, while they themselves mostly looked on and let this happen as an unspoken entry fee to this exciting world, a favour returned. As Steven careened along on Molly's blue trike while she perched dizzily on the back, she once came a clumsy cropper and broke her arm.

It set badly, and had to be re-broken and set again, under general anaesthetic. Her father's adage about not trusting anybody proved to be true. Would you like to smell some hyacinths, said the doctor, before he fitted the mask on her unresisting nose. She thought she was dying as she drifted inexorably away.

Later they had bigger bikes, and these too were traded for entry into the envied world of the village kids. Molly had been slow to learn on a two-wheeler; her dad had bought her a bike far too big, which terrified her as he wheeled it perilously round the sharp-stoned gravel yard and then let go, when she would wobble and crash time and time again. The grazed knees smarted not just because of broken skin, but because they were shameful evidence yet again of not doing it right. It wasn't till she rode her cousin's much tinier two wheeler that she gained confidence, closer to the ground.

Early each autumn they would all graze on the little golden plums which loaded down the trees at the edge of one of the farm's fields. These plums were another gift to Steve and his gang, and they gobbled them with complicit greed although they knew the price would be paid later with upset stomachs which could last a week.

As they grew older there were stolen hours of sexual exploration in the wood-fringed meadow above the row of farm cottages belonging to John and Molly's father. It was pre-pubertal stuff, looking and poking, doctors and nurses investigating the mysteries, with Steven and Carla enthusiastically leading them all on. At intervals they would sit in a row in the hedge and blow loud farts on thick grasses held tight between two thumbs.

Then at some point when grass-farts lost their zing, someone would suggest a spitting competition: just by spitting, nonchalantly, some way off, but not too far; keeping one's spittle in reserve for when the serious stuff begins.

Steve waits, while everyone else including Molly's little brother has a turn. Pssschewpfahh! No one says a word.

A butterfly lands on the grass nearby and its wings settle, open and blue. So butterflies, do sometimes rest, thinks Molly.

Then, in the silence, with an impressive in-breath, Steve lets his chest expand, swell, grow mighty, while he screws up his lips more tightly and more efficiently than anyone, and lets forth his arc of glittering spray, almost in slow motion. Inevitably it falls far ahead of any of his rivals into the scrub. He just smiles. There is nothing to say. The butterfly shivers and takes off from the shining blade of grass.

Molly was in awe of Steve, they were all in awe of him, eternal King of the Castle to their dirty rascals. He peed an arching yellow bow into the hedge in the same focussed and yet carelessly graceful way as Molly had seen her father do. Now that was where penis envy really made sense. Squatting close the ground, looking down at the beetles and the ants hurrying about their own little businesses, easy as it was for a small girl not yet bothered with niceties, was just nowhere, nothing, in comparison with this consummate offhand skill.

Those green and golden days stretched between one breath and the next, while a stray cat or two basked in the sun beside them, and then they passed.

In her last year before boarding school, when Molly was the only girl in a boys' prep school, cramming for the scholarship exam, these diminutive chancers insisted that they line up in front of her, and that she offer queenly inspection of their parts, so many wee willy winkies dangling before her eyes! Before that time she had only seen her brother's little vulnerable piglet's tail in the bath, because Steve's back had always been turned before he peed. Now she could begin to know something more about a variety which amazed her.

Molly wondered how to link these little tails with the solid packages you could make out beneath the young bucks' swimming trunks at the local pool. Would Steve grow up to be like them? Questions were clearly in all their minds. How on earth did you link this with your own parents? What secret pleasures did they enjoy, locked away from children's prying eyes? Girls the children learned to call 'common' peeked under the raised walls of the changing rooms to spy on women undressing. At the same time Molly struggled to make sense of some strange disturbing drawings of women's bodies which lay shrouded in almost total darkness in a concrete pill-box, remnant of the war defences, that had fallen from the cliff to the sands below. The floor sloped into the sand, was littered with old bags and cans, and the whole dark space gave off a putrid smell. But the drawings had a shadowy, religious quality, like frescoes or icons in an old church. Which in a way they were.

In the late twentieth century a cave was found in France, where luminous paintings of wild animals ran around the dark walls, only to be viewed by torchlight by their makers. There was one human figure: the bottom half of a woman, being entered by a buffalo. Those ancient people worshipped the power and prowess they admired in creatures which maybe seemed superior to them, and they wanted to take on their strengths. The drawings in the pill-box on the beach seemed to have the same spiritual significance, at least to little Molly. There were powerful mysteries here, as there have always been.

Like most children, Molly had a fund of creation myths inside her mind, jostling for a space. Was this a medical matter? Or did it involve some sort of fighting? It might be something to do with the lavatory, she thought, or the woods. But what went on in there was a mystery, and how you joined up these thoughts with thoughts about your parents, and your own body, remained a dark matter. When someone, was it Steve, told her graphically about the mechanics of it all, she felt both cheated and appalled. He saw it on her face. It's all right, he said with a grin, the Queen does it too. But she wasn't sure that this made it all right and chose to lose the pictures he had created somewhere inaccessible in her mind for quite a few years.

What's the time? Half past nine.
Hang your knickers on the line
When the copper comes along
Hurry up and put them on.

The pond opposite the Beartons' house beyond the somersault railing was a whole world in itself, splashy full and teeming with frog-spawn and tadpoles in the spring, sometimes drying like a cracked mud dish with a soggy middle towards a parched summer's end. When Molly was three, washed and bathed and all ready to be a beautiful if rather podgy bridesmaid dressed in yet another of her mother's muslin confections, she strayed out onto the dish to the middle and was bogged down in mud, so that the hero father had to haul her out.

He stretches out a long-handled hoe. Hold on, he says, just hold on and I'll pull you out. All around the summer birds twitter and trill, and the sun sucks at the mud while the cracks grow wider. There's a sickening squelch as she is finally hauled free, and is bathed in many changes of water to get rid of the putrid smell.

Later he made flat-bottomed child-sized boats from old bits of junk lying around the farm, that the children could jerk across the water with sticks. He must have harnessed up a thousand jam-jars with binder twine so that they could catch tadpoles and have them on the kitchen windowsill. The life cycle of the butterfly may be the most romantic example of metamorphosis, but for Molly it was hard to beat the frog.

When she was five or six, Mr Bearton, almost horizontal by then on his two sticks, died (he was the father of Gladys, who cleaned the old house and made the lunch). As with the egg-laying, this being close to someone dead, just across the road, seemed to Molly like a huge privilege, putting her in touch with the infinite, the unknowable. It seemed grand indeed to have known someone now dead, and for weeks she felt exalted and somehow changed by what she saw as this noble passing. Not for Molly at this point the seamier side of dying, or the pangs of loss. The children had buried pets; mice and kittens and hamsters and dogs, but this burial to which she was not of course invited put her in mind of Viking ceremonies. She imagined Mr Bearton distinguished with a halo of burning laurels, sailing out of his grave in the village church-yard and starting his journey across the River Styx, if Vikings could be allowed a Grecian passing.

Many years later, Molly's dear dead Gran, pink and white in life even just before the end, looked after death as noble as a Viking queen, and as proud. She also, as she passed from life to death, grew a small moustache. Horace still speaks to us across the years: *All are thus compelled, Early or late the urn is shaken; Fate will out; a little boat will take us to eternal exile.*

She left Molly her rings. Molly dreams of swallowing them, then having to sift through the shit to find them again. Molly's mother was disappointed at the size of her own mother's quite sizeable opal ring, inherited by Molly, her only granddaughter, after her death. It had been kept in a box for special occasions when Molly's mother was a child. She remembered it huge, flashing fire into the candle-lit corners when her mother played the piano for the local singing club. In reality Gran's ring was quite eclipsed by Molly's mother's own huge diamond and sapphire rocks, which still slipped around her old fingers as she lay dying, not as her own mother had in an anonymous nursing home, but in her own home, in her own bed.

There's nothing better in life than diamonds, said Mae West. They are imperishable, and they don't let you down. They were Molly's mother's hold on immortality.

While Molly's mother was buried on top of her husband in the family plot, her grandmother's ashes were scattered in a municipal crematorium garden. No space for an epitaph as she flew back to join the universal dust. In a local church Molly later found a gentle verse, which she kept in mind so that at least there her grandmother could be remembered.

Tho' Dead, Yet Dear: Tho' Dear yet Dead to Me.
Dead is her Body: Dear her Memory.

Molly and her brother had both been very interested in death and dead bodies, what they looked like, what happened to them, a dispassionate interest quite unconnected with thoughts of their own mortality. Yet they also discussed the ways they felt they would like to be disposed of. Molly had slightly more of a grasp on this and probably led the conversation. At the end, her brother thought seriously for a moment, then breathed a strong sigh.

I think I'll choose to be boiled, he said.

There were other children in their lives: to the vicarage just up the hill from the old house came the Babcocks, a missionary family back from India, with Claire who was Molly's age, Bernard who was John's age, and Beatrice, who was the baby, but blonde and wiry and self-sufficient even as a two year old. They brought new habits and customs and thoughts and words. They didn't talk, as Molly and John did in their house, about spending a penny or tinkling: they did *ka-ka* and *sou-sou*, and these words learned in faraway Africa when the oldest children were babies seemed at once exotic and earthy. The Babcocks lived with the incumbent vicar and his wife, and they brought a bohemian ramshackle blast of air into that formerly staid and dark-green house, where Molly had previously and without enthusiasm joined the Brownies, but very briefly, and then left its rather joyless band.

The idea of little magic people creeping around the house doing 'good turns' was one thing, and you knew that one good turn, or so they said, deserved another, so you could at least wait and see if it was true. But sitting on a lumpy cushion in the vicarage drawing room where the vicar's wife had been a rather gloomy and very Brown Owl, was quite another, as Molly soon discovered. And the constantly present burden of thinking about a good deed for every day! Loving God and serving queen and country seemed simple in comparison, she thought, as she wilted under Brown Owl's stern eye.

Mrs Babcock on the other hand always seemed to be successfully wrestling with excitement and chaos in equal measure, in her untidy kitchen, baking biscuits, potting Beatrice, organising games all the children could play in the big old rambling garden. Mr Babcock was vague and benign in the background, a spectacle loser who nevertheless had a very patient wife, and Molly wanted to live with all of them. Claire and she talked of a tree house where they could live. Molly wanted simply to be near this warmth, which somehow, for her with her own mum, didn't seem to last for long. One day she packed up a sandwich in the red and gold biscuit tin and ran away, to the end of the lane, intending to go, not to the vicarage, but into the world like Dick Whittington, to seek what she so desperately wanted. Then she sat in the hedge to have a think about it, and saw her dad pass by, pretending not to notice she was there. Of course he knew she would run out into his arms, and so she did.

While the Babcocks inhabited the vicarage, Molly and her brother were allowed despite their mother's scruples to go to Sunday school, where they learned about bible stories and sang simple hymns accompanied by the village organist, the young son of the owner of the petrol station. He coaxed wheezing notes from a seemingly unwilling organ, whose panelled and highly decorated lattice work case was an object of Molly's admiration. So too was the stained glass east window in the chancel, where a Resurrection in the central panel gave her hope of life after extinction, which she often felt she experienced on a daily basis. The angel lifts the lid of the stone tomb, and Christ sweeps across the foreground, colourful robes a-swirl, while beneath him the sleeping soldiers miss the glorious spectacle. The window gave Molly comfort even at her mother's funeral, when the organ's soothing tunes were no longer squeezed out by the long-dead son of the petrol station man.

An ironical postscript to Molly's childish admiration was an act of vandalism at the beginning of the twenty-first century, when a memorial vase from her father's grave was used to smash another of the row of stained glass windows that surrounded the Sunday worshippers.

Spring would come at last, and Beatrice would caper under the apple blossom on the trees in the farm garden, now the children were out again, playing games in the mud of the yard with sticks. They were masters of whole mud and water worlds; these were transcendentally mucky games which nobody stopped or disapproved. In Molly's Birthday Book, square and fat and pink, opposite the page marked 'Beatrice's birthday,' was a poem that summed up the particular and absorbed passion they had for mud.

Timothy Trudger on mischief is bent
And nobody knows quite where he went.
He's not in the nursery, not in bed,
Not in the pantry or potting shed.
He's not in the greenhouse, he's not in the loft
Though the apples are sweet and the hay is soft
Tears, calling, searching and sighs,
While Timothy Trudger makes mud currant pies.

In the black and white line drawing underneath this shameless doggerel, the little boy crouches on a stray bit of ground, studding his mud with little stones.

There was a huge and seldom-used iron grass-roller which the children laboriously turned by standing on its top in their rubber-soled plimsolls and forcing it forwards. Nearby was the turkey pen, where the scarlet-wattled 'gobblers' called to one another and terrified Molly. A useful parental threat resulted, 'The gobblers will get you if you're not good'. Maybe Molly knew something about her own wish to gobble up too, that complicated unrequited passion for her mother which had turned to greed for sweets.

They had a tortoise, huge and lumbering under his exquisite umbrella of a shell, and as soon as he had crossed the grassy expanse on his own odyssey towards the shelter of the hedge they'd take him back and make him do it all over again. When he seemed not to want to play the game, they would threaten him that he'd end up on the back of a hairbrush like their mother's splendid example on her dressing table.

The first of two ancient oak trees which stood nearby was felled at Molly's parents' request. Its limbs were sawn off, the helpless still-living trunk was torn up, and she thought in her passionate and vulnerable childish way of its roots screaming as they were wrenched from the earth.

One of her uncles mourned its passing, but her parents said it had blocked the light. This was the first of many demolitions. It seemed they wished to cut off the past, dig it up and dispose of it, rather than sink into the sap of their inheritance, for their own complicated reasons.

On Saturday the Babcocks gave their children pocket money, unheard of till then in the old farm household, a penny for each year of their lives. With sturdy Beatrice in the lead, brandishing her two pennies, all the kids trailed down to the local corner shop, where Mrs Forester looked over her glasses and stroked her ample apron-covered chest as they deliberated how to spend this weekend wealth.

What's your fancy today then, children?

Should it be sherbet lemons, two ounces, or a bar of Palm Toffee, a toffee sandwich with various flavours to choose as filling; pineapple, banana or mint? Should it be medicinally-tinged pear drops, again two ounces, or fiery red clove cushions, shiny hard squares with twisted corners that cleared your passages way down beyond your tonsils? Then there was the constant array of penny chews, in all their flagrant synthetic flavours including peppermint and pineapple. Beatrice could afford a big selection of ten-a-penny tasters, or a couple of long cellophane cones full of tiny little multi-coloured sweets like seeds! After some resistance Molly's parents had agreed to the pocket money ritual, and all the children shared the booty after the tickets had been torn from the ration books. You could, sadly, only spend so much on luxuries like sweets.

There was something about sweets for Molly, they filled a hole, and like Tom in *The Water Babies*, she dreamed of them. Tom lived for Saturdays too, when Mrs Bedonebyasyoudid would arrive and unlock her cupboard full of sea-lollipops, sea-bulls-eyes, and best of all sea-cows' cream 'which never melted under water', and give them out to the good water babies who had spent their week cleaning up the rock pools. Tom, however, had spent his time just idling about, and had fed pebbles to the sea anemones. On Saturday all he got was a cold stone in his own mouth, so he stole sweets from her unlocked cupboard, and gobbled and gobbled till he was sick.

But what did the strange fairy do when she saw all her lollipops eaten? Did she fly at Tom, catch him by the scruff of the neck, hold him, howk him, hump him, hurry him, hit him, poke him, pull him, pinch him, pound him, put him in a corner, shake him, slap him, set him on a cold stone to reconsider himself, and so forth? Not a bit: she just said nothing at all about the matter... but when she looked him full in the face, he shook from head to foot.

When the Babcocks left to convert the heathen somewhere else in the world, the pocket money agreement ceased. During the last years of her time in the convent primary school, Molly stole not sweets but money from her mother's purse to exchange for sweets, the currency for comradeship on the long journey home on the red country bus. She had to lie to her parents about where these sixpences and shillings came from. She 'found' more half-crowns than were ever dropped, and whether she was believed or not, she was never seriously challenged. But she shook from head to foot like Tom as she considered her fate after death according to the Catholic doctrine which she learned at school. She would roast in Hell for this mortal sin, but she would in this life have what she thought was needed to share and be one of the crowd. The everlasting fires smouldered in the future. She read in her encyclopaedia about people being burned, heretics and sinners, only a few hundreds of years ago in England, really burned, till their bodies were reduced to greasy ash. And if the wind was blowing the wrong way, their agony was longer.

Have mercy upon me, O god, according to thy loving kindness; according to the multitude of thy tender mercies blot out my transgressions

Molly had the same mixture of dread and carelessness as Dr Faustus, as she sold her immortal soul for present consolation. On the bus, her chosen penance was to sit next to an old heavily-breathing and unshaven man who travelled regularly at the same time, presumably with a mission in mind. He would pinch her arm and slide his probing fingers up her legs, and she would bear it until she could stand no more, and she'd move to another seat.

Round and round the garden/ Like a teddy bear/ One step, two step/ Tickle her under there

Chapter Eight

In which Molly goes to a local convent school when she is five. While she is eager to be clever and admired, she is also assailed by a growing guilt about her sins, and worries more and more about Hell's Gates opening.

Important: when rolling on it is vitally important that the correct tension between tapestry threads and cotton lining be maintained section by section. But what is the correct tension, and should there be much, or does it form the inevitable backdrop to any project, large or small?

While Molly's mother objected to religion, she didn't object to the education nuns could provide, and when her daughter grew too old for the nursery school at the bottom of the muddy lane, she graduated to the convent school in the local town, navy felt hat and coat in winter, blue cotton dress, straw hat and blazer in summer, she was finally a regular schoolgirl. At school her already over-developed conscience had a huge boost, and so too did her religious fervour. The robust certainty of the catechism, with its questions learned by rote and declaimed with childish zeal, constructed a safe box designed to keep out her doubts and fears. What is a sacrament? An outward sign of inward grace. What are Holy Orders? Molly wanted to be 'Ordained by Jesus Christ', circumscribed by doctrine. 'I believe', she chanted, 'in the Holy Catholic Church, the forgiveness of sins, the resurrection of the body'—*the resurrection of the body?* She couldn't quite get her mind around that one, even then, so she rolled on regardless to life everlasting, such a contrast to the land of the everlasting dead. Many of those who sleep in the dust of the earth, she learned, shall awake. Some to everlasting life, and some to shame and everlasting contempt. A bitter fate. How can anything last for ever? It made her heart race yet again, for fear of what awaited her in the hereafter because of her own sins.

Wash me thoroughly from mine iniquity, and cleanse me from my sin.

We shall not all sleep, the Bible said. We shall be changed in the twinkling of an eye, at the sound of the last trumpet. The dead shall arise, incorruptible, (incorruptible? She looked up the word and it was no help at all) and we shall be changed. Molly hoped she would be, otherwise it would be all up with her.

Wash me thoroughly, she prayed. It made bathing seem like a necessary penance rather than a pleasure.

These sonorous precepts honed her memorising skills and gave her joy as well as fearful awe in their reciting. But the comfort of them soon evaporated into dread. If you stole money, you certainly went to Hell. Unbaptised babies slept their deaths away in Limbo through no fault of their own, but would be rescued by Christ at the Last Trump. There were a hundred pastel-coloured holy pictures of patient saints who had endured unendurable tortures, penances for their own and others' sins. There was even a picture of a martyred saint with her two breasts carried on a plate. Many however were more saccharine, images bordered by creeping vines and faded flowers, and you sent them to your friends with messages written on the back, if you'd had a quarrel and wanted to patch it up. There was a sweet seduction in the making up, and Molly once made the mistake of sending one to her mother. Predictably it just made things worse. Once a year you got to cut out and colour a picture of a little 'black baby', sweet innocents of the wrong colour unfortunately born in the wrong place who needed to be saved. Otherwise they ended up in that Limbo of lost souls, thought to be a disastrous fate, though later on abolished by the church as being perhaps, or certainly, too inequitable.

But Hell, that was Molly's destination. The lashing and the bleeding, the tearing of limbs, she studied it all in medieval pictures. All those man-made instruments of torture, the knives and the racks, the swords and the drills, the choppers and the mincers. The skies were red with burning flesh and burning buildings, and the noise of screams and wild brass instruments seemed to sound in her terrified ears. Skeletons riding skeleton horses dragged the newly dead sinners piled in carts to hell's mouth, where horn blowing devils saluted their arrival. This was undoubtedly a foretaste of her doom, and these were the Christian icons of terror Molly both feared but also secretly loved to look at. She was, after all, a soul promised to Hell.

She drank it all in, and it wasn't until her adolescence that Molly rebelled against the frequently arrogant 'missionary' zeal of Christianity. The Babcock family had seemed to her romantic wanderers rather than pious zealots, and they had seemed to give her some sort of protection against Hell's vicious blasts. It was the patronising air of the Anglican cleric, one of God's more unctuous practitioners of spin, leaning ponderously, white-skinned, grubby-surpliced and overweight over the chapel pulpit at her boarding school which finally caused her eyes to open. The bubble of sanctity which glowed around the convent chapel burst abruptly, and she was transfixed in the cold light of unbelief, blinking and bereft. There was no lord and father of mankind, to forgive her foolish ways. The still small voice of calm was not a comfort. It was a painful flight into clarity. Death, where is thy sting? Scales falling from the eyes can be painful too.

But while she was still at her convent school, her carefully filched pennies ensured that her 'black baby' went quickly up the paper ladder on the wall towards heaven and salvation, while she of course was descending deeper into Hell. Not for her the sweet luxury of confession: some things in any case are best not spoken about. While she had thought before that in some way she deserved the sweets that stealing bought her, this posing as a generous soul tore her apart with its hypocrisy. Our first lies, told to our parents in thought, word and deed, are the seed-bed for a mounting harvest. Molly was overwhelmed with guilt. And who knows the link back to that first guilt, of being born at her mother's excruciatingly painful expense.

At the back of the classroom was an altar laid out on the stationery cupboard, which was full of exercise books and sharpened pencils, and she was careful to position herself in the back row so she could groom the melting candles with spent matches when they were lit for the Angelus at midday, and she could pray for a little bit of absolution. There were so many things she didn't like about herself: but this thieving self sat at the top of the huge pile. Shiver and shake, deny and burn.

I acknowledge my transgressions: and my sin is ever before me. Every tree that does not bear good fruit is cut down and thrown into the fire.

While she knew all about the sinning she was barred from the salvation, holy pictures became taboo in her house, and her secret bedroom altar was dismantled by her mother one day when Molly was out and her mother discovered it. The trembling girl didn't even dare mention its absence and it went into that realm of silence alongside a lot of other events. She couldn't have a First Communion, or a First Confession, and her mountain of sins grew and grew inside her with no possibility of being forgiven. Transgression, confession, penance and absolution: not an option for this heathen child. No matter with what fervour she glided down the polished corridor to the Chapel, no matter how deeply she thrust her fingers into the holy water stoup, to touch a humble sponge soaked with this elixir which seemed so thick with grace, and crossed herself, no matter how often she followed the anguished Stations of the Cross around the walls of that quiet place, testimony to human cruelties, she was a prisoner of her parents' unbelief, locked out from rapture and from peace. Our Lady of the Seven Sorrows, addictive kitsch icon Molly realised later that she was, could be of no help. Molly herself was sorrowful and outside the fold.

Molly wanted, desperately, to be a nun. *I have desired to go/Where Springs not fail/ To fields where flies no sharp and sided hail/And a few lilies blow.* She knew about hailstorms, unpredictable and merciless. She could feel for the desperate Tibetan priest-monks, whom she read about, dancing on the edge of precipices, hurling little pathetic magic pebbles against the stinging multitudes of real hail-stones which threatened to destroy the struggling crops. They took the blame for the storms. Molly put gorse down the back of her dress, prickly to kill, and stones in her own shoes to atone for her sins, to become good enough and brave enough to cross the line between her insignificant life and those of the nuns in their sheltered world. But would any penance in the world wipe away the wrongdoing? Would her burden ever fall off? The scriptural words tolled: *And they shall go out and look at the dead bodies of those who have rebelled against me; for their worm shall not die, their fire shall not be quenched, and they shall be an abhorrence to all flesh.*

Simple faith as Bunyan's Christian had didn't seem to have the same effect for Molly. His burden had disappeared when he believed, and he had leapt with joy. Molly went back to the old fluttering and yellowed pages of her grandmother's book many times, trying to find a way that Puritan teachings could perhaps help her make sense of Catholic doctrines about Hell. But try as she would, each time, to comfort herself, she identified with Ignorance, who had never believed his heart could be so bad, and in the final hour, when Christian and Hopeful had crossed the River with No Name, to the celestial City, Ignorance was found out, like a candidate making up a reference, and was carried off and left at the doorway to Hell. While the fortunate Bunyan then woke up and 'behold it was a dream', these waking thoughts oppressed Molly every day, not waiting politely for the night.

The old Baptist preacher had nailed it, that vicious prison of doubt that was the Slough of Despond… 'as the sinner is awakened about his lost condition, there ariseth in his soul many fears and discouraging apprehensions, which all of them get together, and settle in this place. This is the reason for the badness of this ground.' Mark this, as he said many times in the margins of his mighty work. It seemed to Molly like a pure chronicle of truth, where there was no opportunity to start all over again. Anyone whose name is not found written in the good book of life will be thrown into the lake of fire. Bunyan himself was guilty and fearful. He was addicted to the magnificent noise of the bells in the church tower, but he stood at the steeple door, not trusting to be under the main steeple beam, always anxious that a bell might fall .. 'should the bell fall with a swing it might first hit the wall and then rebounding on me might kill me, for all this beam'.

Q: What is the chief end of man?

A: Man's chief end is to glorify God and to enjoy him for ever.

Our hearts, they say, slow down as we mature. The infant's heart which beats so fast to keep the child alive gradually relaxes, drumming only half as hard by the time that same child is ten. But Molly's heart still fluttered and raced, as she worried her way to nowhere, and she would try to calm it with a shaking hand. Well, I deserve what I get, she thinks. I'm pretty bad. My sins have got together and multiplied, and the number is endless. Then she discovered in later years that reciting four decades of the Rosary, forbidden in her house, measurably reduces blood pressure. No wonder all those nuns held onto theirs, before they met their Maker.

Although the nuns had taught her that every child has a guardian angel, she feared hers might have resigned the post. Sometimes she pretended she didn't care. As for God, when it came to listening to Molly's pathetic little prayers for salvation, he seemed to have his receiver permanently switched off. So how did he choose which prayers to hear, and which to ignore?

The nuns in their black and white habits, like other members of the human race, had distinctive traits and personalities. You could sense, underneath the holiness, the repression and the anger in some, while others seemed truly to have found their vocation and their own version of a good enough way to lead your life. Their white collars were a symbol that they were surrounded by 'community', which may in reality have been a trial to some. The fledgling Catholics in school were told that the wimple represented the soul, that when they sinned it was equal to a nun's having a black mark slashed across her spotless wimple, they must keep their souls as white as a nun's uniform, starched to perfection. This filled Molly's heart with gloom, as dark as she imagined her wimple-soul to be. The nuns' veils were placed irrevocably over the coifs which hid their hair, and were pinned into place at the top of their heads, with a pin too behind each ear. They had belts and matching shoes, sensible and rather grim.

Some had spots and some had hairy faces; others were as beautiful as Fra Angelico Madonnas, consumptive and glowing. Indeed their black and white habits seemed perfectly to mirror the extremes which must have been beating, seething, coexisting with terrifying difficulty side by side underneath their many-layered bosoms.

Molly struggled to swallow the institutional rissoles which tasted as bad as they smelled, in the vast dining room presided over by a Sister Mary Paul, whose white-veiled habit enclosing her menacing pallid face flapped as a living threat over the table when any trembling child lost heart with the watery Irish stew or the slimy lumps of tapioca. On the dreaded tapioca days lines of tearful little children gagged and swallowed and gagged again as they sat in obedient huddles over their accusing plates. Sometimes the room seemed to stink of vomit, and of the vile disinfectant used to mask the shameful deed.

Outside the dining room door lay stacked the iron milk crates filled with little empty bottles after break-time, when the children had sucked their regulation calcium though docile paper straws, mangled and discarded at the end of the statutory third of a pint. It was the Education Act born the same year as Molly which had granted every child in school this free gift of vitamins and minerals, as a shield against the worst effects of poverty and food rationing. It was hard for Molly to link this rather thin and watery offering with that drawn both willingly and unwillingly from the Friesians back home. Did the class sometimes, she wondered, drink the milk from the farm's own grumbling herd, who sent jets of urine down the shed's runnels just as they sent streams of milk from their scraggy udders into the glass tank of the milking machine, warmed from their own bodily heat as the level rose? Manor Belle, Dusty, Ruby and Jane; they fulfilled their purpose well.

The children stood in rigidly defined class lines for registry in the assembly hall, where wall-bars, ropes and benches with leather hooks each end lined the perimeter of the parquet space, and Molly noticed numberless times the touching expressions you could seem to read at the back of children's knees, as they made ready to march off to lessons, dismissed by the Sister Superior.

2A, off you go, now.

Pull your socks up.

No pushing. Walk straight.

No talking, eyes to the front.

While she could stand on her own two feet in the assembly line, she shuddered when she thought of the heavenly assembly to come, when standing up for herself would be unthinkable.

While she was getting used to feeling like a sinner with a permanently discoloured soul, she had the chance to be an angel too, in the Nativity play at Christmas, when her mother, for this precious one time at least like all the other mothers, cut curving patterns of shiny satin with pinking shears, and stuck the curves on cardboard wings in graduated shades of pink and blue. Molly hovered on a dizzy cusp between doubt and hope, as she enacted her silent but decorative part in the annual story.

The nuns supervised the children's moral and physical growth: they played net-ball and memorised the tenets of the faith. And incidentally, it almost seemed, their charges did indeed receive the solid education Molly's mother was seeking.

Sister Mary Finbar excelled at all three tasks. On the net-ball pitch her athletic body betrayed by its vigorous twists and turns how much more supple it was than her enveloping habit, which was slow to follow her and sometimes threatened to trip her up. She looked like a bat trapped in the daylight, whipping itself around to find safety. One moment she was stationary with the ball, as you must be, the next the ball flew through the air and she was flying too. She had the bronze-toned voice of an eagle woman, robust and carrying, as she guided the class through the catechism, still flushed and breathing deeply after the netball match. The satisfaction of belief glowed in her slightly tanned face, with its flat even cheeks below intense grey eyes, themselves below eyebrows which did not arch, but put a gentle horizontal emphasis over the intensity they framed. As St Augustine said, 'if the tongue and the heart are at odds, you are reciting not testifying'. For Molly there was the twisted ecstasy of reciting these precepts, which testified both to her imagined and real guilts, and her eternal persecuted nakedness. She was not able to be clothed in Christ's grace, and lay open to the terrifying scrutiny of both earthly parents and heavenly father.

It was Sister Mary Finbar who called Molly to the nursery class to comfort her sobbing brother, shamed into soiling himself in the anxious first days away from home. She took pride then in being a sister, and the nursery teacher, seductively-named Sister Sabrina, with her round red apple cheeks, her open smile, greeted Molly with frank relief.

Molly's favourite nun was the one that taught the top class, Sister Mary Xavier. Cheerful and robust, with a scarlet face and small wise eyes surrounded by laughter lines drawn in her ruddy folds of flesh, she said without self-pity that she had been chosen by her family to be a nun because being a plain girl she didn't have much hope of a husband. She taught her class the verses of the Welsh National anthem in Welsh, and she came from Rhyl. 'Land of my Fathers'-*Gwlad Gwlad,* Molly carolled, perhaps somewhat tunelessly, but safe in the knowledge then that the land all around her own home did indeed belong to her fathers, her uncles, her cousins... though it was also motherland as well, a more dangerous proposition. 'As long as the sea, your bulwark shall be, to Cymru my heart shall be true'.

Sister Mary Xavier was plump but not placid, she could fire off great shrieks at a spelling mistake and have the class chanting that tricky nine times table over and over if someone, and isn't there always that unfortunate someone, got it wrong. She thought they should be prepared for the world by knowing proverbs, and the children would list in their books the tops and tails of them, putting them together to build a world of certainty and common sense. You can take a horse to water. Every cloud. Look before you. Don't put all your eggs in. Don't spoil a ship for. Don't count your chickens. People in glass houses. Pots and kettles. A bird in the hand. Pride. It goes before a fall, don't you know, and Molly had been told that countless times by her mother, if ever she felt Molly was getting too uppity. Might this have been a time when the pot called the kettle black?

And that brought her smack up against the seven deadly sins. Her mother often quoted pride, but what about the others? Molly did lust after sweets, she was greedy for them, she often felt huge anger but didn't dare express it. She probably envied her mother for being her dad's other sweetheart. The only sin she felt free of was laziness, because she worked like a bee to get things right, to store up honeyed words of praise from the world. But even that seemed not so pure, because of what she wanted in return for all this industry. And pride, there it was again. There didn't seem a way out of this labyrinth, and proverbs? What did they give you in the end?

Some of the wise words were flatly contradictory, and Molly would often puzzle inside her head about how to know when you should look (before you leaped) and when on the contrary you should not hesitate, for fear of being lost. The world of the proverb contained no real guidelines, she sadly concluded, sonorous and weighty as it seemed.

Sister Mary Xavier told stories like an angel, having by heart whole books of Dickens, Austen, Defoe, Bronte. She would stand in front of the class, unselfconscious in her rusty black, bundled up in the middle with her black cord which looked as if it might be keeping the two halves of her together, and out of her flowed such stuff. She could imitate a thousand different voices, go from soprano to contralto to basso profundo, have herself and her enraptured audience surfing on waves of abundant prose, sometimes stormy and exhilarating, sometimes quiet so you could hear the twigs on the trees outside their classroom touching the windowpane. She could make her class laugh and cry at will, a true Sarah Siddons of her order, a heroine to her pupils. Molly loved her. Now she must be entertaining the heavenly throng, alongside her hero Dickens, who could also draw a crowd and keep it breathless to his wishes. Dear Sister, Molly thinks, after so many years your passion and fire live still inside the heart of a grateful pupil.

Later Molly's mother told her what Sister Mary Xavier had said to her parents: 'Every parent thinks their child is a swan, but yours really is'. It was, Molly could see when she finally got to hear of it, a significant pointer towards what was to come: a compliment with teeth. This was a twist on the classic story of the ugly duckling. Swans wouldn't be safe after all. Let sleeping dogs. One swallow does not. Don't put all your eggs.

Swans, they say, keep the ice of the lake open for other feeding birds, but this so-called swan would have difficulty breaking up the floes.

This idea of the swan was also at odds with what that same Sister had written in Molly's little autograph book: 'Be good, sweet maid, and let who will be clever'. This had seemed to Molly to have a deadly ring. Sweet maid she wasn't. She decided that since she'd given up the road to goodness years ago, trying to be clever was the only way forward. Her dad backed this venture up with his own sentence in the autograph book: '2 YYs U R,

2YYs U B, I think U R 2 YYs 4 me'. Her mother, of course, wrote nothing. Perhaps she was never asked, and she would never in any case volunteer to commit herself to paper.

Sister Mary Xavier made a strong contribution to Molly's store of words, encouraged her to write and write, at school and at home. Molly was greedy for words. She devoured overblown words on cereal boxes, minutely printed lists of ingredients on the sides of sauce bottles, even the sparse text on the boxes of shiny hard lavatory paper stacked in the bathroom. Out of the strong came forth sweetness, said the legend on the green Golden Syrup tin, where the bees swarmed in the belly of a dead lion. Molly liked that idea, odd as it seemed, it reminded her of her dad somehow, though not dead, she never thought of that. Years afterwards she wondered whether some copywriter at the advertising agency must have known something about the first bee-keeper, Aristaeus, such a sorcerer in his art that he could even, so they said, generate new bees from the rotting carcase of a cow. Swift sideways move to the noble lion, and a new slogan was born from the old mythology.

Words, as Virginia Woolf observed, do not belong in the dictionary: they live in the mind where they don't form themselves into coherent sentences. They inhabited Molly's mind in seductive whirlwinds. Robust, elastic, delicate words, to construct an alternative world of her own choosing. She loved the very imprecision she discovered later that T.S. Eliot despaired of. What an endless game of chance it was! Words might change under your hand even as you wrote them. Double, triple, even quadruple possibilities; what multiple adventures. If you lean on words they reveal meanings within meanings, worlds within worlds. Perfect little multi-faceted entities were words, leading who knew where, facing different ways. Words which even as an adult when so many childish perceptions fade, Molly could see and remember with the ten-year-old's fascination; like the odd clang between joke and choke, then to choke on food and the choke in the car (and her dad explained later, there was in fact a connection, when she was an adolescent learning to drive a car round and round the farm's circular drive before she had reached the legal age limit).

There had been mispronunciations based on what words looked like, unshed rhyming in her mind with munched, there were nonsense words which rollicked along on their own journey to somewhere or nowhere. While many words seemed tailor made, cut to fit, you could also set sail from accepted norms and see what happened. Crafting these new and unexpected worlds carefully was a joy to her because you never knew precisely where you were going. Thoughts entered, and changed, as other meanings shouted out from above, below, behind, in front, dancing in the wings ready to be called, or pushing forward on their own. Words which might have died in her mouth rather than be spoken came to life on the page. Sometimes, she thought, things ended with a comma, in the dense complexities of multiple plots,

Hitting the coal block to go with the grain, as the poet Seamus Heaney wrote. His mother taught him a lesson in coal; he carried it on in writing.

This was the strangeness of words, which Molly found could only go so far in representing what may in truth be un-representable. There's always a slippage there, between what we feel and what we can say, or what we want to say. Molly had a surgeon's obsessive interest in subjunctive clauses, and in the power of punctuation as well as words to deliver meaning. She developed an irritatingly pedantic horror of the split infinitive. What an annoying child she must have been, as pompous as her heroine Alice. While Alice had been big on 'manners', for Molly, punctuation marks were the manners of prose, gave it a meaning you could control, decide, feel in truth rather superior about knowing while others perhaps did not. Comma, comma, comma, link it all up if you can. The panache of the dash, the space for a query created by that surging line, or how a question mark can be used or not used to make the smallest difference apparent but only maybe to an over-sensitive ear—all this gave her spurious entry into an adult world on which she thought she could have a small hold. The way a sentence could be broken up in different ways, using all these little marks! While the grand George Bernard Shaw could insult apostrophes, 'those uncouth bacilli', for Molly their correct placing was not so much a demonstration of a good education as a way of proving that at least on the page she could do the right thing. The teetering halt provided by: a colon, and in the mark described sonorously by Sister Marie Pierre in French dictation—'*point de suspension...*' And if you could recite how i before e was the rule except after c, it showed at least you knew the form, could show it on a page, even if in her heart Molly sadly knew that the form had truly not been followed in so many known and unknown ways. Full stop.

This gift of what seemed to Molly this cunning punctuation opened up a new world of possibilities and creative potential. It showed her a way to sort out the multi-tracking of thoughts which moved around in her mind, to give them some additional weight, or so she hoped. Layer upon layer of thoughts, private in spite of parental eyes, but more important to her than what they could see, more important sometimes to her than even she could understand. If you don't write it all down, maybe you don't exist? In any case we don't think in sentences, as anyone knows, even if we'd like to kid ourselves we do. We travel many fragmented tracks simultaneously, looping to and fro among the whirling bits, every minute of every ordinary day. And also in the night. If you will still call this a stream of consciousness, it's a very choppy stream, with a language that waits beneath the words. All these thoughts are looking for a thinker, looking for a home, and they settle on someone who can receive them. Or hopes she can. Pirate stations constantly beset the mainline radio, for all of us, as we try to hold that line, but there's usually another thought there jamming the flow.

And there was always 'meanwhile', that word which fixed parallel realities, as Molly pondered while she sat and swung her legs on the lavatory. It seemed like the place you always came back to, but who or what got flushed away was perhaps an unanswerable question. What if, she thought, there were other versions of herself doing quite different things, and the parallel realities of meanwhile sometimes merged into coincidences. All this she would wonder about as she sat with legs swinging, savouring such phrases as 'little did she know'. Little. Did. She. Know.

If growing a language in your mind helps you feel you have an inside to communicate, it also made Molly think about an inside *inside* the inside, which was just for her until she was good and ready. This was a door to her own private world. Speaking your feelings can be a dangerous thing to do. Words can deceive too, and who's to know the truth of it.

She kept for years a small red book, carefully handmade and covered, with precisely cut loose-leaf pages, where she wrote her stories, stapling together the words in her head from diverse sources. 'Telling stories': this meant lies, at home. How did you tell the difference between lies and stories and everything in between? There were definitely stories to be told, and you never knew where the words would go, how a story would end. Collecting them was a comfort. Each corner of this little red book was wisely protected by a green 'photo-corner' and the pages were tied in with a black cord, such precise parental care. She could remember the outside so vividly, touch it and feel it, but not a word of what was in it, how did it slip away into the realm of forgotten and unwanted things? Not so an adolescent exercise book, where between shiny loud blue covers Molly wrote impossibly sad verse, a huge and embarrassing outpouring of the teenage kind, totally lacking in humour and extremely shameful, much better consigned to oblivion than the little red treasure. The unexamined self might be a better aim in adolescence, than all this self-obsessed wailing. 'The whole thing's self-gratification of some sort', said Philip Larkin, who started writing at puberty as many people do. 'It offers something nothing else can, something more than reading'. Molly indulged too in this teenage passion... 'We batter our heads against stone walls to understand the mystery of life. It will still go on whether we understand it or not.' And more embarrassing effluent of a similar sort. But never a fear that her mother would read what she wrote, there was no need for one of those padlocked five-year diaries which were the fashion then, her daughter's feelings were of absolutely no interest to Molly's mother. Molly was one of those innumerable tortured souls who then grow up to be ordinary adults.

But perhaps you could forgive this teenage outpouring, from someone always more than a little prone to—well let's admit much more than healthily engrossed in—self-examination of an unforgiving kind. The pit of self-obsession was addictive and painful. The writing was the beginning of a lifetime's effort to figure out a way through a series of dilemmas; to construct a rope of desperate questioning words to swing above the abyss instead of falling in. And there's no shortage of void, as Beckett's Estragon gloomily said. Molly fancied being a trapeze artist might solve the problem. The soft and frequently damp straw floor of the bullock yard where Molly fell, when her trapeze practice with a stick and an old piece of rope always ended in failure, was as nothing compared with the abyss frontage she stared down into most days, the daily peek into a black hole. To jump or not to jump? We all ask ourselves that old question, as Sartre said, and are sometimes tempted just to give in to the seductive pull. When you stare at the abyss, it stares straight back.

Chapter Nine

In which Molly describes life at home on the farm in summer, and in the village too, when the local holiday camps fill with 'townies': strange speaking aliens who love to play Bingo and sing bawdy songs. The adult world is hard to read, and she tries to understand about life as seen in jolly picture postcards, while Steve encourages her to smoke fag ends they pick up from the road.

You can repair a broken section of your tapestry in several ways: you can use either a weaver's knot, or you can introduce a new warp, but a bit less thick than the original one, carefully now.

While school could have its joys and its heartaches, you came home at the end of the day, on the red double decker bus where the children swung around the stair rail and shoved and giggled on the top deck.

Swop you three refreshers for a bull's eye.

Beat you to the front seat.

Rubbing the ink off their fingers and thumbs, knocking elbows and knees three to a seat till the conductor came to sort it out.

Now then you girls, have your money ready and *be*have.

It was a fifteen minute walk home from the bus stop, and each day Molly said Hail Marys to ward off the frightening barks of the station master's two chained dalmations, who were so different in temperament from the family's own effusively friendly George. If by lucky chance the station master himself was there, smoking his pipe and leaning over his garden gate, dressed casually in a crumpled shirt and braces, but always with a tie to denote his importance, his fierce dogs suddenly became well-behaved.

Hallo young missy, and what have you got in your satchel today?

Some homework and some holy pictures, young missy replies. She's proud of both.

And here's a barley sugar to go along with them, he says, bringing out a battered looking boiled sweet, silver wrapping crushed by proximity with his baccy tin and his grim handkerchief.

Thankyouverymuch Mr Smith, skip Molly's words and Molly's heart, saved from the fearsome dogs to survive another day. Then at home she rushes up the curving drive, lined with snowdrops, daffodils, bluebells or primroses, each in their due season, past the swing and the little triangular pond where the jewelled toads live, lets herself in at the back door and fills herself up with sandwiches of jam and sticky white bread.

On the farm, early summer arrives. The chorus of birds swells in the hedgerows. Their dad teaches the children how to 'birds-nest,' reliving perhaps one of the good things from his childhood as they all three peer together into the thickest of hedges, parting the thorny twigs with care to reveal carefully-made little homes of straw, grass and mud. They whisper in reverence in the very act of plundering each sacred nest, intricately woven testimonies to the sanctity of labour. It is of course an unacknowledged cruelty. They have a huge collection of blown eggs, but always leave some behind so as not completely to deprive the mother, not knowing, or wanting to know, that with human smell on the eggs, most mothers would flee to a safer perch and build a more secret, hidden nursery.

One year, travelling further afield in their quest, the children found a blackbird's nest built over some heated pipes. She'd gone, they waited a while to check, then they took all the eggs. At home when they tried to blow them, they found to their horror that they were hard boiled. Molly could only imagine the mother's grief, when she recalled what a struggle it was to lay an egg, as her researches at the edge of the pond had shown.

She wondered too about the courage or foolhardiness of both the lark and the partridge, who built their nests on the ground. If you disturbed a partridge on her nest, she would rise, whirring with agitation, gabbling with fear, while the lark, trilling in the infinite blue, seemed to say, come up here with me, why don't you, for the heaven's sacred sake, just leave my nest alone. Both seemed so vulnerable in a way which seemed plain foolish, what a curious strategy for ensuring minimum survival it seemed. This was the way that Molly wondered about her own fear of attack, in her own home nest, but not, apart from one time, so huge that she would leave it.

The hedges burst with hawthorn bread'n cheese leaves, and May blossom, great smelly clusters reeking of cat's pee and anyway coming out in June in their cool east coast climate. Once Molly's brother brings some inside the house for their ma. He picks the lowest little branches and ties them up clumsily with a piece of thick grass.

This is for you, he says, thrusting his little scrubby bunch towards her.

No! Take it away!

Now!

He falters, falls back with a blank face, and turns away.

Their mother had shrieked at this transgression of the creed: it was considered unlucky to bring it in indoors. This little boy's gift was quickly thrown out, and maybe it was just one more example of that rejection he too had to bear from the beginning. For their mother, her son's wish to give got quickly translated into an ill-wish from someone, and Molly's brother's feelings were the inevitable casualty of her mother's fears. As Molly discovered, this ancient tree of the hedgerows does indeed have dark links, its heavy perfume was used to mask plague-stench. It is fertilised by insects who mistake its cloying sweetness for dead flesh, and was used by pagan peoples in fertility rituals, then repressed by Christian priests. As is the way of things, it came to be revered by those same Christians, because they said that Joseph of Arimathea's hawthorn staff burst into blossom when he stuck it, weary as he was, into the side of a hill in Glastonbury.

Molly's mother may have spurned religion, but she was often supported by superstition. We must of course preserve our luck however we can. If you find a cast horseshoe, be sure to hang it with the points upwards, her mum warned, so the luck doesn't run out and spill all over the floor. After her mother was dead, Molly found a little silver horseshoe stuck points upwards inside one of the old dresser doors. It was a remnant of an anniversary cake, no doubt, and she left it there.

Early summer days meant tea on the lawn, especially for their mother's birthday, with cucumber sandwiches cut into little delicate white triangles, and strawberries with a blob of whipped cream perched on top of each little Royal Doulton flowered bowl. Drifts of cloudy seersucker had been transformed by the steadily ticking foot of the Singer machine into gauzy dresses for mother and her daughter. Molly can see her mother dressed in clinging voile, white speckled with blue, soft wavy folds tucked in a delta under her legs in the deck-chair. The sky matches her mother's dress. Maybe she arranged it that way. It seems possible. Molly herself, she sits rustling in a shiny dark-pink cotton dress edged with white and embroidered with bunches of cherries, the kind you can make hang on your ears for earrings, while you are busy too with grotesque orange-peel teeth, sticking out in the way you're warned your real ones will, if you carry on sucking your thumb that way.

They ate their celebration tea on the grass in front of the house, just by the old oak tree where hung the swing. No ordinary swing this, but four feet long, sawn from a tree trunk, held up by massive chains and capable of seating Molly, her father and her brother all at one go. He protects them, this father with the motherly streak, his arms strong and brown surrounding them both. Rock-a-bye babies, on the tree top.

One year there was an accident, the chain snapped and they did all tumble down, but not disastrously, as had been the fate of poor Katy. The family swinging was staid and stable except for that one time, and when Molly was young her father would also stand and patiently push her to a decent height to see over the wall and into the bullock yard, then to drop back down again into his waiting arms. But as the years passed solo swinging had a new and fizzy sting. Molly urges the chains to pull her higher, a taste of flying, bursting, cracking through the leafy twigs to reach the ecstatic sky. It is as if she can leave entirely the ordinary mundane business of life and launch into a vaster universe of experience, either in the sky above or back down below, following the pulsing roots of the old oak tree which lies in a mysterious map beneath the lawn, the house, her world.

The cuckoo came in May, and till the end of his life, Molly would ring her dad up when she heard the first one, wherever that might be, just as they would compare notes too about the arrival of the first swallow. Each year you could hear that same binary seesaw cuckoo note, over and over, monotonous yet hypnotising, compressing opposites, up down, in out, here, there. No wonder kids shout 'cuc-koo' in games of hide and seek. Now you hear me, see me, now you don't. In May the cuckoo sings all day, in June he changes his tune, in July away he must fly, in August fly away he must. There was a saying around that an unmarried girl would stay single for as many years as first calls she heard the cuckoo make. And in that contradictory way beliefs play out, that if she took off her left shoe when she heard the call, she'd find a hair which would be the very same colour as that of her future husband. Fancy that, indeed.

The cuckoo, Molly learned later, lays at least twenty-five eggs in other birds' nests, and the giant chick, having rid itself of the competition, runs its parents ragged in its demands for sustenance. This murderousness, driven by the wish to survive by elimination rather than co-operation, remained quite hidden to her, as she admired those repetitive calls. Cuc-koo, cuc-koo, can't catch me…

The Goodalls also arrived in May: an indefatigable camping family, British and intrepid with long khaki shorts and serviceable khaki tents, which they would pitch in the stack-yard beyond the top vegetable garden and the netted soft fruit house. Mr Goodall had a compass and a book of maps. He would solemnly dig the hole for the latrine tent and as solemnly fill it in at the end of their three week stay. Three weeks! It seemed a long and luscious time to Molly, time to play with Jasper, her age, and with Wendy, a bit older, but not with Rupert, who had as a young adolescent with round wire-rimmed glasses already blossomed into adult long shorts, and was too lofty to join in the lounging about, the long walks, the conversations in the hayloft above the stable, where the children would lie it seemed for hours after a full day's dedicated play. The old stable held the history of those redundant heavy horses, the mangers still full of ancient chaff, obsolete as those great beasts who used to sink their ruminating muzzles into the stuff, and scrape their heavy hooves on the cobbles, while Dad and his father before him whispered in their ears. Plough collars, stout harness backs & huge leather straps, all hand sewn and primed for heavy work, lay mouldering above the hay racks, and eventually got sold to a local pub. The group laughed and told achingly funny jokes, never a feature in Molly's household, where childish foolishness seemed not to be enjoyed. Her mother was not a joke teller. The salvation of laughter was rare, and Molly grew up far too serious for her own good. 'That's silly' was never what she wanted to hear.

It was Wendy who told Molly about breasts sprouting, often painfully, and lopsidedly, about secondary school, about a world beyond their village by the sea. Unlike some boys his age, serious Jasper seemed happy to hang out with a girl, and the three of them would creep about the dusty sheds, discovering things, imagining things, what they grandly called 'Exploring' in homage to Mr Goodall and his noble compass. Molly used to encourage hiding from her little brother, which they all enjoyed. Mrs Goodall looked somewhat like her husband though her hair was a little bit longer: she seemed to have no breasts to speak of but was a warm and practical presence. If you were suddenly thrown onto a desert island after a stormy sea voyage and a shipwreck, you would hope that these Goodalls might be on the same boat and get flung up on the same sandy shore. They shared in Molly's mind the robust self-sufficient space occupied by the fictional Robinsons from Switzerland.

Soon after the Goodalls had gravely rolled up their tents and filled in the ka-ka hole, the circus came to town, or, more precisely, to the farm's front meadow! The whole troupe shambled in, and the kids hung on the five-bar gate gawping without shame as they unrolled another tent, but one far bigger and more enthralling than the Goodalls' canvas shelter. You had last year's picture in your mind, and each time they seemed to do things in precisely the same disarmingly casual way, like industrious spiders, with complicated knots and ropes and shouts and then way-hay! It was up, the Big Top, and the children could canter around inside tossing their heads in expectant ecstasy as the friendly men carried on hauling tarpaulins, sorting out boxes of kit and fodder, letting the kids get in the way and poke around and generally make nuisances of themselves. They generated a warm feeling, these 'circus folk' who let the children indulge their fantasies for the few days they were there. Years later Molly met the son of one of the two still famous circuses in a later politically-correct non-animals era: he said his father had employed Poles and Russians to put up the tent, but hadn't allowed them any time off till it was all done because they got themselves blind drunk on vodka at any opportunity. Molly thought privately that they deserved it.

Once the Top is up there is a parade through the village. Molly and her brother stroll on the edges in a proprietorial sort of way, on Dad's Land.

They watch every show. The stained seats with their torn leatherette backs are joined together in rows of six. The kids lurk under the tent flaps, lounge on the ropes and look awestruck to heaven inside the Top while the trapezing couple balance and twirl gravely, but with a safety net, above the heads of the local crowd. There's a baby elephant, horses, and poodles whose spangled costumes rival those of the bareback riders, there's an old and mangy lion, and a smell in the tent of sawdust, shit and sheer magic.

For days after they had left, a melancholy group of local children, headed by Molly and her little brother, would pace around the pale and trampled circle left in the meadow grass, and sigh for next year. Molly used to rig up a primitive trapeze in the bullock yard, in the days following their departure, where she could have a soft landing in the straw, but even with much practice she still fell more than she swooped. It was clearly a profession she was not destined to follow.

In the local holiday town at the end of the holiday season, the family always went to the final circus show at the Coliseum. This was a much grander affair, with barking seals that so frightened Molly's brother that he screamed to be taken out. At the end of the show, oh magical moment, the whole ring was flooded and the performers steered themselves around in multicoloured flat boats, while the music followed their progress in crescendo after crescendo, and the revolving central crystal ball threw enchanted fragments of colour over the whole heartbreakingly wonderful scene. Molly would almost weep with the joy of it.

Second only to the circus in Molly's calendar of joy was the fair, which came around Easter Bank Holiday time. The children's dad and mum would take them to the fairground in the local town, and each child would be allocated money for rides, so unusual this largesse, and they could choose which ones. Inevitably Molly's dad took her brother on the bumper cars, even when he was very young, and there were delighted yells and shrieks from both of them as their father whizzed the steering wheel in a coolly expert way, with a small smile when he too wasn't shrieking with some kind of seemingly transcendent male joy. Foot on the accelerator, drive forward then backwards, veer round and avoid the others, then crash into them when you're ready and wheel away again, showers of sparks falling from the wire grille on the roof. Molly and her mum looked on from the edge of the neon-lit testosterone-loaded stage. Molly herself preferred the huge roundabouts where gorgeous gaudy horses complete at that time with real horsehair tails and foaming manes would gallop and swirl up, down and around as her father held her close on the back of one of them, one leg through the stirrup and one hand carelessly laid on the pommel of the saddle which looked like real leather. The intricately laid radiating thin green boards on which their mounts pranced would swell and soar with the music: Wonderful, wonderful, Copenhagen! The speakers would blare, the Tulips of Amsterdam making way for Che Sara Sara, Istanbul no it's Constantinople, no it's Istanbul... Molly wanted the ride to last for ever, as she got carried away on the blasting waves of sound into a parallel universe of power and exultation. The young man who took the fares, sweeping nonchalantly and magnificently around his empire, was usually dark, handsome and mysterious, at least in Molly's eyes, and she experienced the first stirrings of feelings in her mind and in her body that she would understand better as she grew older.

Neither of her parents shared Molly's wish to peer at monstrosities, so the Elephant Man and The World's Ugliest Woman remained unseen, as did the flea circus where a friend told her you could look through a magnifying glass to see those sprightly fellows walk the tightrope or pull little carts. Just imagine that! Candyfloss was also frowned on, much as Molly envied the pink heavens on a stick wafting by her in the hands of children with more tolerant parents who didn't worry about their teeth. Hers did, rightly so she supposed even then, and she did hate going to the dentist. She had to wait until the boundaries loosened a little around adolescence in order to experience beyond parental eyes the sweet evanescence of floss-in-the-mouth. The children could always persuade their dad to try the hooplas, and as inevitable as the bumper car episodes, would be those when he charmed the often voluptuous pouting-lipped blonde female attendants of the booths, right under the eye of their mother, and win a goldfish for each child. These fish looked half dead already when they received them in little plastic bags, and were often nearly goners by the time they'd got them home. The garish flashing of the lights and the powerful clashing smells would make Molly's heart turn over, she felt full of life and possibilities at the fair, and she wondered briefly whether a career as a show-person would be a wise move.

Once a year perhaps they went too to the local 'Pleasure Beach'. Standing right beside the real beach with its timeless pleasures, this manufactured little world of joy promised to wipe away people's workaday cares, as they entered under the garish gateway to be met by a solid wall of smells and sounds which seemed like a sort of anaesthetic, sweeping you away, just for a while, into a different place. Here too, as with the fair, even though the family went there, there were many treats forbidden to them. There was the pleasure of the roundabouts and the bumper cars again, but Molly felt tantalised by the whole thumping mass denied to her. Wistfully she heard the screams of the people hurled up and down in the carriages of the 'scenic railway'—though how they could appreciate the scene in a state of terror was a mystery to her, even then. The nearest they got to it was when they sat in the parked car on the road outside the showground, licking their dripping Italian ice-creams, or sticks of pink Docwra's rock with the name of the makers written right through each stick. For some reason, these weren't forbidden. But even they seemed a somewhat taboo pleasure, and Molly felt the word guilt written right through her too. Guilty as a stick of rock she was, in so many ways. As they licked, they could see the seamier side of the great 'railway', exposed at the side of the road facing away from the fairground, in all its rather scary flimsiness. It was a scantily covered iron construction, struts of which already floated aimlessly in mid air out of view of the happily terrified passengers on the swooping train.

Back home with her goldfish and her unsatisfied yearnings, Molly was a faithful listener to Children's Favourites on the radio, and she paced around the room in accompaniment when Uncle Mac played her own favourite songs. When Nellie the elephant lost her trunk she said goodbye to the circus! Off she went with a trumpety-trump, TRUMP TRUMP TRUMP! Then there was Sparky, the little boy with the magic piano. Molly loved this because it spoke to her cause of tricking grownups and pretending to do more than you actually could. Sparky has to practise scales on Saturdays, but the piano gets magical and he plays whole sonatas with brilliant ease. What a friend to have, to get you out of struggling to do things, Molly thinks. The piano's seductive multi-echoing voice would sound inside her ear, but her own piano lessons where in reality she struggled with the demands of coordination and memory required, showed her that this was another path she had better not want to follow.

In August the holiday crowds arrived, to redden their skins on the beaches and enjoy a week or so away from their monotonous jobs in their home towns. After the war ended there was more money to spend. Five years after Molly was born thirty million working class town-dwellers took a seaside holiday, whole families would journey to the coast for what became an annual family knees-up. They came mainly from London, but also from Birmingham, from Manchester, and the way they twisted their tongues round perfectly ordinary words intrigued Molly. (Of course they too must have been intrigued by the thick local accents of the village children who swarmed around to cart their luggage up the hill). These campers called the sea 'the wowter'; the women wore triangles of bright material tied over their heads and under their hair at the back, and many walked along singing, with cigarettes hanging out of their mouths. It was Steve who encouraged the gang to retrieve fag-ends from the road and try to relight them to have a puff themselves. Some of them still had bright lipstick gashes showing on them, others were dry remnants of a flattened butt drenched in caked spittle. Molly feared them, but she feared Steve's scorn more.

Picking up fag ends. Well, she was doing that in the dusty road, and in another way in her own shadowed house; the little frayed bits of questions, feelings, phrases which quivered and then disappeared into the darkness. She stowed them all away in the hope that maybe sometime she would start to understand how to put them together.

Steve was hard, implacable. He had a core of steel, no doubt evolved to withstand hard knocks before and later. And he was fascinating.

Goo on, I dareya.

But we've got no matches.

Ooh yes we have, he says, eyes glittering as he fishes them out from the bulging pockets of his short grey trousers. Took 'em from me Nan.

Goo on, gal, have a good puff.

Molly wants him to look away, with his staring knowing eyes, as she shuts hers and sets her reluctant mouth to the task.

Then she opens her eyes and the skies whirl a little, like the swallows whirl around above, screeching. Everything seems in some strange way both blurred and very, very clear.

There were two main 'holiday camps', reservations designed for pleasure, equipped with cheerful prankster staff to keep the spirits high. Each Sunday there was a fancy-dress parade from one to the other in weekly turns. They marched, danced and straggled right past the farm's front gate, those floppy clowns and gauzed fairies, stout grenadiers and giggling harlequins, and Molly and John used to sit on the stone gate-posts frankly staring at these aliens, so unlike their own folk. My old man said follow the band, and don't dilly-dally on the way! In the quiet afternoons you could hear the never defeated loudspeaker voices urging them on to some new merriment, and hooters calling them to their communal meals. Maybe it's because I'm a Londoner, that I love London so, they sang at full lung pitch. They had arrived on trains, right into the heart of the village, or on buses at the end near the big main road. The village kids with their luggage carts got paid well for hauling the cases up the hill. One year Molly and her brother persuaded their father to make them carts and they joined in, but again it was on sufferance and it was quietly made clear that they were trespassing on the village kids' world and their livelihood. But the carts John and Molly's dad made were beautiful, from old pieces of wood he'd collected on the beach, and they rolled defiantly well on little wheels with perished rubber rims.

What an association of flotsam and jetsam Molly's dad collected on his daily beach walks, never the same walk twice he would say: ropes and planks and hinges, rubber tube and bales of string. He would lean into the wind, and Molly leaned in the same way beside him. The sky, often grey, leaned on them both. It was like an area outside time, sky and sea wiping out the other realities back home. Molly walked along beside her father as his eye roved for his own version of what could be useful and thus prized. She was trawling for different treasure: a baby's shoe, a piece of smoothed green glass, a bottle with a foreign name. Once they found the carcase of a porpoise, black and white and definitely dead. When the class was asked at school to write that old story of the wandering penny, Molly chose instead to call up the journey of the little battered shoe, tossed on the seven seas and ending up stranded without its owner or its other half. It was, you might say, a quest for reunion, for the lost other, a hopeless quest that took this little girl across mighty oceans with a feeling that somehow loss could be repaired, always on the lookout for love maybe just around the corner.

Their walks are often quite silent, except for the cries of the gulls overhead. Molly often wonders about gull-speak, as ragged groups cry and moan, banter and challenge one another, or so it seems to her, in their freer element high above. She stands on the hard sand and watches the scrum as they hurtle on the wind. Are they goading each other on to new adventures with their wild cries, or are they retiring defeated in a chorus of mewling and mourning from some raid on the seas where they've ended up hungry? She's sure there's a meaning for them in their strident conversations, as they live these whirling aerial lives of desires, thwarted or rewarded, much like her own. It's a question, too, whether having wings makes much of a difference.

There were more malign objects washed up on the beach; rusty mines left over from the war, which the children were warned on no account ever to touch. Not everyone heeded the same warning, and one day Molly saw from the dining room window the wife of one of her uncle's farm labourers come singing and dancing down the farm drive from the cottage where she lived nearby, only she wasn't singing and dancing but howling with grief and shock, her small daughter scrambling crabwise and terrified behind her. Her husband, a keen fisherman, had brought home a mine and attempted to open it in his back yard. There were not many recognisable pieces of himself and his mate left after the explosion. His wife saw his feet bleeding in his old shoes perched at the top of the hedge, and his daughter talked later of Daddy's glasses hanging in the apple tree. This woman had always had a blank, dazed expression in a flat pale face with dead eyes, as if the disaster had been something just waiting to happen. They moved soon afterwards, and the cottage was pushed down to make way for yet another caravan park for urban trippers.

Her own father's trophies, carried home from the beach, were scorned by his practical wife. But he stowed them away in one of the old sheds, where they lay in scarcely balancing and dust-covered piles until he found a use for them, if ever he did. As an old man, he built whole sheds out of his 'bits and bobs', and then retired inside them to contemplate his own end, as he sat, sorrowful and silent on yet another sagging armchair, with his last dog Tiger sprawled at his feet. Molly's son Sam, when he was a small boy, used to sit with his granddad, and he said it seemed one of the best places in the world to be. There seemed to be a sort of camaraderie in this melancholy.

The holiday camp townies, as the children called them, who were part of what her father was gradually and then finally retreating from, were completely out of their element, and needed the structure of their whistle-blowing laugh-a-minute camp leaders. They apparently had no idea about country ways, and Molly and John's dad would march out with his shotgun menacingly by his side to eject them from cornfields when sometimes they were eating sandwiches in the middle of a carpet of abused and crushed barley, or when he found out that they had stormed a field of peas with baskets and were gathering his livelihood for their tea. Molly feared, and maybe they did too, that he really would shoot someone, as he deliberately roughened his voice and bellowed his scorn as he approached.

How would you like it if I came and sat in your front garden?

Off with you, off with you right now.

Get off my land, you buggers.

Jabbing the barrel of his gun towards their astonished faces. Trespassers will be shot, forget mere prosecution. Forget forgiveness too, as she had recited and requested a thousand times in the Lord's prayer. Molly specially notes that mighty last word he uses with such authority, buggers, so very definitely off-limits for her, as she hovers discreetly behind him.

The campers would quickly gather their stuff together, lob back a bit of abuse themselves, and move off not too hastily, with some vestiges of bravado to face out this thunderous god of the cornfield.

Awright mate, keep yer 'air on.

And when they were further away, feeling safer again in their identity as a group,

Silly old git.

Daft old blighter.

Even though he looks younger and stronger than they do, with their pale skins, their moonfaces and awkward arms and legs, flailing around in the open countryside, out of their city element. He strides onwards, and Molly scampers beside him, proud of his heroism, even if the swearing puzzles her.

The children used to sneak into the campers' Bingo games, and admire the professional bark and sleeked-back hair of whichever previously unemployed male had landed the job of number caller. The job brought its own honour to this lucky man, as he crooned his potent formulae into the microphone. People listened to him. Every ear was cocked, he spoke into a acreage of breathing silence. Half way to Heaven, number seven. Could Molly be the first female representative of the breed? Clickety-click, sixty-six. Two fat ladies, eighty-eight. Eyes down, the jolly campers struck off their numbers, they knew exactly what to do, and at least this was the same Bingo as back home in London or Birmingham, when other things were so odd and new. These strange alien adults sat in silent rows like school-children, pencils poised to win. Key of the door, twenty-one. Two little ducks, twenty-two. All on its own, number one. Bingo!

John and Molly went down to the beach with these holiday hordes, to their sea which got regularly changed into 'the wowter' while the happy campers were there. Their dad provided hugely distended inner tubes of tractor tires, and they pushed them through the breaking waves to the calmer water beyond. The only unsafe thing about them as far as the children were concerned was that sometimes you got stabbed in the back by the three inch long valve which stuck out from the inner side of the rim. They often had only one rather small towel between the two of them, Molly and her brother, and they wriggled out of their wet bathing costumes underneath its sandy cloak after their splashing. Molly never learned to swim in a formal way until she went away to school: it was far too much fun just larking about.

On cooler rainy days they even splashed next to porpoises, who seemed to like the company. And the laughing happy campers surrounded them with their radios and their fizzy drinks and their lollies on sticks, and their congas up and down the beach in a long snaky line.

Show me the way to go home, I'm tired and I want to go to bed.

I had a little drink about an hour ago and it's gone right to my head.

These jolly people crowded round the revolving postcard stand in the village shop. Molly also took many a discreet peek at these cards which showed as much as you could in those days of caricatured breasts and bottoms, coloured bright, jokes about too big or too small, the potent giggly mix brought on by sun, sand and sea.

Doctor to the wife of an invalid: 'I suppose you're giving him all he wants'

Wife: 'Oh doctor, he's been far too ill to think about anything of that sort'

Man: 'Do you keep stationery?'

Female Assistant: 'Oh I sometimes wriggle about a bit towards the end'. Cue Molly's incomprehension.

Breasts and bottoms, bottoms and breasts, 'bobbing up and down like this', was the song the campers sang.

These were supposed to be grownups, but they still seemed like big children, locked in to the annual traditions of the camps and let off from their workaday cares to have an institutionalised good time. Show me the way to go home.

Chapter Ten

In which Molly's wish to know more about the grownups results in uncertainty and pain. She escapes when she can to her grandparents' world in the next village, which seems a thousand miles away from the headaches building in her own.

Sometimes there may be no bright metal thread left. In cleaning tapestries, even the stitches holding down the threads may be destroyed. Once the metal thread is cleaned it must be lacquered to prevent the return of tarnish. Sometimes this is impossible to achieve.

Molly wants a word.

What, another one? demands her mother.

One small stumpy-legged girl just refuses to leave the stage. She still wants to 'hold forth'. That's her mother here, describing the behaviour of anyone except herself wanting a part, speaking what might be in mind.

Still going on. Will she never stop? Does anyone need to know?

Molly's been quite good though, quite quiet up to now, hasn't she. She hasn't really put herself forward too much, do you think? That would be an embarrassment to everybody. So goo on, gel, as your old friend Steve would say, have another go.

Sometimes I don't understand half of what she says. In fact I never understand any of it.

Oh well.

The grownups. There were those improbable alien campers, and there were ours too, the ones in my everyday world. I wanted to trick them like Sparky with his magic piano, but they were tricky, too. I recall one of my aunts, Uncle Albert's wife, leaning on her front door lintel and telling me some untruth, unremembered now, and you could see right through it. Why don't grownups realise, I thought, how transparent they are? Why kid kids? And if the truth be told, as far as it ever can be, there were indeed tricky things going on.

Staying at my cousin's house one night, I remember waking and hearing my father wailing on the back stairs, outside the door of my cousin's room, as I lay quaking in my cousin's second bed. No words, just wails. The hero father was in agony, then. It was all hushed up next day, and I had to wait another twenty-five years to understand the wails, which were about my mother and my uncle, Uncle Albert, brother to my father, some sort of an affair. Maybe not an uncommon infidelity, to turn to your husband's brother. But it echoed down those years, another mystery for so long unsolved and unresolved. All I knew was that the Christmas and birthday presents stopped, the boxes of toffees and the gloves, and so did the thank you letters.

Uncle Albert's wife had been a well-know frequenter of the social events arranged for the American US air force personnel stationed close by, and even as a child I had overhead and half understood whispered tales of wickedness. So in the carousel of rejection and rejected, her husband may have searched around, but not too far, to find a way to pass the hurting on. In the close knit community of this little world, there may have been many opportunities to meet, in an apparently innocent way. Had my mother and Uncle Albert arranged meetings too in deserted windy back roads, where two cars could be parked discreetly behind the hedge? Had there been risky conduct in the meadows?

Even half a century later, a sudden flash of likeness in a photograph can set questions whirring in the brain, correspondences which connect only over years. Who was my brother's father? Who's to know?

The carousel kept on turning, and the next turn would face the queen with something she would never have anticipated.

All the wars in the world were about religion, my ma had said, but this family war was surely not to do with God. Her tight lips spoke of swallowed secrets. A family chasm began to open up and the first casualty was any kind of notion that life was straightforward. There were ellipses and spirals of raw feeling hovering over the life of every day, a kind of dangerous swirl of stars and meteorites and thunderbolts which you could feel but not see. *Under the look of fatigue, the attack of migraine and the sigh, There is always another story, there is more than meets the eye.*

Headaches. My mother had them frequently, and painkillers lay around the house to fend them off. Too many people in her head, clamouring around the queen. Later I had them too, a kind of strange inheritance of feelings, and I woke one morning dreaming that I was swallowing needles, not whole but broken needles, useless for sewing, but just the kind to mount a sharp attack from the inside.

There was an unacknowledged trauma, a raw wound, damaging the tissue of my life, and I took refuge in reading and knotting my hair, pulling off the knotted tufts and storing them alongside gnawed apple cores under the bed. These knots, relics of my confusion, piled one on another and another all on one hank of gathered strands, had a kind of comforting ritual significance, knots that I could make and remake, unlike the family knots which were growing tighter and were so totally beyond my control. They accumulated, piles of half-heard truths and half-truths, beyond sorting, like the clutter beneath the granary stairs in the corner of the old barn.

I took to sitting on the shallow front stairs in the dark at night, straining my ears to hear. To hear what? This sly and secretive child ached to know. I crept down the front hall, to the back hall, to the kitchen and into the pantry where the tins and jars were stored, and hastily tipped sweet Horlicks powder, supposed to be the solution so the advertisers said for 'night starvation', into a glass. Then I trod softly back to my listening post, breath held to stop the stair creaking, sticking my licked index finger into the gluey sweet mess and trying to suck away the empty sound of my heavily beating heart.

When Horlicks proved to be no help I moved on to the harder stuff. Andrew's Liver Salts fizzed at the end of my anxious finger but proved to be no match for the Furies which had been unleashed in my head when I heard my father's anguished cries. Was this an early example of laxative abuse? I was locked in a dark room, alone, and although I couldn't see the face of my despair, it held me in its dead-eye gaze. I worried continually. Worrying, that word which began as a description of what the hound did to his prey, took over and consumed me. I consumed myself, my thoughts exhausted me. My life, from that point, seemed never free from yet another fear, but these were nameless. They seemed to separate me from what I thought of as other people's normal lives.

Only once did I come upon a small silent drama which seemed to embody all I feared. In the dining room, my father is laying a fire in the pale stone fireplace, in his usual careful way, and my mother crouches next to him. Neither speak. I may have stopped breathing. Everything seems poised for an eternal second. They do not see me, and I melt away down the hall, a sad little ghost-girl. What was there in that constellation, my mother, my father and the unlit fire? Dark matters indeed. A cold crime scene, about to unfold, already unfolding, and changing things for ever. I feared I might never be warm again. The word 'divorce' hovered around, not said by anyone, but it was a fearsome word. I could imagine my mother walking off, away from the cold fire, out of the door and down the curved drive, with her suitcase in her hand. I could imagine my father helpless, hands hanging down, eyes finally seeing his own personal abyss. None of this ever really happened, in this particular way, but I replayed it daily in my mind. I went to the edge of the void most days, as I recall, but the time for falling had not yet arrived The power of an event can flow from its dark heart, it can drive you to tell stories to yourself, and then build other worlds you'd rather inhabit than the one where you actually live.

I literally escaped, too, as often as I could, into the world of my grandparents' house. It was only three miles away in the next village. My brother, little absconder too from something unknown and fearful, once rode off there on his own on his tricycle. It was a different pre-lapsarian Eden. You could still breathe there.

My grandparents, my mother's parents, lived in a rambling thirties one-level house, with an outside loo where I sat with dangling legs smelling the odd combination of Elsan fluid, lavender from the bunches hung by my Gran above the door and all our dumped remains. I used to swing my legs, inhale and sing. *Che sara, sara/ Whatever will be will be/ The future's not ours too see,/ Che sara sara/ What will be will be.*

My father's parents had died long before my birth, father of peritonitis from a rotten unrecognised appendix, misdiagnosed as constipation by an ignorant family doctor, as Old Acid always scornfully said, and mother, perhaps, from the exhaustion of continual childbearing. She had made an unpromising marriage for love, and had been virtually ignored for the rest of her life by her rather grand local family, one member of whom had invented shorthand.

There was a tantalising tale, that somewhere there remained an unread will, which left my father's mother the fortune to which she should have been entitled. In the one remaining picture of this woman who followed the impulse of her heart and not her material welfare, she looks a little sad. She could never cook, so my father recalled, had never been taught one might think, in a family full of servants, and there was a family joke that the ducks sank in the pond after eating the rock-cakes she baked which were rejected by her children. But since they had several maids, a necessary succession of Annies, the family didn't starve. While Dad had nothing complimentary to say about his mother's cooking, whenever he had a sore throat he fell back on her tested and ancient remedy for colds. You could tell he was ill as soon as you opened the back door. A wafting sickly smell of vinegar would hit you in your own throat, and my mother, who relied on more modern methods, would look on in frank distaste as he soaked a piece of old toast in a warm stew of vinegar, then wrapped the soggy stuff round his neck in a piece of old sheet.

Oh deary-me, said Mr Goat, I have a very painful throat! Mr Goat apparently boiled his feet in mustard, and took camphorated oil, but for my dad, vinegar did the trick. Mother knows best.

In the last years before her husband died my paternal grandmother had apparently long retired from sex and had been carried up and downstairs by my devoted father, her second youngest son, night and morning, to and from her throne in the living room, where he plaited and re-plaited her hair, winding its heavy coils above her ears. He transferred his allegiance from one queen to another, and it was no doubt a good thing that his mother had died several years before he met his wife. Being in thrall to both would have been tricky if not impossible.

My maternal grandparents had a few acres of land, with a primrose wood and a large vegetable plot out the back, and a series of large and rambling sheds, tarred black, alongside a two-story mansion of a shed, which was my grandfather's workshop. He had been a marine engineer; as well as for some time a joiner making coffins, or 'oak houses' as he called them. He had every kind of lathe you could think of, a whole regiment of tools, some neatly arranged and others from past projects lying in discarded heaps in the sawdust, and curly wood-shavings bagged up but still escaping all over the floor, which gladdened my nose and my heart with their pale sweet-smelling twistings. I sat for hours and watched him work. I swear even today I could lay a wall, so many times did I watch his slow and careful movements, pick up a brick, get a trowel full of cement mixed to just the right soft pudding feel, slap it on the brick, then slap the brick, but slowly, carefully, on top of the last one, press it down, but carefully, precisely, then wipe off the cement that oozes from the join and put it back in the puddingy mass.

Perhaps my grandfather was an obsessive. He would listen to the weather forecast on the radio each evening at six o'clock, and woe betide you if you dared to interrupt the solemn and considered litany of Dover, Wight, Plymouth, Portland, Fastnet and Dogger Bank. What did gale force 8 backing southerly really mean? How does the wind veer? I was never sure. Severe gale force 9 with occasional storm force 10. Moderate visibility, becoming poor. In my child's mind it had very little to do with the real storms out there on the waves, even though we lived by the sea and I knew from the church hymns about those in peril, but I could make a link even then with the kind of tricky weather that could brew up at home. When I grew up I realised that many others too had the same pull towards the dark pictures inside, echoed by the steady voice of the forecaster. Visibility good, occasionally poor.

Red sky at night, shepherd's delight.

Gnats flying about, fine day tomorrow.

Granddad did the football pools every week, and again utter silence had to remain unbroken even by a murmur as he solemnly recorded the radio announcer's news. West Bromwich Albion, Hamilton Academicals, Ayre United… little forests of diagonal lines with the odd little o among them grew on the page as he worked. I knew from the way the announcer's well-modulated voice dipped or soared at the end of each couple of names whether he would pronounce a win, a lose or a draw. These faraway football teams and their often rhythmical names got mixed up in my mind with those from the weather forecasts, Northward Serra, Southward Serra, back home again to our own Dogger Bank.

There was a game he used to like to play with me and my brother, two little dickie birds that we were. He sticks a small piece of paper, moistened with spit, on one finger of each hand. And here we go: 'Two little dickie birds, sitting on a wall, one named Peter, (down comes one papered finger onto the table) one named Paul (and then the other)' He pauses, smiles, and we know every time what's coming next. Solemnly he says 'Fly away Peter, fly away Paul', and he flies them away over his shoulder, then putting down another finger from each hand, no paper attached, on the table. We knew it, we loved it. 'Come back Peter' we would say, 'Come back Paul'. And back they came.

He loved riddles too. He sits me on his knee, while my little brother runs off to see what Gran is up to. He solemnly declaims: Riddle-me, riddle-me, riddle-me-ree, I have a riddle, what can it be? I stare into his eyes, unblinking, as he delivers his rhyme. As deep as a house, as round as a cup, and all the king's horses cannot draw it up. I can hear Granny rattling the tea cups or opening the door of the oven, but I am bound to wait. What is it? What is it? A well, he pronounces, with satisfaction every time. Well, well, he chuckles.

Granddad would sneeze theatrically, then blow his nose hard on his handkerchief after a series of these barks. He would apologise solemnly after what he described as 'breaking wind'. In my house even mentioning this apparently shameful phenomenon was frowned on. It wasn't until I later went away to school that I learned to translate breaking wind into 'shooting bunnies', which is what my dad really did on a weekly basis, and we all admitted under cover of darkness in the dormitory that we liked to smell our own.

It was only in her last weeks that my mother lost her inhibitions about such functions, and did so in a typically flamboyant way, as she lay half-dressed on her bed amid an orchestra of farts, burps, groans and sighs. However it was her visitors, she maintained, who farted, and there were days when she refused entry to any of them.

'He'll fart no more' said the grandmother of Albert Camus, on hearing of a neighbour's death. My mother is unaccountably silent here.

Granddad had a moustache rather like Hitler's and he sleeked down his hair with some sort of smelly pomade, he wore suspenders with his socks, and arm-bracelets to keep his shirtsleeves trim. Where are my gig-lamps? He would demand when the daily papers arrived, and he would settle down, serious wire spectacles on his nose, to digest the local news. He roasted chestnuts on the open fire to perfection. But you had to wait, wait, wait, until he pronounced them absolutely perfect. His small, precise writing seemed to reflect his character. In my little autograph book, crammed full of such immortal lines as 'By hook or by crook, I'll be first (or last) in your book', he wrote an impressive two lines in this meticulous script, precious but incomprehensible to me at the time:

As you mount the ladder of success, May you never meet a friend coming down.

I worked out that the one coming down would tread on the fingers of the one climbing up, and then, painful transition over, the gap would widen for ever. Why did he choose this image? I didn't know then how this might apply to him and his notion of a life lived according to the inescapable law of gravity. But my mother told me many years later that he had been offered a promotion as a skilled marine engineer, which meant moving to Scotland. But he had stayed in the village where he was born, and perhaps despite this being his own free choice, he may have felt with part of himself as though he had in some way descended the ladder.

If you came this way, you could start from anywhere, it seemed, at any time or at any season, it would always be the same.

My house seemed perpetually to echo with doors just closed, and halls draughty from sucked–in breath and sighs, singing floors to trap the intruder, the poisoner, the murderer; floors whose creaks and squeaks warned me of unseen enemies about. My grandparents' house, so aptly called 'The Retreat', held all that was certain and warm and without hard edges. This little house which had felt so confining to my mother, and far beneath her aspirations, was my haven. Red sky at night, shepherd's delight. Red sky in the morning, shepherd's warning. Gnats flying about. Fine day tomorrow?

My grandmother, Flo, was warm too, and soft. 'I have three Florences', my grandfather would say, 'my wife, my daughter and my stove'. I think he loved them all. This modest couple never went to Florence, or even very far at all out of their own patch of the earth. But Florence Nightingale, that noble nurse, had been named after her birthplace, and as her fame spread, so did this name, not much used since medieval times, when it had been a name for women and for men. My grandfather was named after a king, the noble Alfred, with James to follow on. 'Edgie', Gran called him, and it wasn't till my son pointed it out years after their death, that I realised this as an affectionate corruption of the initials of his stolid Victorian name.

There were in fact two more Florences in my grandfather's life: his mother Florence Louisa, who had eleven months after her marriage given birth to another Florence, Florence Chrisanna. But she died, that little one, less than a month after her birth, and less than a year after her parents' marriage. My grandfather, perhaps a replacement child, was conceived six months after she had been buried. All this is recorded in the tiny dark-blue leaf-embossed leather book given to the first Florence by her fiance, and left to me by my grandmother. We cannot always trace the way, runs the verse for little Florence Chrisanna's birthday, where thou our gracious lord doth move. But we can always surely say that thou art love. What a breathtaking contradiction of the feelings which must have been around when that baby was snatched away by death.

My brother would sit on my grandmother's knee when he was a little boy, kneading her breasts which were squashy and welcoming, calling them 'her buns'. She laughed with tolerance, and love. Her bedroom smelt of lilies of the valley talcum powder, which she let me use too, sprinkled on a large and soft pink powder puff, which lay ceremonially with her silver brush and comb and mirror on the top of the large mahogany dressing table. While baths at home were mostly strictly about cleaning until I was considered old enough to do it for myself, baths in Grannie's soft pink and cream bathroom were languid and warm, as I sat and made huge air bubbles on the surface of the water with her flannel, and exploded them under water in a thousand little beads, so that the flannel seemed as lively as a fish swimming in a heated aquarium.

Gran taught me to knit, and I struggled proudly with the thick needles and dropped many stitches, to make pathetic little scarves for my dolls and teddy bears, lopsided and inadequate, which she examined with a critical but kindly eye. My continually imagined projects of perfection as mother of my little family never failed to disappoint me with their sad reality, but she encouraged me to persevere.

She called me 'duckie' and 'pet' and made marvellous caraway seed cake, which we sometimes ate on the lawn, where she warned me not to sit on damp patches under the acacia tree, for fear of getting 'tick dolleroo'. When I learned French at school later, I recognised this as a version of the French '*tics douloureux*'. So I used to sit on her doorstep, tracing my finger over the smooth sunny sill with one hand, a piece of still-warm seed cake in the other, talking and carelessly munching with my mouth open, if I wanted to. There is a cutting from *Woman's Life* in Elizabeth Craig's book of 'Economical Cookery', dated 1919, with a recipe for this 'excellent seed cake'. It had margarine and golden syrup in it, brown sugar and one and a half teacups of sour milk, added a very little at a time, and three teaspoonsful of caraway seeds, those useful seeds that had been used to make the gripe-water which had soothed my infant stomach.

There were two crab-apple trees in the primrose wood, and in Gran's cookery book, in a small yellowed envelope carefully marked 'Crab Jelly' is a handwritten recipe, not her own careful script, but neat enough, from a neighbour maybe, who advises washing the crab-apples but leaving the stalks so that they just 'peep out' of the water. She uses a strong pillowcase, she says, to drain the pulp all night over a bowl. Squeezing, she warns, must not be done on any account, or you will have a murky result. Next day you boil the juice with a pound of sugar to every pint, and test it as you go to prove its jelliness. You must skim it continuously. Those saucers of gelling jam set out so long ago strike my inward eye immediately, when I read these words. I used to stand by my stirring Gran, balanced on a chair next to the old Florence stove, and badger her to test the jam, raspberry, strawberry, marrow or crab, every few minutes, so I could pronounce on the progress of the jam and even more important, lick up the wrinkling contents straight from the saucers as they stood in little rows by the open window.

I loved burnt bits on Granny's cakes, and I used to persuade her to scorch one side and cut it off especially for me. That meant going against Elizabeth Craig's exhortations about turning the cake for even browning— but Gran did it anyway. I would recall too from my book of historical tales the story of King Alfred, who had the same name as my grandfather, and who was a great defender of England against the Danes. This beleaguered man sheltered one day in a cowherd's cottage in the West Country, and he didn't notice the evidence of his nose as the oven's heat grew and the cowherd's wife scolded him.

'Cas'n thee mind the ke'aks, mon? I'm boun thee's eat 'em vast enough, as zoon az tiz turn!'

I felt as grand as the lax King Alfred as I sat on the door-sill looking at the mesembryanthemums in the flower bed opposite the door. They had little spiky wax-petalled flowers that opened, like I did, in the sun. Although they can grow vigorously in poor but well-drained soil, they open only in that summer sunshine. I sucked in my grandmother's nectar, encased in her soft body like the sugared centre of her favourite Newberry Fruits, full of colour and sweetness.

And how was it, I can wonder now, that I found her so empathic, when something had gone so wrong between herself and her one and only daughter? Was it simply the mellowness of age, which made my grandmother so accessible to me, or had the fit between mother and daughter never been good enough? Perhaps I gave her a saintliness which was a contrast with what I experienced at home, with my mother.

Gran used to take me on the train from her own small village to the local town. The village was reassuringly solid, as we walked to the station side by side without talking very much at all, in the dry and dusty air which blew around my feet as I scuffed it up with my sandals. Names like Station Road, Cliff Walk, Kennel Loke, and Main Street, both sewed it into normality, a place on the map, and gave it for me a sort of mythical status too, like a little settlement at the foothills of Mount Olympus. I sat in awe with my legs dangling on the firm seats of the closed carriages which led straight onto the platform of the village station, well-kept and spruce in those days, with only the odd stubborn bit of red valerian challenging life at the foot of the wall outside the ladies' waiting room. The station and the station master were both in those days necessities, before the wholesale arrival of the car and the death of this honourable railway life. Each carriage on the heavily breathing train had six water colour reproductions fixed above the seats, often of local scenes, the marshes and the windmills and the skies with their endless spaces, and little nets above the seats to keep your hat and brolly in. The windows opened and were fixed by a strong leather strap. The station master's firm timetable of whistles and waves gave me great comfort; a sense of something in the world going to plan.

Each station stop was marked by the calm announcement of its name, several times, not by a recorded voice but by a Someone in one of the little station offices. It seemed to me like an honourable job, to mark the pilgrimages ordinary people made, and I wondered whether that might be something I could aspire to, in later life.

On rainy days I crouched by the bottom brass-handled drawer of the huge and shining walnut bureau, poring over the old copies of *Picture Post* and *Illustrated London News* which packed the drawer to the brim, making it hard to open. There were pictures of conflict around the world, of politicians and film-stars, and of those two fairy-tale princesses Elizabeth and Margaret, who seemed in their cuddly cardigans and buttoned shoes so remote and inscrutable and yet, strangely, as near to me as the sisters I had never had. When my dissatisfactions, real and imagined, with my real parents grew to unmanageable proportions, I would dream of being royal too. Perhaps I shared my mother's aspirations. These little girls, whose pictures had been re-released when their nanny decided to tell her story, were in reality quite a bit older than me. Indeed the Princess Elizabeth, fourteen years old at the beginning of the war well before I was born, broadcast her empathy to displaced people everywhere, saying she was glad her home, even though it was a palace, had been bombed too, so that she could look the people in the East End of London in the face.

Granny also had a scrap-book full of picture postcards, saved all down the years from when she was a girl, recording the treasured holiday moments of the to-me unknown old friends and relations, which must indeed have contributed somehow to the sum of human happiness. My dad too had saved all the postcards I had ever sent him, but bundled haphazardly and held with an elastic band. When my mother died and I had to clear her house in a hurry, I sighed, put them in a black plastic bag for the dustman and have regretted it so many times, not for what they might have told me, but because I was throwing away something he had cherished. And in her own way my mother must have cherished them too, moving them from house to house.

Relegated to the lumber room in Gran's house, and I never knew why, was the little old blue upholstered armchair which my mum had sat on when she was smaller than I was then. I used to go and sit on it in secret. It had a melancholy feel, and whatever history it hid, I felt I could ask no questions about it.

In the main living room, the sitting room they called it, along with little gold-framed oil paintings of marshes, dykes and windmills, landscapes where melancholy music seemed to seep from the shadows, hung her beautiful collection of pale blue painted Chinese plates, fluttering with butterflies and small birds, etched with twigs of extraordinary delicacy, and amassed throughout her married life. When she was an old lady she offered them to me, and in my ignorance I refused, saying I could not think of it while she was still alive and they ornamented her life. So she thought them not worthy of any attention, directed in her will that all her goods go up for auction, and my sister-in-law bought the lot. Because of the family rift which plagues each generation of our family, I can no longer even see them now.

Could I have asked you, Gran, about what was going on? Would you have said, there there, pet, don't you fret yourself? Could I have let you know what was eroding me from the inside, invading even the softness of my night's sleep in the billowing folds of your second best feather bed? I dream of straining to hear Gran's voice above rushing water, but can hardly make out what she's trying to say.

There there, pet. I'm still here.

Just outside the back door of my grandparents' house mounted on the fence was a tin food-safe which kept things cool behind its wire-mesh door. In summer time too there would be a wasp trap or two hanging from the adjacent tree; a jam jar with a spoonful of some sweet bait at the bottom and a paper lid with a one-way-no-exit hole. The greedy wasps buzzed in eagerly and drowned in the nectar they had so desired, and as they died you could hear their mournful buzzing recitative. They can fly forwards, backwards, upwards and downwards, those canny wasps, masters of their little universes, until they are defeated by the baffling inward shutters of a paper lid.

Over the fence was a well-tended orchard plot, where another Mr Smith, this time an old man with teeth stained almost black from a lifetime of tobacco chewing, pruned his apple trees and leaned his bent body on a rake to admire his tidy work. I would kneel on a chair looking out of Gran's dining room window and watch him, raking and chewing, up and down the lines of little trees. If I gave him a small friendly wave, he would nod briefly, and carry on.

Why doesn't he speak to me, Gran?

His wife is dead, duckie, and he's probably very sad.

But his garden is lovely.

Yes.

Inside the house just next to the back door was the cupboard under the draining board where my grandfather kept the shoe cleaning stuff: a battalion of little circular gold-lettered tins and graded wooden-backed brushes, all neatly labelled. Black Polish, Black Off, Brown Polish, Brown Off. The smell of that cupboard intoxicated me, it was as magical to me as my old friend linseed putty, and I would watch as he gravely worked up a shine on a row of his stout shoes, Gran's well-worn high heeled lace-ups (the nigger brown as it was called then, and the navy pair), and my own current pair of buttoned bar-shoes too, if I was lucky.

Next to the cupboard and the kitchen sink was the pantry, a walk-in cornucopia of tins holding buns and cakes, jars of jams and marmalades, and a great big white porcelain pot which held the pickled eggs and smelt of brine. There were neat piles of green and white china—the best bone china pansy teacups were in a separate china cabinet along with the silver teapot, which I now don't keep as shiny as she once did—and mugs hanging from hooks along the length of the shelves. It was all painted cream, like the kitchen, and reminded me of Caroline's finest cream rising in the yellow bowls at home. It seemed to smell of baking, and I could feel satisfied just standing in there, without needing to eat a thing.

In the post-war cookery book that was evidently my grandmother's bible, as I suppose from the cuttings and jottings she left behind in it, the author offers this sage advice: 'when choosing your culinary wares, let your text be: *Everything in this Kitchen will have to be cleaned*'. The average kitchen, the writer maintains, contains too many things. With the demise of domestic servants, her maxim is to buy little and replace each broken article only where necessary. Her list of kitchen equipment for a household of about four people looks extensive, but my gran had all these things from china jelly moulds to fish slices, mincing machines and fish-kettles, all neatly stored away in her own little palace kitchen where she was both queen and servant maid alike.

'What a lot of odds and ends accumulate in your kitchen!' One of the advertisements at the end of Granny's cookbook advises throwing them all into a saucepan and stewing them for half an hour with a packet of Edwards' dessicated soup, made in three varieties, brown, white and tomato. This, or so the spin had it, would turn your useless scraps into 'a dish of dishes'. The little circular inset picture of a self-satisfied woman in bib and bonnet somehow set the seal on this sinister advice. I can't imagine my Gran ever having to stoop so low.

Granny was a member of the Women's Institute, and I too faithfully
went along to the local village hall to hear about local history and flower
drying, and to sing Jerusalem at the top of my off-key voice. I shall not
cease from mental fight, nor shall my sword sleep in my hand. I bathed in
the warm attention of granny and her neighbours, and when my own
attention wandered I could wander too, out to play ball on the grass below
the high windows, where I could say hallo to passers by. Jam and Jerusalem,
a cliche now. What would she have made of WI members posing for a girlie
calendar, or Spit the Cherry Stone competitions? Spitting was for kids and
we had revelled in it—but for grownups? Gran wore a little oval badge,
with the letters W and I entwined in its centre, a Tudor rose on the left and
a maple leaf on the right, to salute the movement's beginnings in rural
Canada at the end of the nineteenth century. This W and I seemed a
harmonious knot to me, just like the reef knots my father used to teach me
about: 'left over right, then right over left'. If you crossed the ends the
wrong way, what you got was what he called 'a Granny knot', but to me,
a Granny knot was good. She, who had the powerful gift of being
remembered well by many people, lives on in me.

Night night, pet, sleep tight, don't let the fleas bite.

A friend at my convent school had shown me how to make a 'false
knot'. First you make a circle of string, just about the size of a skein of
wool. I'd seen my father patiently hold these skeins while my mother
swiftly rolled off the wool into loose balls and stowed them in her knitting
basket. She could do the same job by stretching the skein between the
backs of two upright chairs, but it was something both she and my father
seemed to enjoy, the rhythmic gentleness of it, somehow binding them at
least in those moments into a functioning whole.

This false knot intrigued me from the start. You wind the string circle
around and around your fingers, so it looks as if you're binding them up
beyond escaping. Then you lift the two intertwined strands from off your
little finger, give a gentle pull, and the string against all logic untwists into
your original circle. I practised for weeks till I got it down to a certainty,
then did my magic over and over again as a comfort when there were other
knots which weren't so easy to master.

Above and below the valiant logo emblazoned on the W.I. brooches which decorated the tireless breasts of British women were inscribed on dark green enamel the words 'For Home and Country'. It seemed a good enough aim to me, at the time.

The village fete was held once a year on the pleasant pasture they called 'The Meadow' at the front of the house, my own home and country of the heart, bordered on one side by the village school and on the other by the Methodist chapel and an area of tangled blackberry bushes, all now vanished in the thrust of development. All that remains is the stained glass lantern from the chapel, saved from the demolition by my granddad, and now hanging in my own hall. Because this was my grandparents' land, I felt a pride of ownership, as with the circus on Dad's Land at home. There was a live pig which people threw hoopla rings for, a tombola, stalls and stalls of village produce, a tug o' war and a Beautiful Baby competition. Each year the same old characters emerged and it felt as if this could never change, that I would never be grown up, that there would always be a front meadow and a fete, and there were early photos of my ma, same age as me, child-mistress of the same occasion twenty-five years before.

If you followed the straight little dusty path beside my grandfather's huge vegetable garden, always with a scarecrow or two on guard, where the grass and the dock-leaves and the dandelions would brush your toes in summer, and cover your shoes with a kind of heavy penetrating dampness in the winter, you could take a short cut up to Kennel Loke, where the fish shop was, kept by a Mr Snowling, who had relations in my own village close by. A dog seemed always to be barking somewhere in the distance. Mr Snowling's tweed cap sat firmly on his thinning hair, he had an apparently permanent drip on his narrow blue nose, and a mournful cast to his steely grey eyes. I have to try very hard each time not to imagine the hovering viscous drip falling onto the fish that he carefully selects from his slimy marble slope and wraps up in yesterday's newspaper for Granny to take home. Then we go back the same way, through the little wicket gate with its satisfying click when you shut it. There. That's done. Home again.

To the left and in front of the house, beyond the primrose wood and edged by tall trees, was another meadow, where the blackberry bushes were more accessible and where we would all hover and gather in baskets and punnets the fruit that Gran made into jam, into pies, and solemnly sealed in vacuum jars which were warmed and ready in the oven on bottling day. My Dad and Grand-dad hauled down the more inaccessible clusters with their long sticks. Purple lips gave me away and I used to get fed up with the command to pick more and eat less. I would grizzle, groan and stagger my way theatrically around the field, and the adults tended quite rightly to ignore me. My brother was too little to be required to do anything beyond being there, under their eye. Gran would pack the fruit in the jars, fill them with cold water and screw the caps down tight onto their rubber rings. They would sit in polite rows in a pan of water in the slowly heating oven for an hour, or maybe two. Then she would remove them, one at a time, and give each cap an immediate and final screw. It was a satisfying hoarding of the world's bounty.

In her battered post First World War cookery book, one of the batch of advertisements at the back, all couched in courteous language now long since abandoned in the world of the hard sell, proclaims 'a revolution in fruit bottling'. For one and ninepence you could get a batch of thirty seals and 'adaptable parchment covers' to use on any old jar you happened to have around. But Granny, proud in her kitchen, used only the best, her fruit didn't need to 'keep indefinitely', pies and crumbles would be scoffed soon enough.

But there's something in me still which responds to the need in those days to preserve and conserve. In the same cookbook are extolled the virtues of a hay-box, and instructions how to make one. This fireless cooker came into its own as domestic labour became scarcer after the Great War and when fuel was rationed. You brought your pot of porridge or your beef stew to the boil, and then nested it into the hay-box where it could go on cooking gently in its own cocooned heat. Redundant newspapers and fine hay in a mattress made of old flannel kept your dinner snug, and you could even, it was suggested, make the outside of the box gay with paint and cretonne, tra-la!

Briefly, I had a Shetland pony called Nimbus who grazed in the field next door to my grandparents' house, just beyond the primrose wood. It

166

was a passing passion, and I used to ride with my cousin, daughter of my father's younger brother, a slightly larger girl than me, with a slightly larger pony. Plump blonde-haired children both, we would take our mounts to be shod at the local smithy, watching silently with freezing hands deep in our pockets as the blacksmith sizzled the shoe-shapes he had made in the white hot heat of his furnace onto the ponies' feet, after he had cooled them in a bucket of water, and the bitter air was filled with sinister blue smoke. A bigger pony bought later, called Puck, proved to be as nervous and unstable as I probably was myself. He bucked and bucked, and after many falls and parental exhortations to get back up there, I gave up the idea of being a show-jumper too, and Puck was packed off in a horsebox to a new home where a small girl more determined than I was might be able to manage his frisky ways.

I loved the stand of trees at the edge of Nimbus's field, where I would go with my grandparents' *Daily Express* to read about lovers and murderers and girls of sixteen who seemed like women to me. When I was sixteen, I thought, as I sat on a fallen tree-trunk in a sun-swamped glade where life teemed overhead and underneath my feet, I'd have no more problems, I'd really be a grownup after all this counterfeiting since the age of three. But my mother, seeing a spot of blood in my knickers, had told me about periods. I sat under the kitchen table as she too baked cakes or pies, and said with shock and disbelief, so this will happen to me every month until I'm fifty? Her mute legs led upwards from under the table to further mysteries.

It was another insurmountable hurdle it seemed to me, and being a grownup became a more problematic project. Then she taught me to dust, sitting me with a duster beneath a row of chairs. I flicked the rag in disbelief and thought, there must be more to life than this. And since dusting as far as I can recall was something the women did who cleaned the house, rather than my mother, I wonder what message she was trying to convey. My thoughts about this idea of 'being a woman' were confused by the scattiness of Gay Gambol, the cartoon character on the lower back page of the *Express* under the Sports section. Gay as her name, fluffy and *insouciante*, an airhead, she would arrive home carrying a toppling pile of parcels, proclaiming to her husband George how much she had saved in the sales by buying another pile of needless nonsense.

I had no idea how my little girl's body was supposed to be transformed into the angular knowingness of the models drawn in the *Vogue* magazines my ma pored over for new dress inspiration. The jut of their hips, the set of their chins, their regal gaze stretching over and beyond the ordinary world… Questions rose inside my mind and dissipated like smoke as I marvelled at my ma's concentration on this task, and the fierce eagerness in her eyes. I was only ever allowed access to these magazines when the next monthly issue had slapped onto the mat beneath the front door. Just like the queen in her palace, my mother never touched a paper or magazine that had been touched by anybody else before her. But the next one always came, and then it was my turn to drink in last month's images. I copied the drawings with some accuracy, but the states of mind such poses were supposed, I thought, to represent, were beyond my understanding. The way the gently swelling curve of a calf slimmed down to an ankle which rose above the elegant heel of a high-heeled shoe, I drew it over and over, that fluid line, as if the drawing would reveal something to me about the mysteries and sexual powers of adult women. Alongside dresses, my ma's passion was for shoes, and there are shoes of hers I still keep but can't wear, they're so high-heeled. Shoes made of snakeskin, of shiny leather with little saucy toe-or heel-bows, where the heels might make you soar in fantasy, as I think she did, above the others, the lofty queen of all hearts. A stiletto can be a weapon even on a shoe, and Ma had an armoury of them.

Other little girls I knew from my convent school had dressing up boxes full of their mother's old clothes and shoes, and I would love as they did stalking loudly around and stumbling over extravagantly long skirts, in their more permissive houses. But I never dared put a foot in my ma's shoes. Many were especially made, from crocodile and python, and she travelled up to the Bond Street shoe shop which also sold shoes to the queen of the land, by appointment of course. Ma too would sit in 'The Royal Box'-a little red velvet curtained enclosure discreetly tucked away at the back of the shop, and turn her ankles critically over and over as she pondered on the creations which emerged from a stack of boxes piled by the side of the deferential manager, a man with a well-trimmed moustache and heavy black spectacles, and a permanently concerned air to do his best for his royal customers, who recognised no limits on their own spending power.

If Ma ever threw any of her clothes away, they never came my way. Either she really had no idea this is what girls (and boys) tended to like to do, or she would have considered it a blasphemy to allow her grubby little daughter to have presumptions about even cast-off finery.

Oh Ma, maybe I didn't understand you properly, even just a little bit, and that I have to accept, but you also did not understand me. Can we make peace now, now you're dead? I still wish I might have done better: do you ever wish the same? It was always a question of too close or too far away. You used to look forward to my weekend visits, suffer them while I was with you, then weep just as I was leaving.

At my grandparents' house I slept in a large double feather bed, sinking into its mountain folds as I listened to them listening to the Palm Court Orchestra on the radio on Sunday nights in the next room. They had an old record player, just like the one the dog listened to on His Masters Voice black shiny records: you wound it up and you could listen to *Scenes from a Persian Market* or Kathleen Ferrier's drowned-soul lament *Blow the wind southerly, southerly, southerly*, or my favourite *Being a Chum is fun, that is why I'm one, Always laughing, always gay, Chummy at work and Chummy at play…* what a crashing bore this chummy person must have been. I would wind up the handle, put on the disc and stomp around the room in a trance of dance—*Fare-thee-well for I must leave thee, Do not let the parting grieve thee…Adieu, adieu, kind friends, adieu adieu adieu, I can no longer stay with you, I will hang my heart on a weeping willow tree, and may the world go well with thee…*Then I'd collapse in exhausted delight onto the brown leather settee (they weren't called sofas in my grandparents' lower middle class milieu).

The brittle black discs with their coloured central labels were each carefully stored in a brown paper wrapping, which seemed to smell of something both comforting and at the same time new when you opened the lid of the inlaid walnut record box where they were stored, with its green baize lining just like that inside gramophone itself.

There was a yellow chamber pot just peeking out from under the bed in the spare room where I slept, so I didn't have to go outside to pee in the night.

In the morning I would dress and admire myself in the three sections of the dressing table mirror, a pier glass I think it was called, and I certainly did a lot of peering, apprentice narcissist that I was, adjusting the mirror sections so I could see every angle, every facet of myself, and then playing my own game with infinity. Mary Mary, quite contrary, how does your garden grow? I had a bucket with a picture of contrary Mary on it, and she herself held a similar bucket. I stood in front of the central mirror, holding mine. Try as I would I couldn't quite make out the picture on her bucket, but I knew it was there, Contrary Mary and the bucket receding infinitely, like Alice getting smaller and smaller and ending up in a totally different dimension. Here the impossible union of spheres of existence seemed to be mysterious, tantalising, but potentially actual, if only I could figure it out. This struggle with unknowable questions is the province of all small children, future philosophers and evolutionary biologists maybe, but also just ordinary enquiring kids who grow up and forget they asked the questions. Truth seekers all, in the beginning.

It was a future leading mathematical scientist who, when he was a young child, lay in his cot for his enforced afternoon nap, already bored with the restriction. Sleep was replaced by mathematical calculation, and starting by adding one plus a half plus a quarter plus and eighth plus a sixteenth, and so on with different fractions, he discovered infinite series of numbers, in a cot made of mahogany bars so he couldn't climb out. 'I don't think I talked about this' he said seventy years later, 'It was just a game'.

My questions kept coming up, as they do. Well within the normal range of the average enquiring child's mind. Why does a chair have arms, where does the sun go, if the world spins how do we stay on it, what makes us die. Are we nearly there, where do our dreams go when we wake up, and do you love me. Why does the wind blow. Why? 'Because God made it so' declared exasperated even though flagrantly non-religious parents when I was young, shutting the door on this quest for why, so I kept my struggle inside myself and had to wait for years to know the eternal human-ness of these preoccupations. Was someone infinitely larger than me, I wondered, holding a bucket with me as a picture on it?

My grandparents kept chickens, and each day my grandmother mixed up in a galvanised pail a warm steaming mash of spuds and bran, it smelt good enough to eat myself, and just as I had chewed on calf-nuts at home, once I sneaked a finger-full when she wasn't looking. But not a second one.

By the chicken shed was the dog kennel, inside a wire run, built by my grandfather, where their old black coated mongrel Curly barked at strangers and friends alike. Each evening he was loosed from his pen to run —run—run as far as he could, lost in the early evening dusk, but, hungry for his dinner which he had waited for all day, he would come back maybe half and hour later, when my granddad whistled... whistled... whistled... into the fading melancholy twilight.

In the next of a haphazard line of black-painted sheds were our white mice: my grand-dad built elaborate cages for them with wheels and ladders and separate rooms, truly stately homes. Later they went back with us to the farm, and even later still when we had tired of litters of pink babies and the responsibilities of feeding their parents, my father let them go. Generations afterwards, you'd see the flash of a mouse in one of the sheds, piebald from his semi-domestic ancestry, grander maybe but more visible and vulnerable.

I had a little rocky garden plot—just a raised mound of rather unpromising ashy soil next to Curly's dusty run. More interesting to me than growing plants whose pale-green and undernourished stalks sprawled helplessly over the soil and almost never bore flowers, was upturning the stones and watching the wood-lice, pale grey and unhealthy-looking, curl into balls or lumber for cover. If you sat quietly you could start to sense a whole new world, an insect world where ants with agenda crawled officiously about, hoverflies cruised over the landscape like monitoring gods, and little red-coated ladybirds, bishy barnabees as the local children called them, landed briefly before shaking their episcopal finery and opting for more propitious horizons elsewhere.

By the side of this mound ran a path deep into a tangle of what was called 'the plantation', I imagined it full of creeping monsters and hobgoblins, and never went down there as far as I recall. In reality I believe it just led rather prosaically to the boundary fence.

Chapter Eleven

In which the two worlds collide, the box of secrets overflows, and Molly is sent to boarding school. It is an attempt at escape, but soon proves to be of no help in keeping at bay the drama of life back home.

There are several ways to mend a broken warp. You can either use a weaver's knot, or you can replace the break with a newer, thinner, thread. If you have by your own carelessness cut into the canvas, you can turn it over, and clear the break from its surrounding stitches. Then you have to carry on, tease it out a little more.

So there were these two worlds, separated only by a few miles, but seeming miles apart in emotional territory. Gold, if pure, does not tarnish. As Molly lay in the huge feather bed at her grandparents' house on summer evenings listening to the purling coo of the wood-pigeons, all felt right with the world. Their call could comfort her throughout her life, wherever she was. There there, pet, they said, there there. When she fell asleep on those warm nights at The Retreat, she could still hear outside the rooks bickering over sticks to build their nests in the high elms, shouting Shame, Shame, Shame, over and over into the dusk. Rooks may seem dysfunctional with their eternal family quarrels, squawking aerial soap operas, but they were the ones who could tell far before the experts which elms had been stricken with the Dutch disease, and they refused to nest there, even when the trees still looked sound.

Rooks too, however sensitive, were not sympathetic to any bird who dared to build a nest elsewhere. These nests, built high in a different treetop away from the noisy tribe, and able to withstand gale-force winds, would quietly disappear as soon as the calmer weather returned. You would see the odd rook carrying twigs back to the main rookery. Careful dismantling, then obstinate rebuilding—being a rebel clearly was not tolerated in the rooky world. Rules are rules.

Back home, it wasn't only Germans that lurked behind the door, but unknown gusts of feeling surged around the staircases and down the halls. *'What is that noise?' 'The wind under the door.' 'What is that noise now? What is the wind doing?' 'Nothing, again nothing.'* But the floors still sang like malignant nightingales.

And then, just before her tenth birthday, Molly's grandparents came to live with them. Her grandfather's solid building skills were needed to convert agricultural land to something more profitable, tourist-land with a club-house and a shop, to serve the caravan sites which had already covered over Molly's beloved meadows, heaving, throbbing with the natural life which had existed there for so many generations. It was the beginning of an end. This was the way in which her parents, perhaps without knowing it then, were obliterating themselves from the map. The grandparents left their wonderful retreat and came to the country of uncertainty, where the landings in the old house creaked louder and louder.

Later came the split. This disaster split Molly's life in two terrible pieces, not solid tectonic plates but pieces that split infinitely, a catastrophe never mended. This was not between mother and father but between parents and grandparents. It involved strange hinted-at liaisons, this time between her grandmother and her father, and yet again Molly had to spend years as an adult trying to piece it all together.

It came out in such a sudden way, when Molly's mother had flared out at her over the telephone, but Molly, growing braver as she grew older, had simply put her mother in her place, put the phone back on the hook, cut off the cut, only for a new one to open up. She had phoned, her mother declared, at 'the wrong time', 'Surely you know we always have our tea at six o'clock'. The Snow Queen as icy as she had ever been.

These weekly phone calls were demanded, as a right, by the queen, while Molly's dad was the letter-writer, and was never invited to the phone. The calls were less about communication than about the failure to communicate, and Molly dreaded them. Her mother however seemed to thrive on them, and indeed told Molly, when her daughter had once been at the other side of the world and unable to communicate by the then available means, that this had been the loneliest time of her life. She told Molly the smallest details of her own life, while requiring, and giving, nothing in return but that Molly should listen.

Why did you put the phone down? Why?

Why did you shout at me?

I'll tell you why, shall I tell you why? Because of what happened to me.

What happened to you?

Your father, your father, had an affair with my mother.

The childhood dreams of a box-full of something unknown high in a cupboard in a dark house came gushing back. But now the secret had a name. The old queen and the jack could be together in Bezique, gaining maximum points, but in life, in all their lives, it spelt disaster not victory. Like the larger universe, it seemed that only a small percentage of Molly's had been visible, much of it had been unpredictable, and a large part unimaginable until this breaking news arrived. There's more to any universe than meets the naked innocent eye.

Hallo, hallo, who's your lady friend? Who's the little girlie by your side?

Later still her mother told her more, of catching her husband years before the final split, holding Molly's grandmother's breasts as she bent over John's cot.

Night night, duckie, sleep tight.

Molly sees her dad there in the half darkness of John's softly curtained room, straining into her grandmother's body as she leans over the cot to place the sleeping baby gently down.

Her buns. Loved by both grandson and son in law, it seemed. In contrast to the Snow Queen, Molly's gran seemed warm and as freshly baked as a caraway seed cake, and Molly's first thought was to understand the transgression. Her father, like his daughter and her brother, was drawn to Gran's lacy cardigans, her pink satin petticoats, her strong hold on life, on her grand-children, and on him too. Although mother's and daughter's birthdays were only a day apart, they were profoundly different, a challenge to the maxims of astrology. He was mid-way between them in age, both older and younger than the two conflicting objects of his desire.

But of course it hurt Molly's mother, cruelly, and maybe it was his revenge, to strike her at the heart of her life with her mother as she had struck him, embracing Molly's uncle, the baby brother who had supplanted him on his mother's knee so many years before. In the world where history and imagination fuse and confuse, there remains no certainty of this. And who knows about that old devil the unconscious, was this too a way of getting at his own incestuous longings by another route? The first woman any man touches is his mother, and the desire remains.

Incest: that illegal bond, defined in different ways in different cultures, whether the forbidden fruit lies on a marriage line, an adoption line, or a line of consanguinity, or just simple but profound affinity; same-household liaisons which can sabotage a clan, but liaisons that had been permitted in the old Norse culture of Molly's ancestors.

I've seen you, with a girl or two,

Oh, oh, oh, I am ashamed of you.

And how is little Georgie, Gran would ask Molly about her six-foot father, when the grand-daughter dared to visit her grandmother in later years, but not often enough. She was mad for me, Molly's father had apparently told his wife. It was a mortal blow for Molly's mother. But she didn't die, just carried it in her heart like a poisoned sliver which added its strength to the bitterness she felt, and the bitterness she then handed out to her children.

During one of his last illnesses, Molly's dad in his hospital bed had introduced Molly to her own mother as his mother. There seemed no end to the confusion between the generations, in all their minds. In her mother's final days, Molly dreamed that her mother sat by Molly's bedside, dressed in Molly's clothes, what a mix-up it was. Perhaps the mother identified her daughter with her own mother too; envy and understandable hostility against a mother who has a husband, but also wants her daughter's mate. A bitter history indeed, however common, or so it's said, in reality. It was inherited but not then re-enacted, by Molly and her own mother in the female line. 'Leaving Home' had been a protection as well as a deadly sin. This was a way in which Molly could try to smooth out this painful wrinkle in her mind.

Tarnish can be caused by atmosphere. The encrustations can be chipped away with the curved blade of a scalpel, or they can be rasped and sanded with a special brush. Protective goggles are essential. Bits of fibre can break free and spring into the eyes. She's not crying, just blinded with tiny filaments as things fall and fly apart.

But first, and this is where this story begins to end, or at least begin another chapter of 'life afterwards', was Molly's separation from both these worlds. She was to go to boarding school, only twenty miles away it's true, but it could have been a hundred or a thousand. The bright child-swan, if that was what she was destined to be, owed it to them all to fulfil her potential, it seemed, and this meant going, pulling away from all the ties that bind, from the entangled threads that made up the fabric of her remembered and felt childhood.

What would such success do for her? Would it rescue her by magic from her cares in the ordinary world? *Che sara, sara…* Her father, for all his frequently old fashioned views, was committed to Molly's education even though she was a girl. But she would end up, he thought, at his fantasied destination: 'some big man's secretary'. It was only later that Molly yearned to be, not a silk purse with obligations, but a comfortable sow's ear. This separation, seeming so small, would actually be the beginning of pushing her further and further away from them all, making her somewhat of an alien in their eyes. There are distances which may be impossible to bridge. There exists, at least for some, this melancholy side to the great gift of education.

Just after Molly's fantasy sister Elizabeth had been crowned Queen, Molly was about to lose her own princess's crown. It was the end of sweet rationing too, but just in time, as she discovered a little later, for her to have them rationed again in boarding school. Five sweets a day, no more no less. Intricate bargaining was sometimes involved; a large butterscotch wrapped in crackly gold paper was equivalent to several dolly mixtures. Counting all the minute sweet small bricks in the Pez plastic dispenser was something many of the children forced the house mistress to do, to find equivalents with Spangles or Toasted Tea Cakes, those brown, squashy coconut delicacies which reminded Molly of tea with her gran. Later her dad, to

Molly's shock, had someone make her for her birthday a blue plaited work-basket with a secret compartment, to 'smuggle' sweetness into her boarding school life.

Everest was conquered the same year as she conquered this mountain of achievement for her parents' sake. On the world's stage, Stalin died and so did Dylan Thomas. Deep in a cave, paintings of animals, luminous witness to prehistory and to our ancestors' preoccupations, so similar perhaps to our own, more than we know, were discovered in France. When Picasso stumbled out from the darkness of those caves at Lascaux, he declared with awe and humility 'we have learned nothing'. 'I saw Mummy kissing Santa Claus' revolved on the electric record turntables in England and America.

Molly was prepared to sit for the scholarship, and she walked through the little wood next to her grandmother's old house (now let to tenants when the grandparents moved to Molly's house) to see Mr Denny, a retired teacher who became her private home tutor, sucking his pipe comfortably as the small girl wrestled with maths and answered page after page of 'general knowledge' questions. The walk through the woods, the spinney they called it, small as it was, felt dangerous, space without boundary, who knew what wolves lay in wait behind the snow-berry bushes, but at Mr Denny's house the ticking clock held the rooms in place, and Mrs Denny brought them hot chocolate and Chelsea buns. Molly would unravel the bun's length of dough to pick out the currants first, her appetite for work grew, she enjoyed the knotty problems, the tricky questions, the space to display her knowledge, and the struggle with what she didn't yet know but wanted to learn. There were more answers than she yet had questions for.

The exam was passed and the interview was requested. Molly sat in a waiting room with strange small girls some of whom would in fact be her classmates and companions as they grew up in a world without parents, which would be a vicious and unprotected place. There was Jane, sharp, bright and nervous on the edge of her chair, who would a few years later be asked to leave because of her revolutionary Sapphic tendencies, which might have been more in the teachers' minds, as she liked walking hand in hand with a particular friend. And there was Hester, who lived near Molly and was to suffer equally with the leave-taking, soiling her bed for nights in a row as she struggled and failed to hold on to her misery and her anger in the echoing dorm.

What was she reading at the moment, the headmistress asked. The question emerged from lips as severely cut as her impeccable short iron grey hair. Yet somehow Molly recognised something indefinable, something she was seeing maybe for the first time, about a concerning but also enticing widening horizon symbolised by this hair so different from her mother's carefully permed head, and she didn't feel intimidated. *Gulliver's Travels*, she said. Different contradictory world of big and small, joining up with her dreams.

Who were her heroes? Molly told her Marie Curie. But fired as Molly then was by Curie's discoveries, perhaps the attraction also lay in her fine partnership with her husband. Together, she read, they went on bicycling holidays, with their little daughter carried in a seat at the back of Pierre's machine. It was for Molly the ideal family scenario, harking back to a time when there had been no brother. Later, after the little bangs and coloured flashes, after the noxious smells had been reduced on the black-board to minute hieroglyphs laboured over by the tiny chemistry teacher, again with grey hair cut as short as a man's, the realities of chemistry defeated her.

A few days later the letter came, Molly had done it. She had a new role now: a 'scholarship girl'.

The scholarship swan was about to broach difficult waters; encounter different perspectives, make contact with new minds. Something about difference would sow the seeds for a lifetime's guilt, a family vendetta where independent minds would be seen as a threat and not a development.

Then too began a puzzled preoccupation with relativity in the social universe. The girl with the curl, called a 'snob' by the village children by whom she so longed to be accepted, became the scholarship girl whose father collected her from school on the all-too-infrequent exeats in an old black Zephyr car often trailing bits of straw, such a contrast to the sleek Bentleys and Rolls Royces which glided in to the school entrance to gather up her peers, who in this respect were definitely not her peers.

There was a Clothes List, sent in advance of that first term at boarding school, forbidding in its length and its requirements. Side by side, Molly's mother and grandmother worked together at this clothes list, almost as if it were a trousseau, even if in other ways they were working as still unacknowledged sexual adversaries, before the final split. They sewed on the blue Cash's name tapes and carefully, artistically, made bags with different coloured bias binding in swirls and embroidered tails, labelled 'Shoes' and 'Linen' and 'Shoe Cleaning'. This last held an arid little couple of brushes quite removed in smell and style from Molly's grandfather's armoury. There was a wooden mushroom for darning socks. If you unscrewed the top there was a hollow in the stalk to hold your needles for different kinds of stitching.

Was Molly stitched up? Now there can be a stab of pain for their naivete and their goodness. These two women genuinely believed, or did they just hang on to it in the face of other thoughts, that they were kitting her out for a brave new world, not knowing of the abysses and the crevasses and the raging storms that lay ahead for her, and for them all, in the next years. These forecasts of difficult weather were already present in their adult lives. Molly's mother hauled the handsome sewing machine off the shelf and made her daughter a dressing gown, as she had made one for herself years before at the birth of her own new life as a wife and mother. And perhaps she was confusing them and their aspirations? The dressing gown was pink and had a fake leopard-skin sash: somewhat *risque*, no, downright inappropriate, for life in a chilly English boarding school for girls.

Apart from ordinary daily navy knickers, with their own separate white linings, there were green silk knickers to go under the best green silk Sunday dress, green slimes the girls called them, bought on a special trip to Harrods, such an urban excursion, an unfamiliar city stage-set so fiercely exciting for Molly the country girl. She discovered later, they had to line up and lift their skirts to prove they were actually wearing the things. She minded this much less as time went on, when the green slimes heralded going to a concert in the large school hall. There she could be immersed in the complex tides of conversation between different instruments, smoky, spiky, mysterious. Quite eminent musicians came to play. She seemed to have another life in these passionate talks which might have mirrored those with her mother, or with some other version of her mother who might have listened much more than she was willing or able to do.

There were two pairs of walking shoes for beating the roads on Sunday country walks, after the Sunday Service where 'forgive us our trespasses' had a hopeless ring, far less exciting than her dad's stormy accusations in the pea fields. There were six pairs of thick brown lisle stockings and two spidery suspender belts, whose mysteries Molly had to wrestle with alone.

A celebrated early twentieth century poet had written the school song, and as the pupils sang it lustily, Molly too sniggered with her companions when they came to the line about 'wondering what we were'. 'Wondering what we *wear*', these little girls chirruped. The trial of the suspender belt seemed like an initiation ritual into a new world, one far removed from Eros. Here in this house where we are singing thus, long generations will come after us, all faced with the same slithery task of attaching stockings to little fiddly pink plastic fasteners, so that the seams are straight. Worlds away from Molly's father's lyrical descriptions of his wife at her own graceful toilet.

There was a camel-hair coat, a box-pleated navy gym slip, two school ties, certain recipes for more wrestling, navy games shorts and a grey jersey and scarf that you were never allowed to wear on the games field no matter what the temperature. How Molly's poor ears ached in the icy Suffolk blasts. Neatly lined up on the bed for a solemn prefect's later inspection were those six navy-blue knickers with elasticated legs, and the six pure white knicker-linings, which would later be stained with menstrual blood.

'I must be dying!' sobbed one little girl later in the large dormitory at night, far away from maternal support, terrified of the stains on the sheet. These were the first signs of the birth of a new adolescent body, and a portent too of giving birth herself. Molly, whose mother had let her know about periods at least, explained as best she could the burden of Eve's curse to her frightened little friend, under cover of darkness, after the matron had prowled officiously around, sweeping her torch over the apparently sleeping forms of twelve small girls who were just waiting for her to leave the silent breathing room.

But each morning when the light returned, every little girl had to stand to attention by her stripped bed, after breakfast, so that a house prefect could ensure it had been thoroughly aired. This practice was of course a perfectly sensible one. If the prefect deemed the bed not stripped back far enough, the whole lot was then seized, pulled off and thrown on the floor. There would often be an unmistakeable gleam of satisfaction in the prefect's eye, and it was a version of torture for the unfortunate sinner, especially if she was a 'new girl', who would have to put it all back together again before the bell for lessons sounded throughout the three floors of the echoing Victorian house. If by chance an under-sheet was blemished by menstrual blood, this was revealed for all to see. Eve's sin, 'the Curse', indeed. 'The curse has come upon me!' cried the Lady of Shallott. Her mirror cracked, from side to side as the poem said, and once most girls in the class had crossed the boundary from unsuspecting childhood through the blood rites, they would snigger knowingly at her dismay.

And there were twenty-four handkerchiefs. Each had to be marked with a blue name-tape. Should that have alerted them all to tears ahead? Everything had to be ticked off and accounted for, first at home by these two women seriously heaping up their industry as a surety against difficult times, and then again by that stony-faced prefect, light years away now from her own first day as a new girl, on that first agonising afternoon.

Molly could take some photos and a teddy bear: but instead of letting her take her old worn Ted that her ma had made her from upholstery fabric, her parents bought her, from the kindest of motives, a new shiny white dog with a plastic nose, the obverse of Dad's dear black Bonzo. This dog sat up and begged in perpetuity, his mouth slanting sharply down at each side of his nose, and his legs as unbending and rigid as Molly secretly felt was her fate, in spite of her parent's enthusiasm. Philip Larkin, notorious poet of depression, had a toy rabbit when he was a child, it sat on the table beside him as he ate, and one day it fell into the mint sauce ears first. 'It was hung out many days to sweeten and was washed and scented, but I never felt the same about it'. Deprivation, as he observed, became for him what daffodils became for Wordsworth. There was an ill internal breeze which set in, it seemed, for ever. For a long time that was so for Molly too. She felt she was the one being hung out, losing touch with all the old odours, having to put on a shiny white plastic face.

If you go down to the woods today, you're in for a big surprise: If you go down to the woods today, you'd better go in disguise. Today is the day the Teddy Bears have their pic-nic.

She played this comforting song over and over, on the grandparents' wind-up gramophone which had ended up at the old house, when she went back home after the first term. But this was no picnic. It was a leave-taking where she felt bereft, not left with much, taking little. The anxiety of leaving was covered over, eclipsed, by the hope embedded in the departure. There was such conviction that this parting was right, that this so-called swan had to sail away, that no-one ever mentioned being homesick. Angela Brazil and Enid Blyton never mentioned it in their jolly tales of boarding school, full of midnight feasts, laughter and endless, endless fun. Little cruelty tarnished their stories, which were airbrushed to show small parentless human beings in the most favourable but unreal light.

Molly's father of course, in his accustomed charismatic way, swung her trunk with heroic strength off the tailgate of the car, and swept up the elderly house mistress into his charmed circle of attention. Before each term, they would spend some time in her room, door only partially open, discussing life. And if that crusty old woman was grudgingly drawn in to his ambit of folk wisdom laced with something almost godlike, the pretty under-matron, giggly and plump, was completely captivated. Molly's father's *droit de seigneur* it seemed, this power to enslave, could go on right under the eyes of Molly's mother.

On the first morning after the first night away, tossing and rigid in the stiff bed with its unfamiliar horsehair mattress, Molly cried into her pale scrambled eggs as she perched with other girls on a long backless bench in the high-ceilinged dining room. There were so many chewing, swallowing mouths, and they bewildered her. She was led away, snuffling apologetically, by the resigned senior house matron. She wondered if she would ever get used to it.

She wore the new stiff clothes and gradually became accustomed to them, and to this strait-jacket of a life with conduct marks and order marks, ticks or crosses for when you 'opened your bowels', having your toenails cut by the stern matron, all life's little intimacies hauled out on show as the under-matron watched you bath properly on the single evening a week you were allowed one. Molly learned a new language, where lavatories were honks, where the communal bathroom was the slosh, where the least composed thing to do was to get 'baity' as the some of the irritable teachers did. Splish splash splosh, washing in the slosh.

Molly's parents, who were of course not her enemies, had marked her out for this. She was in shock for months, and so maybe were many others, though they kept their mortifications hidden. As Molly rediscovered, with guilty relief, thoughts at least were private. Years earlier she had been dissuaded from sucking her comforting thumb because it would make her teeth stick out. Thumb abandoned, she had gnawed her nails to little pink and mangled stumps. Now these stumps blazed, beacons of her unhappiness, above the grey knitted cylinders of the fingerless mittens her ma had knitted for her to wear on wintry days. While Padre Pio's mittens covered up his stigmata, Molly's wounds were advertised for all to see.

Ladybird, ladybird
Fly away home.

If only she could have done, like those ladybirds who had simply cruised off from her little garden plot at The Retreat, to find a better place to be.

Again the puzzling and apparently contradictory world of proverbs did not help. Absence yes indeed maybe made a fond heart grow even fonder. But out of sight out of mind? Whose sight, whose mind… She thought of home every day, and secretly that old self-centred self was shocked to think that it could go on without her.

The memory of Sister Mary Xavier still lay warm inside her. The range of teachers in this secular school could not replace her old heroine. Even Molly's new coloured pencils, all twenty-four of them, in their saccharine carton emblazoned with a splurged picture of the Lake District, and her mysterious set-square and protractor, could not console her. But she learned to draw intricate patterns with a pencil firmly screwed into the shiny compass, and she stabbed its point determinedly into the cover of each of her exercise books, to make a reassuring similar pattern of circles and triangles within them. She began to experiment with different handwriting styles, in an attempt to make her own decisions about who she might be. Shall her name be written with large swirls and curves? Or neat and tiny, hiding her real self underneath small marks? Her signature changed from day to day, until it came to rest a few years later. She liked collecting shiny new facts too, and stored them away for future use, well you never knew.

There were some teachers who possessed a little romance. The English teacher, Miss Potter, was a fiery Irish woman whose fiancé had been killed, they said, in the war, and who read Chaucer's verse with what she assured her pupils was an authentic pronunciation. *A povre widwe somdel stape in age, Was whilom dwelling in a narwe cottage, Besyde a grove, stonding in a dale.* She was of course never destined to be a widow herself. Her hair, though streaked with grey, still curled abundantly round her shoulders and she half pinned it back with decorated slides and combs. She wore long sweeping purple skirts, and velvet shoes. Later in an interview for a university place, Molly was to charm the Middle English professor as she read those same lines, imitating Miss Potter's accent with confidence and naïve pleasure. She had mentioned the readings done at school, and he had swiftly produced the very book from a drawer in his desk, like a triumphant conjuror. I also admired your purple costume, he said later, in one of her tutorials, and Molly understood that he meant her suit, it's my favourite colour. The purple suit, perhaps an echo of Miss Potter's skirts, she had borrowed from her mother, who when she heard of this seemed just a little proud to know that her colour and style had an influence beyond her own small sphere.

Miss Potter also introduced them all to Malory's *Morte D'Arthur*, and was Molly the only one who thrilled to her teacher's romantic voice? *And they rode till they came to a lake. The which was a fair water and broade. And in the midst of the lake there rose an arm, clothed in white samite, mystic, wonderful.* The sword in the hand seemed like a solution and an aspiration. Malory had written this when he was in prison too, as Molly often felt herself to be in some obscure way.

Not all the teachers were romantic of course. There was History Higgins, as they called her, the teacher who stuttered and rocked her way through the significant dates in the world, but only those which ended at the end of the nineteenth century. Still maimed they said by shell shock, she stood and stared at her mesmerised class through her thick glasses, reflecting the world outside which was evidently so much more intact than her own. Her brown pleated tweed skirts did their best to keep her together, but she was frequently un-tucked at the waist, and not only at the waist, it seemed.

The maths teacher Mrs Box, so clearly a widow and thrown onto hard times, with a kind voice and yellowish smoker's eyes also hidden behind huge circular glasses, was sometimes to be seen weeping in the chapel. She wore beige cardigans, which matched her eyes, and these loose knitted tents dragged vaguely round what had been her hips in former days. She was often it seemed moved by the bible lesson of the day, especially any which mentioned love, read from the huge book on the chapel lectern in front of all the rows of little to middling to large girls, many making plaits in the long strands of their gymslip girdles, as was then the rage. Molly liked maths, was talented at it as Mrs Box told her, and she assembled all these bright new mathematical facts like well-sharpened pencils. But then things changed. Molly was put off, even outraged, by Mrs Box's assertion that parallel lines met in infinity. First she protested, but the world according to Mrs Box refused to change just to suit her, so she drifted away from mathematical calculations, which had been her pleasure, into more literary waters. It was over forty years later that a maths professor said Mrs Box had been colliding facts herself, mixing Euclidean flat-plane geometry with Reimann's three dimensional discoveries. 'She shouldn't have told you that', he said. Molly also wondered later about those parallel lines, her sense of shock that they should meet, when unknown to her then, the lines between the generations were meeting at home.

The geography teacher Miss Halton must in her own turn have put off many of her pupils from learning about the world as she droned on in an unstoppable monologue, studded with a 'very-very' almost it seemed in every sentence. Her words were accompanied by expansive arm movements, and the class cruelly called them her breast exercises, of which she was definitely not in need, as her breasts nearly reached her waist.

Before each lesson, one pupil was chosen to count the repetitions, and they were listed secretly term by term, until Miss Halton herself got very-very old and had to retire.

Body image, when less than perfect, was mocked in these teachers, as the small girls struggled to manage their own often mysterious changes with precious little help. The Latin teacher, large and sweetly over-plump, like a grown up Renaissance cherub, had a surname which could easily be warped into 'The Sow'. Molly loved Latin, however, where again rules of conjugation and declension made things either right or wrong. Subject, object, it was all spelled out: of the table, to the table, by the table. *Agricola amat puellam.* The farmer loves the girl. And she, of course, loves him. A temporary English teacher, ponderous and with a rolling walk to manage her size as she walked into the classroom declaiming Wordsworth, became 'Poetry in Motion'.

There were two well stocked science labs, with sheep's hearts, fossils and speared butterflies lining the grey walls, where girls giggled surreptitiously when Miss Dean, the serious biology teacher with short dark hair like a boy's cap exhorted them to watch her 'while I mount an amoeba'. The pictures of seminal vesicles they were instructed to draw in their blue-covered biology exercise books bore a striking resemblance to the patterns that Mrs Miniver, the town's birthday cake maker, drew on the sides of the chocolate heavens she produced for lucky girls' birthdays. The whole territory of sexuality was one where every girl pretended to know more than she did. They all did, and yet they did not. Looking up 'prostitute' in the dictionary to find that this was a woman who sold her body produced mystification. And that puzzling word 'adultery'. Was it about being an adult? If so what was the shock there? The adulterers who took and the adulteresses, by and large, who were taken: was this the inevitable adult route? Two sisters surnamed Stern were called Big and Little Sperm—the teachers perhaps winced but allowed this to continue because to prohibit it would have meant explanation of things they weren't prepared to speak about. And when a serious school prefect who unfortunately had an uncertain stammer stood in front of the whole school and read, quite unintentionally or so it was thought, the 'wrong' bible excerpt, teachers and older girls looked at the floor either in embarrassment or to prevent hysterical laughter, as the entire assembled troupe heard about Onan, son of Judah, spilling his seed on the ground.

Molly became used to the ordeal of communal eating; it became almost tolerable unless you were seated at the central table, where the pupils changed places each meal so you got a turn sitting on either side of the stony-faced house mistress. You had to have prepared in your mind at least four subjects of conversation. It might have been a pleasure, but clearly was not so for the house mistress, who would bark a single response to each of your tentative little questions, shoot it down quickly so your quiver was soon empty and you were left naked, silent and ashamed, with unborn topics dying in your mouth.

The dictionary, while being sometimes gnomic, also had other uses. For a while the three or four 'top girls' in the class, including Molly, a little revolving, wary group, quick to notice signs of impending attack from another of their number, set themselves a tricky little challenge. Each would provide another, a process decided by tiny initialled scraps of paper, with two or three words from the dictionary, words way beyond the normally accepted knowledge of their age, and these had to find their way, however unlikely their meaning and connection, into the next essay assignment. It was always an exciting task, to find the words. From covercle to dromomania, through peripraxis, raptus and sanify, all the way to zeugma, a tricky part of speech where one word refers to two. If anyone on the staff had their suspicions, these were never mentioned. The girls wondered if the teachers too had to look the words up. It gave Molly another Holy Grail to aim for, verbal triumph when really she knew very little about a lot, and she developed an enjoyment of exams, of approaching a triumphant edge which seemed to free her thoughts and her pen. Even though she dreaded exams, like all the rest, in the usual way, once she was in the room she felt launched, invincible. These words from the dictionary had given her a sense of power. But underneath there always lurked the dread of being exposed.

The pupils tried daily to summon up drama into their lives, by playing such tricks as Vaselining the blackboard before the French teacher, an elderly woman clearly well past her prime, came in to write out the French phrases for the day. It took Molly some years to be affected by Mam'zelle's hurt dark eyes, and to regret the casual cruelty meted out in the classroom. Cruelty was dished up to the more vulnerable girls too, where names would be wrenched and stretched in order to undermine identities already made uncertain by the sadism of growing up in this parentless world. Mary Ford, unfortunately large, became Fairy Maud, and of course there was Diana Deacon, known as Dors, whose breasts sailed before her on the hockey field. She was not supposed to feel proud of her assets, while others were still anxiously wondering when their own breasts would emerge. While Molly, with the perhaps feigned innocence of hindsight, couldn't recall being a bully herself, neither could she recall standing up for those unfortunates whose unprotected selves invited attack.

Sometimes drama and tragedy struck from the outside. Somebody's mother was killed in a head-on car crash the week before the Christmas holidays. 'She had our presents in the back of the car' mourned her traumatised daughter. The beloved brother of one of the middle-school girls was killed when his head was kicked in during a rugby match at his own boarding school, far away, so it seemed, in another part of the country. His little sister, verging then on adolescence, seemed on the surface to take this philosophically, but she stopped obeying any school rules. She walked about with head held high, and calculated contempt blazed in her eyes. She had emerged out of the little circle of hell which school structures tried to build, and into a larger sphere of agony. She looked down on her fellow pupils from another plane, and Molly felt a grudging admiration for this girl's daring, which was in reality a response to the kick in the head she had received herself. The girl was sent to the bench outside the staffroom most days, because of some insolence or refusal to conform, and she would sit there, not crying, not ashamed, but looking around her with flat eyes which held some hint of sad amusement at the pointless efforts of this little world to control her fate. It was a little breeze of bravery which rippled into the stifling world of rules largely conceived of and imposed it seemed by frustrated, dissatisfied or bereaved women.

Despite the school's wish to control thoughts and feelings, they went on underground, and would erupt in mysterious symptoms. There was the girl who had to be led away many times from the dining room table, where she could not stop wringing and washing her hands, over and over, between every mouthful. Then there was the case of the phantom pregnancy, when one adolescent girl grew stout and breathless, and then disappeared, to return sadder and flatter the next term. Nothing was ever said about such events, and they drifted away on the currents of everyday school life, neither marked nor mourned.

Physical illnesses also struck. There was the Russian girl whose surname, Molly discovered, ironically meant 'freedom' in her own land. She arrived as a full blown diabetic, and this fate, which meant she had to be injected twice a day with insulin, injected enormous fear into the other pupils, who prayed at night not to be stricken in the same way.

One morning the whole school was assembled to hear from the rigidly controlled lips of the head teacher about a pupil who had collapsed on the games pitch some weeks before.

'I have some sad news for you all. Rosemary has been in hospital, as some of you perhaps know. But she has died, of a brain tumour.'

Dead? Rosemary had had frequent and extreme headaches, been off games almost continually, apart from that fated day when she had collapsed, to the scorn of many of her fellows, who thought she was faking it. Everyone knew about faking, but hardly anyone dared actually do it. Molly, never a games fanatic and one who had always rather wished her own headaches had been as bad as Rosemary's apparently were, was devastated both by the unknowingness of her own failed wish and this girl's fate. While death had been considered as a remote concept, it certainly didn't figure inside the school. Dying hadn't been invented for children. Molly had yet to appreciate that you're never too young to die, and there was no way of talking about this particular event after that one announcement in the school hall.

So their lives went on: when lessons were finished and 'homework', done in one of the echoing classrooms under the strict eye of the teacher delegated for the day, was completed, games of balls thrown against the wall that Molly had loved back home in the dusty road by the pond were replaced by more intricate games of fine motor control. The little five pointed metal Jacks which came in a drawstring bag were tipped out on the floor, or on somebody's prep desk, then thrown up high in the air. You inverted your hand to see how many of the original ten you could capture. The remaining fallen ones had to be retrieved in ones, or in twos, or in threes, between the bouncing of a small and hard rubber ball. Here was an art that some could master, others not, usually the clumsy girls who also had difficulties reading and adding up. Hierarchies grew everywhere, and were inescapable. The box of multi-coloured pik-a-stiks were twisted and cast in a towering muddle all over the floor, and then again you had to pick each one up, without moving the pile crowded underneath, on peril of losing your turn.

There were holidays from school, and Molly made friends with little girls who asked her to stay with them. It was here, in more expansively affectionate homes, that she discovered such marvels as mothers who tucked up all the children, even Molly herself, at bedtime, and gave each one a goodnight kiss. Goodnight, darlings. Darling. A word she had never heard her mother use. Sleep well, sweet dreams. But at most holiday times, Molly sat beside her dad in the old Zephyr Six as he negotiated with his usual flair the twists and bends in the road that led back home. Despite all the anticipation, as she lay in her narrow dorm bed on the night before he came one particular Saturday morning, when she reached home, she fairly soon discovered that something had been ruptured. It was in the air, immaterial knowledge ungraspable but still palpable. All too soon there was the family rupture too, when parents and grandparents split irretrievably.

The shock of the news that they had gone, how it was broken and by whom, was something that Molly could never recall, even in dreams. The only image she found was of a floor suddenly giving way under the condemned victim's feet, and the noose tightening around the neck. Trapdoor into agony, not death.

'You'll understand one day,' she recalled her mother said, 'when you're grown up'. Growing up transformed in that instant into something to be feared, not hoped for. This was a thousand times worse than Eve's curse.

Her grandparents had left behind their windup gramophone and their stack of black records, but the songs gave no more comfort to Molly, only pain. They lost their power to lift her up, but were holes she fell into and down, down, every time.

Perhaps Molly's going, and her brother's too as a boarder at a small local prep school, from which he frequently escaped to walk home, seemingly possessed by dromomania or the addiction to running and roaming, as the dictionary had told her, left an unfilled space for this to happen. In any event it was a seismic shift.

Her letters from the world beyond the school were censored, to make sure her grandparents didn't contact her. *Don't go breaking my heart.*

Hearts can be broken, from external blows. A huge impact can cause the electrical signals to flutter and scramble. But even when this happens, if you keep the chest pumping, the blood keeps flowing, until a machine arrives to shock the heart back to normality.

Each Saturday after morning prep Molly would rush back from the classroom to search through the mail laid out on the black shiny sill of the window outside the common room. There would be the familiar letter in her father's large round hand, with news of the farm and the animals, but nothing in her granny's copperplate or her grandfather's careful small script. What had happened?

Time passed in an obscure cloud. At least the grandparents survived in Molly's mind, and they really did too, though she never found out how, survive this transgression of the generations, the affair between son and mother-in-law. Molly's granddad maybe forgave his wife, had to, just to keep on living, but never his son-in-law, his daughter's handsome husband, so much taller and more elegant than he was, that dapper little moustachioed man. The grandchildren were shipwrecked in the middle of this perpetual storm, waves and particles in a perpetual and sickening synaptic whirl.

Molly wrote to her grandparents, but found out later that these letters too were stopped in their tracks by the house-mistress on her parents' instructions. It could not be spoken of at home, and such was the prohibition in the very air they breathed that she could not bike the few miles to her grandparents' house for fear of being asked where she was going. Her brother and she didn't speak of it, though he too must have missed them cruelly. Then when Molly's grandmother rang the school to say her husband had died Molly was at last allowed to speak to her.

'Oh duckie, your granddad's dead. Tell your mother. He's dead. He had the operation, but he died. There was a clot in his blood, it stopped his heart. Oh duckie, duckie.'

The line went dead, and something emptied itself out, unfurled and flew far away.

Heart-stopping.

Molly's heart crashed into something dark, maybe an ocean, bubbles were the only sign of where it fell. She joined the dead people, gasping and retching. No boundaries here, but infinite sucking night. Somewhere became nowhere—where why and when were questions that slid off the cliff into the darkness. These are the dramas which can go on apparently undetected beneath the face which masks them.

Maybe, she thought, this is a test. If I keep praying, help will come. But she was completely torn apart by grief and loss, gnawing at her stomach, pushing her backwards and forwards, turning her inside out.

All this went on in Molly while she half-heard the house mistress's quiet words somewhere very far off from where she stood. She leaned against the wall of the house mistress's drawing room, and the bewildered woman looked at her, helplessly. This was perhaps beyond her experience as well as Molly's.

I think you should ring your mother, was what the woman said.

Only the previous week Molly had been ill, and had received as she lay weakened but mending in the school sanatorium one of her grandfather's meticulously written letters urging her to get well soon.

Somehow the ban on letters had been lifted, perhaps temporarily, because she was unwell. In any event she had been recovering when the letter came, under the somewhat stern but always containing motherliness of a Sister Flitch and a Nurse Bonham. Even in the sanatorium, a little hierarchy was in place which kept the world understandable. Sister Flitch wore a navy nurse's uniform and her starched collars made perfect pointed shapes above the slope of her kindly chest. Nurse Bonham's overall was a more restrained grey, and her collars were softer and rounder, although she actually had a much sharper tongue, a narrow disappointed face in contrast to her superior's full cheeks and ready smile.

Ring your mother, a tricky thought. Little girls were allowed to use the telephone when there had been an upsetting event at home. These in Molly's experience usually concerned pets that had died, inconsiderately, in term-time rather than in the lavish affectionate days of holiday. When she rang her ma, even being allowed to dial the numbers herself, as she stood weeping and supported by the dark window-sill of the house mistress's sanctuary, she gulped out her sad tidings in a voice choked with grief and also fear. 'Granddad's dead, mum. Gran told me. He had an operation and-.' Her mother said without a pause or so it seemed 'they have both been dead to me for many years'.

Where was the comforting mother in this tale? Molly could only in the repeating circle of adult thoughts feel any anger, before some understanding tempered her passion, but at the time, all she had felt was grief. This mother left her daughter to bear the thought of her grandfather's death on her own. And from the mother's point of view, cutting out feelings had been her own defence against the pain of her husband's betrayal with her mother. Molly felt no anger then, only unspeakable pain.

Maybe the house-mistress felt it for her little pupil, as she continued to stand, perplexed, while Molly died and wept and died again all in a few moments. How many feelings can be freighted in one sentence? How could she carry this additional burden?

Dead for many years.

Well, her mother had killed him off in her mind, to put this plainly.

Though that may have been true then, Molly's mother did go to her own mother's deathbed years later. John left a note tucked under the windscreen wipers of her car, she came and this normally undemonstrative woman held Molly's hand tightly as they sat in a distant circle around the labouring old lady, whose hand the matron held, so that Molly felt torn apart and unable to go and sit on her Gran's bed, to help her with her final breaths. She breathed—and paused—and breathed—and paused—and breathed—and died. She took another great piece of Molly's heart with her and Molly was powerless to stop it. An old lady in the next bed was watching the Grand National in heroic denial that it would be her turn soon.

But her own mother lived on in Molly's mother's mind. Mum! Mum! Let us pray! She shouted it over and over in her own last days, so her carers said. Deep in her heart she still needed the solace of forgiveness, it seemed, was as guilty as she often made her children feel. Although she had thought she lived without her mother, within her it was a different story. Perhaps she played back over all those little instances where she had done things 'wrong' and God and her mother were needed to sort it out a little. The revenants, the returned ones. Maybe they come back to claim their dues, or they never go away, they're there all the time, like stars only revealed in the night sky of ending. They rise, float out of their boxes, whispering.

There was a sharp gasp from several mourners at the crematorium when Molly's ma appeared after all those intervening years, for her own mother's funeral, dressed in white as was her habit for all significant occasions. She walked with her nose held high down to one of the front pews of the chapel at the crematorium. She spread a perfume around her, expensive but deadly cold.

'They have both been dead to me for many years'.

Edit it out, please, please. Screaming in the wilderness. He had died just before his birthday. Molly walked and walked around the school perimeter, a headlong, headless course, past the lacrosse pitch and the tennis courts, past the swimming-pool abandoned to winter leaves and the windswept hockey fields, trying to make sense of her shattered world.

On the edge of a tiny Scottish island, she once found a dead lamb, curled white and small at the very back of a dark cave, squeezed against the wall. Had he taken himself there, giving up on the struggle to find a life without his mother? His plight reminded her of something in herself that day, abandoning itself to a shadowed fate.

Walking, walking, walking, to avoid falling apart. Molly felt she had been propelled beyond all known limits, she didn't any more know where home was. If disorientation is thought to be loss of the East, the point you sail by, one small girl on the east coast was all at sea with compass smashed. The wind blew through her and she was hollow. Her chest cracked, her head broke apart. Pieces of Molly were catapulted outwards, hitting and clanging against the iron rim of the sky. If you think this is dramatic, just remember that you can't see what is going on in other minds. If you can see, then they may already be broken beyond repair. As new girls, Molly and her peers had 'beaten the bounds' with a prefect, and later they played on the gorse-covered perimeter slopes, called 'Paris', a rather windswept place with little holes and crannies to creep inside and hide from authority, and smoke Menthol cigarettes and practice 'film-star kisses' on the mouth. But now all bounds were broken in Molly. Bearings were lost, gone, blown away, she was fearsomely possessed of some ancient vertiginous terror, spinning in space.

Back-shot of a distraught eleven year old girl, stumbling and tripping in the folds of her long purple velvet school cloak, whipped by a wind which had torn up her tent from its pegs and sent it hurtling into the iron grey sky. She is trying still to gather together in a bag the bits that are blowing and going. Sticky bits unstuck, fragments so tiny and pathetic but she is desperately clutching them as evidence, evidence of something which had once seemed whole. But the bits unfurl into chaos, in spite of her small whimperings. Tight-shot to tears and tears and tears. Twenty-four handkerchiefs all bunched together could not cope with this flow. There was a great gaping hole in the neural net, the horizontal warp and the vertical weft, all of its eleven billion pulsating cells, and there was no-one to help.

The following Sunday the whole school assembled in the big hall, as they did each year, to listen to the service of Remembrance for the Fallen Dead, in the two world wars. Molly survived the two minutes' silence, she even survived the ten buglers' haunting notes as the Last Post echoed down the years. But are the dead glorious? Even then she wondered, as the cruel separation from her grandparents crowded in on her. Beethoven's Funeral March was her undoing, and as on her first day at school she had to be discreetly escorted out of the hall by one of the teachers.

Pull yourself together, little girl, from these fragments. She feared there was no more self to pull.

Is it even possible to begin to sew this all together? How could Molly take the wooden darning mushroom and thrust it deep into the sock of her own insignificant life to cobble up the holes? Could she unpack it and rearrange it like her gran and her ma patiently rearranged her school trunk so that you could shut the heavy lid with her initials bravely stencilled on the top? It was impossible to get rid of the lumps and the bumps of unanswered questions, half understood perceptions, indigestible shocks and the agony, the irreducible agony, of something gone for ever. This was a permanently altered state.

The very landscape itself, already under-laid and mined with uncertainty, came apart into fragments. It was a broken country, not ploughed so that you could at least stumble over thick clods, but blasted beyond recognition. Motherland, Wonderland, No Man's Land, the icy pieces blinded her. This was the soil, dangerous unpromising ground. Floes turned to shards, sharper than the heart could bear. Somewhere inside it was winter for a very long time, and the great sighing soughing tide of the grey North Sea pushed her and pulled her, a sobbing undertow to the new life. Somewhere it sucked at her for her whole life long.

But look, listen just a minute. Can you, as Larkin said, climb clear of a wrong beginning? All our ordinary lives are full of holes and rents and scars and puckers where the skin heals over the ruptures, the fine lines of pain which mark all of our origins. Under the many masks there lies an often artfully concealed tracery, and we survive, unless the fault lines are stirred up too dangerously. Scars can be dressed, can be nursed, can be fed with resentments or can fade. Precious duelling scars, if you can see it that way, unless there are too many. Molly had cracks now, which like hair whitening with trauma, seemed to come overnight. But, and though that 'but' can sometimes seem to be a very long short word, the truth is, there's usually an end to falling. It might have taken half a lifetime to land, an overlong first act it's true, but land Molly did, as most of us do. Life's little ordinarinesses and pieces of sheer good fortune alongside the dramas eventually balanced the picture, giving it a more realistic cast. Grit has its place, in the making of something, maybe not a pearl, but of value just the same if you can let it do its silent work.

Chapter Twelve

In which the weaving, which never truly ends, reaches a time when it's finished enough to be hung. The house is swept away by change, but the babble of voices is not so easily subdued. And is every step you take forever? Molly's voice joins the never-ending line of wondering words.

Textile conservators need a profound knowledge of the factors which lead to decay. They also need to understand how to slow it down. They have to cultivate a deep understanding of how the original objects were made. It's not the only occupation where it helps to understand the context.

Now we've got to have a go at hanging this tapestry with all its imperfections, in the best available light. Starting from one end, gradually unroll it. It takes two people to hold the bottom of the roll, and one to fasten it to the rail. That makes three.

Stand back and look at it. There's the North Sea, sea of Molly's infancy, where she began, enthroned inside her mother, queen baby at the beginning, in the usual way. Two hundred and twenty thousand square miles of it, ranging in depth from a hundred feet to two thousand. Sea, the onlie begetter of everything. The scene of arrival, the point of departure. The sound of its advancing and receding waves lives inside Molly as close as her own heartbeat. At its extreme edges crouches the great Norse giant Hrae Svelga the corpse swallower, who sends blighting icy winds over the face of Molly's tiny plot of earth as he beats his eagle arms. Here be germs, and Germans, dragons and a good deal else, as the old maps used to say. Dusty little secrets carried away by storms into the deep. In its depths in some protected cave sit the three old women, the Norns, spinning the never-ending threads of life. Molly sees her youthful father, who didn't learn to swim till he was an old man with a heated pool installed on his own patch, jumping and tossing in the great brown rollers of this huge North Sea. *Time's toppling wave.* She sees herself as a little girl, running away on stubby legs from the pursuing waves up the sands of the beach.

Where is her brother? Not yet born when she fled the waves; in the idealised state of being the Only One. Perhaps neither of them could fully cope with the idea of siblings, a failure inherited from their own parents. Molly's young parents, her makers, watch her on the hard beach sand, as she runs. Their arms are kindly linked, at least in Molly's mind. This was the mother she had, though not the one she might have wished for. She too was the daughter her mother had. Forgiveness and thanks must be stitched in here. The road leads back to you, as the song says, and maybe all tried according to what they could manage at the time. Shadows on the wall in Plato's cave, far removed maybe from ideal parental forms, but these are the parents Molly can see. The feel of the cave remains. She's still stitching. Who owns our memories, she wonders.

How briefly they touched, do we all touch, after the before, and before the end. Molly loved her parents passionately, in different ways, as children do. She loves them still, and love of course is not outgrown with death. But in truth, they were often all at sea, living by powerful unwritten contracts signed and sealed within each self, each past, each present, each future. Self-pity is a potent trap, but self-love, far from being a sin, is vital in every life, a healthy way to grow and a parental gift from the beginning, if it's given. Even though she's dead, Molly's mother keeps on grumbling, and Molly too keeps up her worrying and guilty ways.

I told you you've got this all wrong.

Why don't you ever listen to me?

All this flapdoodle over nothing.

The sea still gnaws the cliffs, eroding the land, and slowly it took a whole chestnut wood that stood exposed on the flank of a hill-face flushed with scarlet pimpernels in early summer when Molly was a child. Sand-martins still nest in what remains of the fallen cliffs, where children used to dig holes, until a holiday-making boy was buried alive in his own private tomb, and the digging was forbidden.

One minute he was a small boy, digging alone in the side of the cliff. Was he thinking of what a hero he was, digging his way to somewhere, or of what he'd done to his little brother earlier that day? Then his cave caved in, and he must have panicked, fighting and struggling in the despairing darkness, before the weight of the sandy clay crushed his chest, broke his body completely, and he suffocated in the blackness and the silence. No time to shout Mummy! Sand or grain, both are as easy to be drowned in as the sea. As easy too, as an excess of despair when hope is too far away.

The sea defences, stout wooden constructions braving out the waves to protect the cliffs, have now toppled into the very sea they were meant to keep out. Molly's father broke his neck once, when he was climbing on their slippery seaweed covered surfaces while his dogs swam around them and barked in concern. He crawled his way back home. In that very sea, out where the seals played on the sandbanks, there now exists a wind farm, where thirty mighty sails catch energy from the air Molly's father once breathed in and out, even as he struggled on.

Should the sea continue to swallow up the land, then those houses built where once the old house stood will in their turn be drowned and doomed. Like the once-thriving town of Dunwich a little further south on the Suffolk coast, where a medieval port's twelve churches sank slowly beneath the swell, the last one slipping over the edge just before the first Great War in the twentieth century. Deep down, the legend goes, the bells still toll. When the bones of civilisation so swiftly float away, on tides borne from the implacable east, perhaps to be buried facing westwards as Molly's parents were has its own sad logic. We fly from our inevitable destruction, then slip over the cliff.

We create our parents, we kill them, we restore them. We're just the latest in the never-ending line of little children. Perhaps it's hubris to want to give parents a new life. Do they haunt us or help us? Do the shadows fall between us, or are we ourselves only shadows? It's a whole life's work to see yourself, and even then you might be on the wrong track. There may be these unanswerable questions always, but still we ask them. Perhaps children and parents only dreamed one another, perhaps still do. Maybe the

dead still love us, or are indifferent to us, in their own way, when words
have had their day. Perhaps we can only know our parents when they die. As
someone once said, many parents do not fulfil the promise of their early years.

That's enough of 'perhaps'.

Molly's mother doesn't give up, does she? There she goes again. The
past persists and so does she.

It didn't happen that way.

Didn't it?

I shall just rewrite it.

Maybe she should. If only she could.

How would she rewrite her lines, or would she leave them as they were?

Is there ever a moment when people find out who they are?

Science in the nineteenth-century demolished previously established
truths. We're all merest sparks in the impossibly vast history of the earth's
existence. Accidental outcasts from an accidental universe, disinherited now
from comforting prophecies. This is scary stuff. What we know is that
change is continual, never-ending, and we are part of it. Whatever the final
plan of living things, or lack of plan, we're all included. Gnats dancing in a
sunbeam, skylarks ascending; we all saw death there but chose to ignore it,
what you will. But is nature, as Tennyson's aggrieved complaint rang out,
really so careless of a single life? He was indignant, refusing to accept the
banal reality of it, where however long the game goes on, creams and
cryogenics notwithstanding, the outcome is the same. Get a grip, Alfred
Lord Tennyson, as everybody must.

The old farm house where Molly and her brother lived, and her father
and grandfather before them, was bulldozed, saleable bricks laid in pallets in
tidy piles, no room left now for the shades of those it housed, either to
mourn or to settle old scores. She was born in that house, and it was borne
in her, then it was swept away. The Domesday record was finally obliterated
by the wave of new development, as inexorable as the wild North Sea. That's
just the way it is. The houses are all gone, as the poet said, under the sea.

Demolition. How was the old house in all its beauty and its ugliness
reduced to untidy piles of bricks, some whole, some cracked, some falling

in helpless dull red shards from the wooden pallets? How could it translate itself, in all its concreteness, into memory, Molly's and those, so few now, who had remembered before her? How could anyone read the rubble? *Show me the way to go home,* that's what the jolly campers had sung. What had lived in that space no longer had a home. The proof of this presence has disappeared, like the cliff-side churches, over the edge. Houses, the humble ones and the great ones, and the haunted ones, die too. Not even their skeletons remain, as they sink to oblivion under the earth.

When the second son died in the Great War, was that when the first slate started to slide down the roof? When the first-born did not, in time-honoured tradition, inherit the broad acres, driven off to Canada because of his affair with the dairy maid? What intricate patterns the generations weave, when each actor, however minor, influences the other actors, in the past, in the present, in the future. Einstein himself stubbed his toe on this idea of randomness. He could never accept how small scale happenings dissolve into a cloud of probabilities.

While everyone slept, it seemed, the house was demolished. Away went the roof, slated and fine-chimneyed. Away went the upper storeys, previously facing the western glow of the sun slipping behind the old church tower on summer evenings. Like a victim before execution, did the walls wait, bowed and silent, for the deadly kiss of the iron wrecking ball? And who loosed that ball?

Molly sees a great brood of presences from many generations, silent and watchful, an assembly of shadows, wistful hungry wraiths, gathered on the lawn to say goodbye to the house they loved. Crowds of puzzled little children leave their balls and hoops and jointed dolls forgotten on the grass, as they gaze in wonder at this sight. Then they fade. They drift away for ever. Poor un-housed ghosts, helpless witnesses to a destruction swift as fire, but not even leaving a ravaged shell, only a pile of rubble still breathing dust. A little lump in the throat might be forgiven her here. Or could it? Don't we ever grow up to the facts of life? There's no way to reverse the film and have it jerk back to life, it's gone in a minute. A baby's first lexicon of words often includes the word 'gone'. Gone is a backbeat to every life. This is the latest loss in a line of losses for Molly. And of course there will be more.

Was a sin committed? If so, by whom? And does it matter now? Maybe even asking this question means she's trespassing—but whose ground is it any way, and who is the gatekeeper?

Who was betrayed, by whom, and why, remains an unanswerable question. Do we really need to know? There are multiple voices here, and broken images, and no certainty of truth even if we try to tell ourselves another story.

How can you begin to get to grips with the random nature of it all; not progressive development but progressive decay? The frozen music of that one old house, surrounded by a lake of frozen tears, plays its cold melody in a blank space right on the sharp edge between reality and imagination. It's a twisted legacy, fractured and dispersed by family splits. Many children share this sort of fate. Some make pictures, some sculptures, some hold fissures in a void inside, telling no-one, some kill... To recover our lost loves is a wish that we all share. Even though somewhere we know from the beginning, that everything grows and then goes.

Years passed before Molly could mourn the lost marks which had ascended the too-brilliant orange walls of the narrow back hall, measuring her son's advancing years.

Dreaming, she lets herself in to the garden by the side gate, and to the infinitely sad sound of a woman singing, wakes in tears.

Returning to the way things were remains the privilege of dreams. Each return brings something new.

One timeless time, she's walking from the top of the hill where the old farm cottages still show their simple architecture beneath an eruption of balconies and sun-porches, past the now-derelict holiday camp, where rotting divans and sagging armchairs lie discarded on the raised path above the road, past the old vicarage where the Babcocks so briefly stayed, and now old people nod their way out of life in a nursing home. The old meadow is restored, there is a circle of children. Sitting, laughing, in a random casual tousle on the ancient grass. But Molly wakes before she can turn the corner to see where the old house would have been.

She can walk down the curved gravel drive, lined with snowdrops and daffodils and bluebells each in their own season, and see her name still written in cement on the mended wall. She can come upon the warm red walls of a house facing that sliding red sun in the west, catching a glow from the weeping copper beech planted in the kind slope of the lawn. She can walk round to the back door and see the scarlet roses crowding the wall next to the iron water tank where mosquito larvae, scarlet too, wriggle and wait for metamorphosis.

Molly remembers this, but still it fades, even when hauled into the mind on the strong rope of memory. Recovering the lost object in the mind is the work of mourning, so Freud said. This is an individual orison, repeated for ever. There's a 'lost house' in every life. Perhaps it's the penalty for being born at all, as we're inevitably expelled from our first house, the womb: displaced persons from the beginning. Molly dreams of a map, showing that dear old house as a small square on the small coast road. It's marked there still, in the mind, the only way it can be, now. This is how the dead live, not in the artifice of eternity, but here and now, and now, and now, in us. Perhaps they too are works in progress, as myth turns to allegory, and back again. We meet them at night, in the dark mineshafts of the underworld, and we talk, we argue, we call names, we justify, we regret, and sometimes we might understand. It's a perpetual conversation, made against a background of static interference from our different selves, and the imagined selves of others.

But just down the road, by the railing around the old pond full of everlasting teeming life, Steve and Molly are still smoking, spitting, and careering wildly round the corners on an old blue trike, just before the fall.

'Ere we goo, gel!

Hold on tight!

Epilogue

There are two old photographs which tell a small part of the story. In one there is a little boy, born when the twentieth century was new, standing serious in his sailor suit. In the other sits a little girl with a flop-eared rabbit, called Wilfred, she told Molly, propped against her stool. He clutches the arm of a chair, a little nervous it seems of the photographer's scrutinising lens, and she has a chubby hand fastened on a ball. Is she going to throw it? She did and it went on rolling. It started as a soft sewn ball, and ended up as an iron weapon, the wrecking ball. Fading, fragments, all this rolls and wears away. Father Time and Mother Earth keep on and on with their relentless coupling. Forgettable creatures all, we feel compelled to tell our stories, such as they are. Often they may be, no they are, a tangle of revisions, a thinnish skin of words to cover something dark and maybe unknowable, the final meaning of our own part. Even if we stress and strain and puff and indulge in this drama of self-discovery, there are no real answers. There is a self who seeks, and a self who hides, and others more besides. Coo-ee, as Gladys the housekeeper used to say, now you see me, now you don't.

We had the experience but often missed the meaning, as the poet suggests. Approach to meaning restores the experience, he said, but in a different form, beyond happiness. Yes indeed. The dead exert a hold over the living, they inhabit our lives, and who can tell if we inhabit theirs. Matisse talked of looking into a formless world, which was begging to be ordered and shaped… 'I see into a whirl of shadows of human figures, who beckon to me to weave spells to redeem them'… Dante thought love moved the sun and the stars. Maybe hate has its part too.

This is the ultimate plot, the inexorable theme that takes all the characters down the same slow road. Try as we may to appease our ghosts, finally, we just join them. 'I imagine the earth when I am no more: nothing happens, no loss, it's still a strange pageant, women's dresses, dewy lilacs, a song in the valley'...

Human memories are fragile, easily covered over with the plaques and tendrils which obliterate the act of remembering. They sprawl randomly like plants in a long-overgrown garden much in need of a prune. But if you prune them, they grow again. Anxieties, like hope is supposed to do, spring and sprout eternally. Verily as the Book of Wisdom said, every person living is altogether vanity. It's only when the last human being disappears that we will have unloosed our departed dead forever. The broken melodies will drift away, a stream of unconscious information from all those dissolved people, distant fading music, punctuated with random cries lost in the wind; cosmic strings aimlessly tossing in the expanding, careless universe. *Exeunt omnes* as the playwrights say, actors and extras every one, in every little life.

Though they may stay hovering in the shadows for a long time, providing a kind of deep focus even when they're gone from central stage. Like little neutrino ghosts, passing through our bodies and our minds, one hundred trillion times a second, or so the scientists say. Until we can let the dead go deeper still and far away, still dreaming their own dead dreams. Is it an accident that the most sophisticated neutrino detector is designed like a breast?

Born and falling,
Into this world, within this world,
Under this earth.
'Ere we go, gal.
Way-hay!'

Appendix

Molly's Great-grandmother's Christmas Pudding Recipe

(This amount makes 5 medium puddings)

6 oz. plain flour
18 oz. white breadcrumbs
12 oz. suet finely chopped
6 oz. sugar
12 oz. seedless raisins
24 oz. currants
16 oz. sultanas
4 oz. mixed chopped peel
1 apple, grated
1 nutmeg, grated
1-2 tsp. cinnamon
1 tsp. salt
1 tbs. golden syrup
1 lemon, grated rind & juice
1 orange, grated rind & juice
8 eggs
Old Ale to mix
Brandy to taste

Mix all dry ingredients; add fruit juices, syrup, eggs. Stir well. Put in enough old ale to make a moderately soft mixture. Cover & stand overnight. Next day add more old ale & brandy (to taste) to make a fairly soft mixture. Fill buttered basins within 1 inch of tops, cover with buttered greaseproof paper & either pudding cloths or foil. Boil for at least nine hours. When required for use boil a further three hours.